Fishing
in the
Tiber

Fishing in the Tiber

ESSAYS BY
Lance Morrow

HENRY HOLT AND COMPANY   NEW YORK

Published by Henry Holt and Company, Inc.,
115 West 18th Street, New York, New York 10011.
Published in Canada by Fitzhenry & Whiteside Limited,
195 Allstate Parkway, Markham, Ontario L3R 4T8.

LIBRARY OF CONGRESS CATALOGING-IN-PUBLICATION DATA
Morrow, Lance.
Fishing in the Tiber : essays / by Lance Morrow. — 1st ed.
    p.   cm.
Essays which appeared previously in *Time* magazine from the
mid-1970s to the mid-1980s.
ISBN 0-8050-0635-4
1. United States—History—1945- 2. History, Modern—1945-
I. Title.
E742.M67   1988
973.92—dc19   87-29525
                                                    CIP

First Edition

Designed by Beth Tondreau Design
Printed in the United States of America
10 9 8 7 6 5 4 3 2 1

ISBN 0-8050-0635-4

For Janet Heussner

CONTENTS

INTRODUCTION   xi

REPRESENTATIVE MEN   1

John F. Kennedy   3
Sightings of the Last New Nixon   16
Ernest Hemingway   21
Lindbergh: The Heroic Curiosity   24
Who Is Buried in Grant's Tomb?   29
The Bishop of Our Possibilities   32

ADVERTISEMENTS FOR ONESELF   35

Advertisements for Oneself   37
The Shoes of Imelda Marcos   40
Scribble, Scribble, Eh, Mr. Toad?   43
The Island of the Lost Autocrats   46
Changing the Gestures of Passion   49
Invasion of the Body Snatchers   52
Why and When and Whether to Confess   55
Last Words   60
Daydreams of What You'd Rather Be   63
In Praise of Older Women   66

Waiting 70
At the Sound of the Beep 73
Ranting 76
Exaggeration 79
The Morals of Gossip 82
Snobs 85
If Slang Is Not a Sin 90

AMERICAN DREAMS 95

The Shuttle 97
Reimagining America 99
Dreaming of the Eisenhower Years 103
Excellence 108
The Return of Patriotism 111
An Elegy for the New Left 114
Is the Going Still Good? 117
Are Children Necessary? 121
What Is the Point of Working? 126
Downsizing an American Dream 131
Vietnam Comes Home 137

THE WAY OF THE WORLD 147

The Dance of Negotiation 149
The Falklands 154
The Dynamics of Revolution 157
Israel's Moral Nightmare 161

THE HALL OF MIRRORS 165

The Decline and Fall of Oratory 167
Public Vanishing 173
The Perils of Celebrity 176
The Politics of the Box Populi 180
The Art of Weathercasting 183
Goodbye to "Our Mary" 186
We'll Always Have *Casablanca* 189

METAPHYSICS   193

   God and Science   195
   They're Playing *Ur*-Song   200
   The Temptations of Revenge   204
   The Importance of Being Lucky   207
   A Time for Every Season   212

HARD QUESTIONS   215

   What Does an Oath Mean?   217
   Abortion and the Unfairness of Life   220
   The Powers of Racial Example   224
   Bringing the Vietnam Veterans Home   227
   The Poetic License to Kill   232
   "Forgiveness to the Injured Doth Belong"   235
   Living with the "Peculiar Institution"   238
   The Fascination of Decadence   244
   The Lure of Doomsday   250
   The Lebanese Dance of Death   253
   The Start of a Plague Mentality   256
   Thinking Animal Thoughts   259

THE ANIMALS OF AFRICA   265

   Africa   267

INTRODUCTION

Once, after a day's wandering in Rome, the young Henry James wrote to his brother William in Cambridge, Massachusetts. "I've trod the Forum and I have scaled the Capitol," he reported exultantly. "I've seen the Tiber hurrying along, as swift and dirty as history."

I wrote these essays for *Time* magazine over a period of ten years, from the mid-seventies to the mid-eighties, from the early days of Jimmy Carter to the last days of Ronald Reagan. That stretch of history has often been swift, sometimes murky and squalid. These essays deal with wars and politics, with presidents and dictators: big fish. They fetch up more modest and private things as well—strange moments and customs, old boots and tires. There are also lovely fish in history, and the waters now and then run miraculously clear. They have their graces and redemptions. In any case, not everything that breaks the surface is to be taken seriously.

The essay is supposed to be a meditative form. Sometimes working for a weekly newsmagazine, one is forced to meditate very fast—in a few hours on deadline on a Friday afternoon, before the magazine's weekly closing. I wrote many of these essays in such circumstances. I sometimes even prefer to write that way, a little scared, under the agitation of a deadline. It seems to give some energy to the writing.

Sometimes I have had the luxury of weeks to prepare an essay. For the article on African animals that concludes this collection, I traveled for two months in Kenya, from the Northern Frontier District to the Tanzanian border in the south, under Mount Kilimanjaro. I lived for nearly two weeks with some tribesmen of the Loita Masai, herding cattle with them in the hills during the day and at night prudently sleeping inside their *boma*—the tall fence of thorn and cedar that the Masai build to keep out lions.

I love the essay form, which I find almost endlessly flexible. It can achieve intimacies, a transparency much harder to accomplish, I think, in a conventional newspaper or magazine column. A columnist is somehow enacting his personality, a public version of himself, and that seems to me to reduce the range of his instrument. Anyway, I have almost never used the first-person singular pronoun in these essays (it appears only in the African piece).

All of us who write for *Time* are forced to discipline ourselves to be concise, to work within the confines of the magazine's available space. The piece on the African animals was allowed to run at generous length, but normally one must fit the essay into a page, or two pages, of the magazine. Over the years, I have learned the pace of the form, like a runner who instinctively knows how to run a 220-yard race, as opposed to a 440 or a mile.

One of the pleasures of working for *Time* is the extraordinary intelligence and talent of its editors. I am most grateful to them—above all to Henry Grunwald, Ray Cave, Jason McManus, Edward L. Jamieson, Ronald P. Kriss, and John Elson. In writing most of these essays I have had the help of Anne Hopkins, who has provided not only research but hours of thoughtful conversation as we closed in on a subject. I am most grateful to her as well.

Representative Men

John F. Kennedy

In an essay on Napoleon, Ralph Waldo Emerson wrote, "He was no saint—to use his word, 'no capuchin,' and he is no hero, in the high sense." Napoleon had fulfilled an earthly career, at any rate. His life went the full trajectory. One could study the line of it and know, for better and worse, what the man was, and did, and could do. He inhabited his life. He completed it. He passed through it to the end of its possibilities.

John Kennedy's bright trajectory ended in midpassage, severed in that glaring Friday noontime in Dallas. The moment when one learned the news became precisely fixed in the memory, the mind stopping like a clock just then. It is Kennedy's deathday, not his birthday, that we observe. History abruptly left off, and after the shock had begun to pass, the mythmaking began—the mind haunted by the hypothetical, by what might have been.

And the myth overwhelmed conventional judgment, as if some wonderful song prevented the hall from hearing the recording secretary read the minutes of the last meeting, or the minutes of a thousand days. Today, Kennedy still occupies an unusual place in the national psyche. His presence there in the memory, in the interior temple, remains powerful, disproportionate to his substantive accomplishments. He probably was not president long enough to be judged by the customary standards.

Kennedy had his obvious accomplishments. Merely by arriving at the White House, he had destroyed forever one religious issue in American politics. When Edmund Muskie ran for the Democratic presidential nomination in 1972, his Catholicism was only a minor biographical detail.

Kennedy presided over a change of political generations in America, and did it with brilliant style. He brought youth and idealism and accomplishment and élan and a sometimes boorish and clannish elitism to Washington. He refreshed the town with a conviction that the world could be changed, that the improvisational intelligence could do wonderful things. Such almost ruthless optimism had its sinister side, a moral complacency and dismissive arrogance that expressed itself when the American élan went venturing into Vietnam. But Kennedy, when he died, was also veering away from the cold war. He made an eloquently conciliatory speech at American University in June 1963, and he accomplished the limited test-ban treaty. He had many plans, for Medicare, for civil rights, for other projects.

But after November 22, the record simply went blank. An anguished and fascinating process of canonization ensued. The television networks focused their gaze on the story almost continuously from Parkland Memorial Hospital to Arlington National Cemetery, as if in professional tribute to the first President who understood the medium and performed perfectly in it. In sanctifying his memory, videotape became Kennedy's Parson Weems. The reality of what the nation had lost was preserved with unprecedented, unthinkable vividness: his holographic ghost moving and talking inside every television set, that American dreamboat campaigning through the primaries among leaping and squealing adolescent girls, the snow-dazzled inaugural ceremony, the wonderfully witty press conferences replayed endlessly, the children, the family, the one brief shining moment shown shining again and again in counterpoint with the Book Depository and the shots, and riderless Black Jack fighting the bridle, and the widow, the little boy saluting, and the long mahogany box in the Rotunda—the protagonist and the irretrievable mystery of the piece. The death of John F. Kennedy became a participatory American tragedy, a drama both global and intensely intimate.

The event eerily fused, for a moment, the normally dissociated dimensions of public life and private life. And so Americans felt Kennedy's death in a deeply personal way: they, and he, were swept into a third dimension, the mythic. The ancient Greeks thought that gods and goddesses came down and walked among them and befriended them or betrayed them. The drama—bright young life and light and grace and death all compounded by the bardic camera—turned Kennedy into a kind of American god.

In any case, for a long time, some thought forever, it seemed almost impossible to look objectively at the man and his presidency, to see what he had done and left undone. Not long after the assassination, Gerald W. Johnson wrote, "Already it has happened to two of the thirty-five men who have held the presidency, rendering them incapable of analysis by the instruments of scholarship; and now Washington, the godlike, and Lincoln, the saintly, have been joined by Kennedy, the young chevalier."

Ronald Reagan has been in the office almost as long as Kennedy. It is fascinating, though complicated, that the youngest elected President, who occupied the White House for the shortest (elected) term since Warren Harding—and who had a problematic tenure, very much a learning process and a mixed bag of one fiasco and many missteps and some accomplishments—should be thus elevated, by the force of his presence, his vivid charm, to the company of the greatest Presidents, as if the inspirational power of personality were enough for greatness. Perhaps it is. Many Americans make the association. Yet what sways them is in some sense the strange coercive power of the martyr, Kennedy's great vitality turned inside out. He came to have a higher reputation in death than he enjoyed in life. And in a bizarre way he even accomplished more in death than in life. In the atmosphere of grief and remorse after the assassination, Lyndon Johnson pushed through Congress much of Kennedy's program, and more: Medicare, civil rights, and the other bills that came to form Johnson's Great Society.

Three million visitors still come to his grave at Arlington every year. Although fewer photographs of Kennedy are enshrined in bars and barbershops and living rooms around the United States than there once were, they can still be found in huts all over the Third World: an image of an American president, dead for over twenty years, a symbol—but of what exactly? Mostly of a kind of hope, the possibility of change, and the usually unthinkable idea that government might intercede to do people some good.

Is it possible now to detach Kennedy's presidency from the magic and to judge it with the cold rationality that Kennedy tried to bring to bear upon his world? Or is the myth, the sense of hope and the lift he gave thereby, a central accomplishment of his presidency? W. B. Yeats wrote, "How can we know the dancer from the dance?"

Kennedy would have found the solemnity and mythmaking amusing, and hopelessly overdone. His intellectual style was sardonic and self-aware: wonderful lights of satire played across it. If he sometimes labored hard at being a hero, or *seeming* a hero (before his election in 1960, he listened intently to recordings of Winston Churchill's speeches, picking up the grand rhythms of the language), he knew the limitations of everything, including himself. His instruments were sensitive to the bogus. He might even have had some mordant crack to make about that Eternal Flame.

As the years have passed, Kennedy has been inevitably caught up in the pattern of idolatry and revisionism. All presidential reputations ride up or down upon wind currents of intellectual fashion and subsequent history, the perspective of the present constantly altering interpretations of the past.

First the murdered president became saint and martyr. But then the sixties arrived in earnest. In a study of tragedy, George Steiner wrote, "The fall of great personages from high places *(casus virorum illustrium)* gave to medieval politics their festive and brutal character." The real sixties began on the afternoon of November 22, 1963, and they turned festive and brutal too. It came to seem that Kennedy's murder opened some malign trap door in American culture, and the wild bats flapped out. His assassination became the prototype in a series of public murders: Malcolm X, Martin Luther King, Jr., Robert Kennedy. His death prefigured all the deaths of the young in Vietnam.

The sixties eventually turned on Kennedy. The protests and violent changes of the time jarred loose and shattered fundamental premises of American life and power. From the perspective of Vietnam in the late sixties, some of Kennedy's rhetoric sounded incautious, jingoistic, and dangerous. The Arthurian knight talked about building bomb shelters. The extravagance of all that the hagiologists claimed for him now seemed to make him a fraud. His performance on civil rights came to seem tepid and reluctant and excessively political. Stories about his vigorous sex life, including an alleged affair with the girlfriend of a Mafia don, brought into question not only his private morals but his common sense. At last, the revisionists wondered whether his presidency belonged more to the history of publicity than to the history of political leadership.

Presidential reputations are always fluid. Dwight Eisenhower, for example, was regarded during the sixties as a somewhat vague golfer with a tendency to blunder into sand traps when attempting a complicated English sentence. Now he is enjoying a rehabilitation. His watch was essentially peaceful and prudent, his revisionists say.

• • •

At the end of his terms, though, Ike seemed archaic and gray. The virile young man in top hat who rode with him down Pennsylvania Avenue in 1961 had promised to "get the country moving again." That bright Inauguration Day, Kennedy brought Robert Frost to read a special poem for the occasion. The glare of sun on new-fallen snow blinded the aged poet, and so he recited another poem from memory. The poem he did not read that day contained these lines for the Kennedy era:

> It makes the prophet in us all presage
> The glory of a next Augustan age
> Of a power leading from its strength and pride,
> Of young ambition eager to be tried,
> Firm in our free beliefs without dismay,
> In any game the nations want to play.
> A golden age of poetry and power
> Of which this noonday's the beginning hour.

Frost had caught just the spirit of the venture, with a confidence about the uses of power and ambition that now seems amazing. Kennedy took office with extraordinary energy and the highest hopes. He seemed in some ways the perfect American. As the historian Doris Kearns Goodwin points out, he embodied two contradictory strains in American tradition. One is the immigrant experience, the old American story of the luckless or disfavored or dispossessed who came from Europe and struggled in the New World. Rooted in that experience is the glorification of the common man and the desire for a common-man presidency, a celebration of the ordinary. The other strain is the American longing for an aristocracy, the buried dynastic, monarchical urge. "Jack is the first Irish Brahmin," said Paul Dever, a former Massachusetts governor. He had both Harvard and Honey Fitz in him. He was an intellectual who could devastate any woman in the room and devour *Melbourne* in a speed-reader's blitz and curse like the sailor that he also was.

Kennedy's critics sometimes wondered whether he was animated by a larger, substantive vision of what he would like America to become, or simply by a substantive vision of what he wanted Jack Kennedy to become. His rhetoric was full of verbs of motion and change, but his idea of what America ought to be—other than wanting it to be an excellent place in all ways, not a bad vision to entertain—was often murky, crisscrossed by his own ambivalent impulses. When Kennedy came to the

White House, his main previous administrative experience was running a PT boat. He had a great deal to learn.

One New Frontiersman who became a minor patron saint of the Kennedy revisionists was Chester Bowles, the career diplomat. He thought that he had located a central problem with the Kennedy Administration. He feared that it deliberately, almost scornfully, detached pragmatic considerations from a larger moral context. To discuss the morality of actions was evidence of softness, and intellectuals with power in their hands cannot bear to be thought soft. Everyone carried the Munich model around in his head. One talked in laconic codes, a masculine shorthand; one did not, like Adlai Stevenson, deliver fluty soliloquies about the morality of an act. After the Bay of Pigs, Bowles wrote: "The Cuban fiasco demonstrates how far astray a man as brilliant and well-intentioned as President Kennedy can go who lacks a basic moral reference point."

Kennedy's inaugural address bristled with a certain amount of cold war rhetoric, tricked up in reversible-raincoat prose ("Let us never negotiate out of fear. But let us never fear to negotiate"). To a nation reading it from the far side of the Vietnam War, the most alarming passage was the one in which Kennedy promised to "pay any price . . . to assure the survival . . . of liberty." The revisionists have always seen that line as a précis of the mentality that brought on the war. But both Arthur M. Schlesinger, Jr., and Theodore Sorensen reject the notion that the inaugural speech was a prelude to cowboy interventionism. "It was," says Schlesinger, "in part an overreaction to a speech two weeks earlier by Khrushchev that was read in Washington as being very truculent." Sorensen, who drafted the text, insists, "the speech isn't as bellicose as the revisionists have made it. It was really a call to negotiation. But he knew you didn't get there with just appeals to the other side's good will."

One of the central dramas of the brief Kennedy Administration was his passage from a sometimes indiscriminate anti-Communist hard line to a deepening awareness of the real dangers of nuclear war. It did not help Kennedy in this passage that he assembled a staff of war-hawk anti-Communist intellectuals (McGeorge Bundy, Walt Rostow, and Robert McNamara, for example) who were brilliantly nimble and self-confident and often disastrously wrong about what counted most. They could be overbearing men, and curiously disconnected from the realities of American life. Once, after Vice President Johnson talked wonderingly of all the brilliant characters Kennedy had brought into the White House, House Speaker Sam Rayburn remarked to him, "Well, Lyndon, they may be just as intelligent as you say. But I'd feel a helluva lot better if just one of them had ever run for sheriff.''

Kennedy's team of White House men, according to historian Joan Hoff-Wilson, began the pattern in which Congress and the federal bureaucracies became adversaries of the White House rather than partners. ''That kind of privatization and centralization of power in and around the White House clearly begins with Kennedy,'' says Hoff-Wilson. For men who put such a premium on brains and information, the elite around Kennedy sometimes seemed either exceptionally naive (about the Bay of Pigs, for example) or ignorant (about Vietnamese history and culture). Some of the same men stayed on with Johnson, and presided over the escalation of what became in some ways the nation's hardest war.

The Bay of Pigs fiasco, however, came early. Kennedy had inherited the plan from the Eisenhower Administration which, according to Arkansas Senator J. William Fulbright, had already sunk forty million dollars into the training of a band of Cuban exiles who were supposed to sweep ashore in Cuba, join forces with the grateful, disenchanted islanders, and dislodge Fidel Castro. Kennedy was skeptical of the idea, but allowed himself to be talked into it by men who seemed so sure of what they were doing. The mission, of course, was an utter disaster, and it taught Kennedy several important lessons. One was that truculently self-confident experts, such as generals and CIA men, can be ludicrously wrong. After the Bay of Pigs, Kennedy came to mistrust military solutions.

The botched invasion also revealed an attractive trait in Kennedy: an openness and candor, and a freedom from that neurotic, squirming evasiveness, the deflected gaze or outright mendacity, that one came to expect from one or two subsequent occupants of the White House. Kennedy made no effort to escape blame for the folly, to cover it up or excuse it. We made a terrible mistake, he said. Let's go on from here.

As an administrator, Kennedy was intense, but also casual about the forms—improvisational, never rigid. Eisenhower favored a formal chain of command, with orderly, predictable structures. Kennedy's mind was extremely orderly, but his techniques in office were sometimes heterodox and unexpected. They might have struck an outsider as being somewhat chaotic. He constantly bypassed the chain of command. He telephoned assistant secretaries or lesser military officers in order to seek information he needed. His press secretary, Pierre Salinger, once remarked that the back door of the White House always seemed more open than the front door. He understood the dynamics of meetings, and sometimes mistrusted them as a way of doing business. He thought that his presence might intimidate people. He liked to get information orally, in small groups or one-to-one, or else in memos from those people he trusted and admired—his brother Bobby and Arthur M. Schlesinger, Jr., for example, or John Kenneth Galbraith, whose elegantly intelligent reports he always enjoyed reading. Kennedy detested long, tiresome memos from the bureaucracy. He complained that the functionaries at the State Department were incapable of getting to the point, to the essence, in their reports.

He did not keep rigid office hours. If he wanted to take a little more time in the morning to play with Caroline in the family quarters of the White House, he did so. He had a sort of seigneurial ease about the day's routines. When he went for a swim, when he had people to dinner, when he went away for weekends at Hyannis Port, the world he thought about and tried to control was always there with him. It also kept him up late on many nights.

Kennedy's tenure was littered with messy crises—in Laos, Cuba, the Congo, Latin America, Algeria, Vietnam, and Berlin—and his record in dealing with them is decidedly uneven. Revisionists like to say that Kennedy was a cold warrior who sought confrontation, but in the early sixties, the Soviets busied themselves around the world in ways that no American President could ignore.

Too quickly after the Bay of Pigs, Kennedy went to Vienna for a summit with Nikita Khrushchev who, judging Kennedy to be callow and inexperienced, ranted and bullied. Khrushchev followed the meeting by building the Berlin Wall and then, within a month, interrupting the informal moratorium on nuclear testing in the atmosphere.

Kennedy's strategy in world affairs was a mixture of gestures. The founder of the Alliance for Progress and the Peace Corps, those aggressively idealistic enterprises, could be by turns imperial, bold and assertive, and restrained. He learned eventually to define American interests and hold firmly to the line he had drawn, as he did in the Berlin crisis and, most notably, in the Cuban missile crisis. The Bay of Pigs had taught him caution and the exploration of options.

The missile crisis, more than any other single event of his presidency, demonstrated the way in which Kennedy matured in the office, the way in which he could master complexities of process, could orchestrate alternatives. He had learned to wait and to question. The Bay of Pigs had instructed him to rely more on his own internal deliberations and less on the hormonal instincts of his military and intelligence advisers. During those thirteen days in October 1962, the world held its breath; it waited in a real sweat of nuclear panic. Never, before or since, has global annihilation seemed a more intimate possibility. Kennedy rejected the idea of direct strikes against the offensive missile sites that the Soviets were installing in Cuba. Working in the extraordinary partnership that he had developed with his brother Bobby, the president imposed a naval quarantine on Cuba and allowed Khrushchev time to consider. When the Soviets sent two somewhat contradictory replies to his ultimatum, one hard and one more accommodating, Kennedy simply ignored the hard message and replied to the softer one. It worked. Khrushchev blinked, and in the memorable denouement, the Soviet ships turned and steamed away from Cuba. Harvard political scientist Richard Neustadt stated, "The Administration set a new standard of prudence in dealing with the Soviet Union. The standard of prudence, the hard thought given about the crisis as the Soviets would see it, thus giving our opponent as much room as possible—these were a model of presidential conduct."

But there were deep contradictions in Kennedy's foreign policy, conflicts in which an old view of the world and an emerging view competed with each other. Part of him retained the mentality of the cold war, a kind of Dulles-like brinkmanship. At the same time, a succession of crises convinced him that a new course was necessary. At American University he declared, "What kind of peace do we seek? Not a *Pax Americana* enforced on the world by American weapons of war. Not the peace of the grave or the security of the slave . . . not merely peace for Americans but peace for all men and women—not merely peace in our time. . . . Let us re-examine our attitude toward the cold war, remembering that we are not engaged in a debate. . . . We must deal with the world as it is." It was the American University speech that began the long process of détente between the United States and the Soviet Union. Ironically, the man who brought Kennedy's policy to its fullest bloom was Richard Nixon.

And yet Kennedy would ask for nearly one thousand new ICBMs for the American nuclear arsenal, which eventually triggered what has become the greatest arms race in history. He acquiesced in the overthrow of the Diem government in South Vietnam in 1963. And he ordered sixteen thousand American troops into that country.

Would Kennedy have become involved in Vietnam to the extent that Johnson eventually did? The answer is unknowable. Many Kennedy loyalists think not, though their opinion is not disinterested. They point out that Kennedy was eminently a pragmatist; he would have seen the morass that lay in wait. Kennedy was a superbly self-assured man. He had already proved himself in war and had no need to do so again. With his keen sense of public relations, his loyalists believe, with his knowledge of the uses of the media, he would simply have decided that Vietnam was not worth the dreadful publicity, which is not a very principled notion to put hypothetically into Kennedy's mind, but still a plausible one.

At home, as abroad, Kennedy's performance was mixed. He was a fiscal conservative. The economy was robust during his thousand days. Economic growth averaged 5.6 percent annually. Unemployment came down by almost two percentage points from the nearly 8 percent level when he took office. Inflation held at a prelapsarian 1.2 percent.

The central problem was confrontation between blacks and whites. Kennedy's approach to civil rights at the beginning of his term was slow and inattentive. Arthur Schlesinger writes in the *New Republic:* "If anyone had asked Kennedy in 1960 how he really felt about civil rights, he might have answered something like this: 'Yes, of course, we must achieve racial justice in this country, and we will; but it is an explosive question, so let us go about it prudently.' " Like most other white politicians, he underestimated the moral passion behind the movement. The protests of the Freedom Riders on the eve of his departure for the 1961 meeting with Khrushchev irritated him.

He appointed some Southern judges who proved to be outright racists. But the civil rights movement was becoming an urgent presence in the nation; it demanded Kennedy's attention. He was not a leader on this subject, not for a long time, but was led by events and historical pressures and by figures like Martin Luther King, Jr.

The South was filled with agitation and change. There were riots at the all-white University of Mississippi when a black man named James Meredith tried to enroll. Two people were killed. Kennedy was forced to call out federal troops to install Meredith in the university. In Birmingham, public safety commissioner Theophilus Eugene "Bull" Connor turned loose police dogs upon a march led by King. The news photographs of that spectacle—the fire hoses and the snapping dogs and the beefy Southern lawmen—outraged Americans and turned the public mood. In the spring of 1963 there were two thousand civil rights demonstrations in more than three hundred cities. Kennedy now faced the civil rights cause directly. "We are confronted primarily with a moral issue," he said. "It is as old as the Scriptures and is as clear as the American Constitution."

Eight days later he sent Congress a civil rights bill that would assure equal access to public accommodations and fight discrimination in schools and jobs and at the polls.

But as in foreign policy, Kennedy's performance was somehow deflected, inconsistent. While pronouncing civil rights to be a moral issue, he acquiesced in an FBI investigation of King. FBI Director J. Edgar Hoover, for decades the lord of his own almost independent principality within the American government, said that King was associating with Communists. Kennedy and his brother Bobby, then Attorney General, allowed the wiretaps of King to clear King's name and thus disarm Hoover, to see for themselves whether Hoover's suspicions were correct, or both. They did not, however, authorize the bugging that amounted to a much broader invasion of King's privacy.

Kennedy died before his civil rights bill could become law. His relations with Congress were not good, one of his failures as a leader. His program also suffered because he lacked a working majority on the Hill. Eventually President Johnson, that consummate creature of the Congress, obtained a comfortably functional Democratic majority in 1964. Johnson pushed through the Civil Rights Act of 1964 and the 1965 Voting Rights Act. His Great Society went well beyond what Kennedy envisioned. "He's done," wrote Walter Lippmann in April 1964, "what President Kennedy could not have done had he lived."

Kennedy all along had calculated that his first term would be a period of developing programs, for sowing seeds that a second term would allow him to bring to fruition. He might have run a modified version of the Great Society much more successfully than Johnson did, without the middle-class entitlements and the immense and inflationary burden upon the economy.

It is sometimes difficult to know whether Kennedy was a visionary or simply a rhetorician. He did have a high sense of adventure, which he combined with patriotism in the launching of his plan to put a man on the moon and thereby repay the Soviets for the technological humiliations of Sputnik. He did imagine a better America, a fairer place, a more excellent place. He even believed that it was part of his task as president to lift American culture. He and his wife, Jacqueline, brought Pablo Casals and Igor Stravinsky and Bach and Mozart to the White House. His own taste may have run more toward Sinatra or Broadway musicals, but Kennedy believed that it was his duty to endorse the excellent in all things, to be a leader in matters of civilization. That was a novel notion in American politics, novel at least since the days of Thomas Jefferson.

A judgment on Kennedy's presidential performance inevitably ends in a perplexity of conditional clauses. If he had lived and been elected to a second term, Kennedy would have become, at age fifty or so, a world leader, with unprecedented moral authority. Perhaps. One of Kennedy's strongest qualities was his capacity to learn from experience, to grow. His first six months in office were nearly a disaster. But by 1963 he was far maturer, riper, smarter, still passionate, but seasoned. It is interesting to wonder what his second inaugural address would have sounded like. It would almost surely not have reverberated with the grandiloquent bluster that one heard in the first.

It is possible, in any case, that the manner of Kennedy's leaving the office, his assassination, much more profoundly affected the course of America than anything he did while he was in the White House. There was a kind of dual effect: his death enacted his legislative program and at the same time seemed to let loose monsters, to unhinge the nation in some deep way that sent it reeling down a road toward riots and war and assassinations and Watergate.

One Kennedy revisionist, Garry Wills, argues that the extraordinary glamour and heightened expectations that Kennedy brought to the office have crippled all of his successors. They cannot compete with such a powerful myth. It is equally possible, of course, that Kennedy's successors simply do not measure up. Kennedy's was a mind with all of its windows open and a clear light passing through it. That has not been true of anyone who has sat in the place since.

Robert K. Murray of Pennsylvania State University has surveyed one thousand Ph.D. historians as part of a study on how such authorities assess American presidents. The thousand rated Kennedy thirteenth in the middle of the ''above average'' category. Those considered great: Abraham Lincoln, Franklin Roosevelt, George Washington, Thomas Jefferson. Near great: Theodore Roosevelt, Woodrow Wilson, Andrew Jackson, Harry Truman. Above average: John Adams, Lyndon Johnson, James K. Polk, John Kennedy, James Madison, James Monroe, John Quincy Adams, Grover Cleveland.

Kennedy was in the White House so short a time that he almost cannot be judged against other presidents. The first twelve or eighteen months of any presidency are a learning period during which the man in the Oval Office must get his bearings and put his Administration in place for the work he hopes to accomplish. That would not have given Kennedy— elected in a squeaker, with no clear mandate and no working majority in Congress—much time to prove himself.

American political moods run in cycles. Periods of activity and reform, of idealism and change, alternate with more quiescent, complacent, even cynical times. Schlesinger believes that the activist cycle comes around every thirty years or so. Thus the era of Teddy Roosevelt at the turn of the century, then the New Deal beginning in 1933, then Kennedy in 1961. By Schlesinger's hopeful calculation, the United States will be ripe for another time of idealism and political innovation toward the end of this decade.

The wave of negative revisionism about Kennedy may now be receding. But the myth of John Kennedy will undoubtedly outlive the substance of what he achieved. History will remember not so much what he did as what he was, a memory kept in some vault of the national imagination. In the end, the American appreciation of Kennedy may come to be not political but aesthetic, and vaguely religious.

Sightings of
the Last New Nixon

*We'll survive. Despite all the polls and all the rest, I think there's still a
hell of a lot of people out there—and you know, they want to believe . . .*
                                    —Nixon to Haldeman, April 25, 1973

It was not a re-emergence to compare with Napoleon's journey out of
Elban exile to try to regain France. Nor was it precisely the great soap
opera of redemption that occurred in the mid-fifties when the American
people decided that Ingrid Bergman, disgraced adulteress, might be restored to favor. But somewhere in the historic procession from the majestic to the trivial, one might plausibly place Richard Nixon's trip to
Hyden, Kentucky, over the Fourth of July weekend in 1978.

For the first time since he said good-bye to the White House staff and
flew away to his self-imposed house arrest in San Clemente, Nixon came
to speak at a fully public occasion. He had rejected one hundred thousand
invitations. He chose Hyden carefully: a remote eastern Kentucky coal-
mining town of five hundred, Republican since the Civil War, where the
virtue of loyalty has been toughened into a kind of clannish defiance.
Nixon rightly sensed that there he would find, unregenerate, some of the
believers he described to H. R. Haldeman in the spring of 1973 when his
Administration was in the first stages of its slow-motion collapse. "All
Nixon did was stand by his friends," said the local motel owner in Hyden. "And that is one of the traits of us mountain people."

Hyden and the rest of Leslie County had reason to think well of Richard
Nixon. His revenue-sharing program had, among other things, helped to
build a new $2.5 million recreation center (gymnasium, swimming pool,
community center, and tennis courts). Gerald Ford was invited to dedicate
the center but his schedule was full. To Hyden's surprise, Nixon accepted.
Flying into a tiny nearby airport in an executive jet, Nixon may have

imagined himself in a time warp, transported back ten years to an old campaign. He found a crowd of 1,000; some of them had waited for three hours in ninety-degree heat. They wore Nixon campaign buttons; some lugged his 1,120-page memoirs, the size of a small steamer trunk, hoping to get an autograph from the last president they truly and fully liked. "He should get around the country more and speak out," a local Republican committeewoman said with wistful truculence. "Other Presidents have done as bad as he ever did." But a friend of hers was not so sure. "He wouldn't ever want to run for public office again," she said. "He should just lead a quiet life from now on." Four satin-shirted high school musicians played "Hail to the Chief." Nixon plunged into the crowd, pressing flesh, absorbing adulation like a man breaking a long fast.

As a limousine swept him into Hyden, a dusty, red-brick collection of small shops, two pool halls, a drive-in movie, and a motel, Nixon read banners that said THANKS FOR REVENUE SHARING, NIXON IS THE ONE, and NOW MORE THAN EVER. After a night in the motel, Nixon rode to the dedication where he sat drenched in sweat in a non-air-conditioned auditorium packed with forty-five hundred people in ninety-five-degree heat. A stream of east Kentucky dignitaries took their bows. Then Nixon, who looked wilted and dazed in those ceremonies, rallied for a forty-minute speech notable for its force and its predictability (the United States needs a strong military and intelligence capability, a strong economy, the will to fight "against aggressors who go under borders rather than over borders"). At last, in a tumult of approval, he invoked the "real America— a spirit you'll find in great cities and small towns, in factories and mines. I know that spirit is strong in the heartland of America, Leslie County, Kentucky."

The Kentucky venture was Richard Nixon's tentative and gingerly staged re-emergence, certainly not into public life but at least, for brief moments, into the viewfinders of public attention. In 1977 he sat for the David Frost television interviews. He went to Hubert Humphrey's funeral. He and Pat flew to New York and the Bahamas, making small banter with photographers at stops along the way. They threw a party back at Casa Pacifica for some three hundred returned Vietnam POWs. Nixon also gave a party to celebrate the publication of his memoirs.

Disraeli once called Gladstone's ministers "a range of exhausted volcanoes." Watergate and its players have seemed similarly defunct: the political passions of the scandals expired, parole boards and literary agents tidying up like janitors, attending to the last details. Then Nixon reappears, one of the strangest, loneliest, most complicated, and interesting political figures in American history. This discreet apparition just dancing on the margins of publicity raises some fascinating questions.

Will Nixon, who has been pronounced politically dead so many times before, be able to rehabilitate himself in the American imagination? Is there sufficient rightward veer in American politics these days to coax along a bit of revisionism about Watergate? If Nixon has by now exhausted the role of American villain, the political Grendel who tape-recorded himself snarling under the bridge, then what role might he still play, if any? An eventual party emeritus perhaps, grudgingly respected and sought out for his savvy in foreign policy?

Politicians of both parties agree that Nixon could never run for public office again. One California Republican who was asked about Nixon's future grimaced: "Bringing him up again is like poking a dying frog to see if you can get one last jump out of him." But the man undoubtedly still arouses extremes of feeling. Distaste, contempt, and even hatred rise almost reflexively in many Americans at the sound of his voice. The late Stewart Alsop, attempting to explain this automatic reaction to Nixon, once told the story of an argument he had about Franklin Roosevelt. Young Alsop had his collegiate defenses of F.D.R. demolished by a rectilinear old Republican who declared: "A man who does not dislike and distrust Franklin Roosevelt by instinct, without asking for reasons, is no gentleman." Plenty of Americans feel that way about Nixon: it is an allergy, a gag reflex.

Furthermore, a devastating disillusion cost Nixon whole brigades of his most loyal supporters, after the tapes revealed that he had lied in his frantic exertions at self-defense and survival. One aide told him bitterly, according to Theodore H. White, "Those who served you best hate you most." Yet there remains in the United States a vague, perhaps unmeasurable feeling that after all, Watergate was not all that bad, that its results were out of all proportion to the wrongs that were done. It is conceivable, goes the reasoning, that he was only defending friends in the White House who had done stupid things, gone too far in their zeal. Or perhaps his only mistake was in getting caught.

The Lasky Syndrome enters here: in his book called *It Didn't Start with Watergate,* the muckraking conservative journalist Victor Lasky detailed prior presidential offenses—what he says were Franklin Roosevelt's uses of FBI to dig up scandal on his enemies and to tap the home phones of his top advisers, the spectacular array of extramarital affairs that Jack

Kennedy paraded through Camelot, the Kennedy wiretaps on Martin Luther King, Jr., and so on. Why was only Nixon driven from office for his offenses when he had such precedents for misbehavior? The three articles of impeachment adopted by the House Judiciary Committee were specific and damning. It takes a kind of ethical myopia not to understand that the accumulated offenses of Watergate *were* different. But in many Americans' minds, the scandal recedes with the years into a small, dark tangle of legalities, a smudge of vengeful newspaper ink.

When Dick Nixon was starting out in California in the forties some Republicans liked to say to one another: "He's our kind of guy." Despite Watergate, despite the acknowledged unlovability of Nixon, he still seems to many Americans "our kind of guy" in rudely definable contrast to "their" kind of guy. It is partly a cultural division—the difference between a sort of Nixon Class (some businessmen, blue-collar workers, large portions of Middle America) and the New Class made up of people who deal in symbols and information, not things: people from universities, government welfare agencies, publishing houses, the communications industry, consumer groups, environmental causes. All kinds of litmus tests can be applied to identify the New Class: What do you think of abortion? Of capital punishment? Do you drive a Volvo? (The distinction is hardly complete or infallible; plenty of businessmen and blue-collar workers detest Nixon.) Some have argued that Watergate was the effort (a successful one) by the New Class to repeal the results of the 1972 election. Well, crime is crime: Congress and the courts, not the New Class, brought Nixon down. But the argument has a metaphorical, symbolic appeal to those who feel Nixon was destroyed for who and what he was, not what he did.

The Democrat now sitting in the White House (in 1978) and suffering his own troubles in the polls is also altering the perspective with which Americans view Watergate. Nixon's foreign policy accomplishments—China, SALT, the Middle East, and the rest—look pretty good against the developing Democratic record. The chiller international weather involving Russia makes many nostalgic for Henry Kissinger. Walter Lippmann wrote several years ago: "Nixon's role in American history has been that of a man who had to liquidate, defuse, deflate the exaggeration of the romantic period of American imperialism and American inflation: inflation of promises, inflation of hopes . . . I think on the whole he has done pretty well at it."

After all sifting of reasons, however, it is difficult for Americans to know what to do emotionally with Richard Nixon. A compassionate and even sentimental people with a kind of friendly compulsion to forgive, they would be disposed to accept Nixon, to leave the past for historians to sort out. But some token of repentance seems to be an informal condition for that. Nixon, in his soft avowal during the David Frost interviews that "I let the American people down" and some gentle self-accusations in his memoirs, appears to have traveled as far as he psychologically can toward contrition. It is possible that he will never forgive either the enemies who brought him low or himself (those given to psychohistory would argue that they amount to the same thing). Perhaps Nixon will grow old in America as a kind of strange, unregenerate presence viewed with indifference, curiosity, or eventually the respect that is accorded, with a short laugh and an incredulous shake of the head, to the unrepentant survivor.

Ernest Hemingway

In 1928 Ernest Hemingway's mother mailed him a chocolate cake. Along with it she sent the .32-caliber Smith & Wesson revolver with which Hemingway's father had just killed himself. Hemingway dropped the pistol into a deep lake in Wyoming "and saw it go down making bubbles until it was just as big as a watch charm in that clear water, and then it was out of sight."

The story is minutely savage in its details and haunting in its outcome: perfect Hemingway. And of course, there is the water. Doctoral theses have been fished from all the waters and fluids in Hemingway—lake water and trout stream and Gulf Stream and the rain after Caporetto and the endless washes of alcohol refracting in his brain. His style was a stream with the stones of nouns in it and a surface of prepositional ripples. Ford Madox Ford wrote that a Hemingway page "has the effect of a brook-bottom into which you look down through the flowing water. The words form a tesselation, each in order beside the other."

It is easier to see to the bottom of the brook than to the dark cold place in the psyche where that pistol came to rest. Ernest Hemingway's books are easier to know, and love, than his life. He wrote, at his early best, a prose of powerful and brilliant simplicity. But his character was not simple. In one of his stories he wrote: "The most complicated subject that I know, since I am a man, is a man's life." The most complicated subject that he knew was Ernest Hemingway.

He was a violently cross-grained man. He was a splendid writer who became his own worst creation, a hoax and a bore. He ended by being one of the most famous men in the world, white-bearded Mr. Papa. He stopped observing and started performing. He sentimentalized and pontificated and lied and bullied.

Still, a long mythic fiesta between two explosions may not be a bad way to have a life. The first explosion came in Fossalta di Piave in northeastern Italy at midnight on July 8, 1918. A shell from an Austrian trench mortar punctured Hemingway with 200-odd pieces of shrapnel. The wounds validated his manhood, which they had very nearly destroyed. The second explosion came twenty-five years later. Early one morning in Ketchum, Idaho, Hemingway (suffering from diabetes, nephritis, alcoholism, severe depression, hepatitis, hypertension, impotence, and paranoid delusions, his memory all but ruined by electroshock treatments) slid two shells into his double-barreled Boss shotgun. *Mens morbida in corpore morbido.* There was a gruesome ecology in the fact that the last creature Hemingway brought down was himself.

Hemingway was mourned mostly as a great celebrity, his worst side, and not as a great writer, which he was. The *Louisville Courier-Journal* wrote in an editorial: "It is almost as though the Twentieth Century itself has come to a sudden, violent, and premature end." He was a genius of self-proclamation. He made himself a representative hero. The adjectives he used did not so much describe as evaluate and tell the reader how to react: things were fine and good and true or lovely or wonderful, or else bad, in varying degrees. As the scholar Harry Levin has suggested, Hemingway sent postcards back home: "Having a wonderful time, wish you were here." He worked hard at his writing, and yet the interval between Fossalta and Ketchum was also a kind of permanent vacation: Paris, Pamplona, Africa, Key West, Havana, Wyoming. Readers chained to their jobs and mortgages and hometowns and responsibilities could pick up Hemingway and taste the wine and see the fish jump, and become Hemingway for a little while.

For a time during the late sixties and early seventies, when the air in America was full of rage and Vietnam, Hemingway came to seem an atavistic character who loved the wrong things: violence and war. But Hemingway's reputation as a writer has survived, and grown. Public interest in the man and his work persists in an age that might be expected to forget the long-vanished ghost of the grandfather of Margaux and Mariel Hemingway. His publisher, Charles Scribner's Sons, estimates that one million Hemingway books are sold each year in the United States alone. A biography by Jeffrey Meyers has been published as well as a memoir by his son Jack Hemingway. Jack and some other relatives have formed Hemingway Limited, which will market the family name for use on such items as fishing rods and safari clothes. Jack has also lent Papa's name, grotesquely, to a line of shotguns.

The Garden of Eden, published in the spring of 1986, is an odd, interesting ingredient in the Hemingway psychomyth. Hemingway began the novel in early 1946, but it ran away from him, swelling to hundreds of thousands of words. He tried over the years to cut it down and make it manageable, but it was still a mess when he died. An editor at Scribner's pruned the manuscript to a tight and coherent sixty-five thousand words.

Perhaps Hemingway had trouble with the prospect of publishing the fantasies he was entertaining. His hero, David Bourne, is a young writer whose wife cuts her hair as short as a man's and dyes it ash-white, and persuades him to exchange sex roles in a way whose mechanics are not explained. The man is to be the woman and the woman is to act the man. In bed, they do "devil things," also unexplained, and the wife brings a lesbian lover into their ménage.

Into the age of Rambo comes an ambivalent Hemingway that he had more or less suppressed. Perhaps it should not be surprising that a man who spent so much of his life being aggressively masculine might (in mid-life, after going through several marriages and two World Wars) wonder what it would be like to take a vacation from his attack hormones. At the end of *The Garden of Eden,* in any case, the usual Hemingway order is restored: the rich, perverted bitch-wife goes crazy and departs and the girl lover, lately lesbian, turns into one of Papa's adoring, delicious, perfect girls of one dimension.

Hemingway should be spared further Freudian autopsy. He was a masterpiece of contradiction. Every element in him had a blood feud with its opposite. He cherished his friends and he treacherously turned on them (on Sherwood Anderson, Gertrude Stein, Scott Fitzgerald, and many others). He adored women and he hated them. His literary program was to write the brutal truth, and yet he was sometimes a liar and a fraud. He was profoundly creative and profoundly destructive. He had a spontaneous gift of life. He enjoyed (that is the word) a lifelong relationship with death. He resolved all contradictions at last by joining his father and his father's pistol in the amniotic deep.

Lindbergh:
The Heroic Curiosity

The air above the North Atlantic, once so lonely that Charles Lindbergh said he communed with ghosts and guardian spirits, is dense now with 747s, the flying auditoriums that are just beginning their summer trade. Passengers doze over their drinks, eat flash-frozen steaks, watch movies through a passage as passive as Muzak. The New York-to-Paris odyssey that took Lindbergh thirty-three-and-a-half hours would be a three-and-a-half-hour streak for the Concorde.

The phenomenon of Lindbergh, the romantic soloist who dropped out of the darkness at Paris's Le Bourget Airport fifty years ago may be difficult for one now to understand. The minute he completed the first one-man flight across the Atlantic, the twenty-five-year-old aviator, boyish yet reserved, became a hero of the world. He hated to be called "Lucky Lindy"—luck had nothing to do with it, he said, just skill. Yet he had intersected with history at precisely the right moment: technology and public mood conspired to endow Lindbergh with an almost primitive magic.

"Every historical change," wrote anthropologist Bronislaw Malinowski, "creates its mythology." Lindbergh was the mythic hero of early aviation. In 1927 flying shone with the innocence of its newness and possibility, with the untrammeled zest of lifting off from the earth. Aloft, wrote Lindbergh, "I live only in the moment in this strange, unmortal space, crowded with beauty, pierced with danger." He was a sky lover. His was a rare moment: personal confidence and skill in partnership with a machine, not overwhelmed by it, as would happen later.

• • •

"Here is a hero," Nietzsche wrote many years earlier, "who did nothing but shake the tree when the fruit was ripe. But just look at the tree he shook!" The significance of Lindbergh was as complicated as his personality. His exploit, proclaimed precisely because he achieved it alone, served to promote a new age of aviation technology in which men and women would be increasingly absorbed into teams, into bureaucracies. Lindbergh rode the *Spirit of St. Louis* on the updrafts of the future, but in many ways he was one of the last individualists. Even in the twenties, he represented a kind of nostalgia. In an era of Teapot Dome and bathtub gin, he seemed to Americans a cleaner, sharper version of themselves, as bright as a new silver dollar, still inventive and vigorous. If, as Frederick Jackson Turner said, the United States ran out of frontier in 1890, Lindbergh opened a new frontier in the air—the United States arching back in triumph to its European origins.

It is possible that from the beginning, Lindbergh was burdened with more symbolism than he should have been made to carry. His flight, for all its significance, was in some ways merely a handsome stunt. It was also one of the first great media events of the century. Frenchman Raymond Orteig had offered twenty-five thousand dollars for the first nonstop flight between New York and France.* Through the winter and early spring of 1927, the newspapers—then in one of the most aggressively competitive eras of American journalism—had promoted the race among Admiral Richard Byrd, the polar explorer, and others. In April of 1927, Noel Davis and Stanton Wooster were killed during a trial flight. Two other flyers disappeared. Lindbergh was the Midwestern dark horse, caricatured as a Minnesota rube, self-sufficient, spunky as a cowlick. The possibility of another death gave the public a shot of adrenaline: Death versus the Kid.

In many ways, the papers were wrong about Lindbergh from the start. Somehow the myth was always askew; up until his death from cancer on Maui in 1974, Lindbergh remained elusive, difficult. Far from being merely a sort of hayseed genius of mechanics, he was the son of a populist Republican Minnesota congressman and a schoolteacher, whose father, Charles Land of Detroit, was a distinguished dentist who invented porcelain caps for teeth. Lindbergh had lived in Washington, D.C., and studied at the University of Wisconsin until he dropped out midway through his sophomore year to take a course in flying. At twenty-five, he was

---

*In 1919, John Alcock and Arthur Whitten Brown had made the much shorter flight from Newfoundland to Ireland.

tough, intelligent, and probably the best pilot in the United States.

Lindbergh was amazed at becoming a hero. His life changed forever. After the Paris flight, people stole his laundry for souvenirs. When he wrote a check, it would be kept for his signature. Once, after a lunch with some pilot friends, a group of women ran squealing to fight over the wet corncobs he had left on his plate. In 1932 came the kidnapping of the Lindberghs's child. He never forgave the mob of reporters who, he thought, had frightened the kidnapper into killing his son, or the pair of photographers who broke into the Trenton, New Jersey, morgue to photograph the baby's body.

The Lindberghs bitterly departed for England; Lindbergh thought it too painful and dangerous to be a hero in his own country. While abroad, he began a strange flirtation with Nazi Germany. In a series of visits at the invitation of Hermann Göring, he was dined, toasted, decorated with the Service Cross of the German Eagle, and led on carefully planned inspection tours of German aircraft factories. As Göring hoped, Lindbergh came away persuaded that Germany's air superiority was overwhelming.

Early in 1939, Lindbergh returned to the United States, now as a preacher. Intervention in the European war, he said at the time, was being promoted by something like a conspiracy of "the British, the Jewish and the Roosevelt Administration." Relations grew strained with friends and even his in-laws, who favored intervention. His hero's luster dulled. Novelist J. P. Marquand, a friend, explained indulgently, "You've got to remember that all heroes are horses' asses." Lindbergh became the most glamorous evangelist of "America first." Franklin Roosevelt compared him to a "copperhead." Lindbergh resigned from the Army Air Corps Reserve, and after Pearl Harbor, F.D.R. refused to take him back. Instead, Lindbergh became a technical consultant for Ford and later for United Aircraft. By 1944, he finagled his way to the Pacific as a consultant and, though a civilian, managed to fly fifty combat missions. On one of them, he shot down a Japanese plane.

Within a decade after the war, Lindbergh's reputation was rehabilitated. Eisenhower reinstated him in the Air Force Reserve and promoted him to brigadier general. He had become a millionaire through his association with, among others, TWA and Pan Am Airlines. Lindbergh wandered the earth for Pan Am, trying out its planes, advising on air routes. But his spirit had changed. He felt far closer to nature than to machines. He wanted not so much his old exhilarations of flight as peace for the blue whales and the primitive Tasaday of the Philippines.

The nature of space exploration is necessarily profoundly different from that of Lindbergh's solitary flight. It costs billions of dollars, as against the fifteen thousand dollars that Lindbergh spent. Astronauts, however highly trained, are nonetheless essentially cargo as they are flung out of gravity on a rocket's nib. The astronaut, says Sir George Greenfield, a literary agent who has specialized in accounts of explorations, "is more like a bus driver than an adventurer." The Viking spacecraft investigating Mars are made of thinking metal. The only humans aboard the Pioneer 10 spacecraft are the little sketches of a man and a woman that are meant to show extraterrestrial creatures what we look like. Still, says Neil Armstrong, the first man to walk on ground other than that of earth, "we are dealing with the spirit of mankind, searching on into infinity."

There are other frontiers. Exploration of the ocean depths may become a new counterpart of the space program. Scientists are engaged in a fascinating search into the structure of atomic particles. "This is a new world of muons, of quarks, and we shall have to invent a new language to cope with it," says MIT physicist Victor Weisskopf. Others are exploring DNA, the stuff of life itself.

Lindbergh's feat was technologically progressive; its trajectory pointed into the future. Much of today's adventuring is essentially regressive—men employing ever more primitive modes of transportation. Thor Heyerdahl's crew sailed in the papyrus rafts called *Ra I* and *II* to show that ancient Egyptians might have discovered America. His 1947 voyage aboard the *Kon Tiki* was similarly primitive.

In the summer of 1975, William F. Buckley, Jr., made an Atlantic crossing—described in his book *Airborne*—aboard his sixty-foot cutter *Cyrano*. Says Buckley: "All adventure is now reactionary." With loran, radar, autopilot, and vintage wines, Buckley was not exactly blown across the ocean on a naked raft. Even the most venturesome solitary sailors today—men like Sir Francis Chichester, who circumnavigated the globe in 1966–67 in his fifty-three-foot boat *Gipsy Moth IV*—have the advantage of sophisticated hull and sail design. Says Tristan Jones, a small, bearded Welsh sailor who has circumnavigated the globe three times, crossed the Atlantic eighteen times under sail, nine times alone: "The boats I sail wouldn't have existed before now. They are fitted with the best technology of our time, from stainless steel to freeze-dried food."

• • •

Lindbergh began as a boyish barnstormer of the new science of flight. "It took me years to discover," he wrote much later, "that science, with all its brilliance, lights only a middle chapter of creation, a chapter with both ends bordering on the infinite, one which can be forever expanded but never completed." That fusion of mystic and mechanic, so American, was what gave Lindbergh his fascination.

Who Is Buried in Grant's Tomb?

Ulysses Grant sat on the porch and marched armies across his memory. He called them up through cocaine and morphine, through the pain in his throat, and into a perfect clarity of prose. He fought the war minutely all over again: Shiloh and Vicksburg, the slaughters of the Wilderness, Cold Harbor, where men were so sure of death that they pinned their names and addresses on their jackets for easy identification when they fell. And at last, the mythy set piece of Appomattox, where Lee came as the elegant last cavalier, and Grant, a shabby cigar stub of a man, appeared in dusty blues open at the throat, one button in the wrong hole, no sword, to embody the victory of some other American principle.

Grant remembered it all on the porch of a cottage at Mount McGregor in the foothills of the Adirondacks in the summer of 1885, one hundred years ago. He was dying of cancer. As he sat in a silk top hat, reassembling the past, tourists came to stare at him from a little distance. He let them watch, even wanted them to. So many planes of the public and the private intersected in Grant: the obscure American failure who saved the Union. Now, at the last, the shabby embarrassment who was also the first genius of industrial warfare made the intimate business of his dying a sort of public spectacle. Grant harbored complications. If he was of all men the typical American, as his friend William Tecumseh Sherman thought, the incendiary of Atlanta also admitted, "I do not understand him, and I do not believe he understands himself." That was the oddness of Grant. In Hannah Arendt's phrase, Adolf Eichmann represented "the banality of evil." In a way, Grant represented the banality of a momentary greatness. Or perhaps the mysterious possibilities of the ordinary.

In the Mount McGregor drama, terminal and succinct, there was a sleazy commercial dimension that savored of the scandals of his White House years. The owners of the resort at Mount McGregor had actually attracted Grant to come and die in comfort there, a sort of publicity stunt. Grant went along with it. But as he enacted that odd humiliation, he was, in the privacy of his mind and on his lined note pad, composing his memoirs, one of the strongest and purest documents of American public life.

Ulysses Grant eventually receded to become a haunting half-mystery of American life. Down the generations he has stayed cocooned, in memory, in a stoical mediocrity. H. L. Mencken said Grant was the kind of man who would say to someone he encountered, "Meet the wife." He possessed an eerie philistine equilibrium, remarking once that Venice would be a fine city if it were drained. What stuck mostly in memory as the decades passed were the shabby things: the scandals and swindles and, ignominiously, the talk about his drinking. He did drink too much now and then, when he was depressed, and especially when he was away from the stabilizing influence of his wife, Julia, whom he adored.

What puzzles is Grant's sudden greatness, his rising to the occasion, and the brutality of his greatness, what might be called the bloody abstraction of it. It was as if Grant had rescinded some logic of cause and effect. Lincoln's best generals failed: refulgent characters like George McClellan and "Fighting Joe" Hooker, who would not fight. Grant, the failure, succeeded. Down the years, if anyone has bothered to think about Grant, he has had to wonder whether the man was a genius (his native genius hidden till the crucial moment) or a nonentity who blundered into momentary success, who arrived at immortality by accident. Ronald Reagan is a leader of totally different temperament and tailoring, but one sometimes hears the same puzzlement over his luck and political successes. In this comparison of qualifications, acting in Hollywood is the moral equivalent of selling cordwood in St. Louis or clerking in Galena, Illinois, as Grant did before the war.

As his death approached, Grant wrote a note to his physician that contained a subtle and accurate conceit: "The fact is that I think I am a verb instead of a personal pronoun. A verb is anything that signifies to be; to do; or to suffer. I signify all three." What Grant said about his dying was true of his life. It was only as a verb, that is, as a warrior, that he found focus. Grant had an animal sense of moment and motion. Mary Lincoln thought for a time during the siege of Richmond that Grant was a mere "butcher," and most of the North agreed. But he was a far better soldier than that. He could march strategies across a landscape the way a cat can walk across a dressing table laden with perfume bottles, never looking at his hind legs and never spilling a drop. That is too delicate an image. Grant spilled a generation or so of blood. Still, he could move armies the way the cat moves its feet, on true instinct, completely self-possessed.

Perhaps if there is something haunting about Grant's life, it is the way that, having achieved military greatness and two terms in the White House, he lapsed toward failure again. He became a parable of the unreliability of American dreams. The American trajectory was supposed to be always ascendant. Grant swooped down, and up, and down again.

And then, at the last, in greatest torment, he launched himself into eternity by producing a work of enduring literature, a parting labor of memory and language from the man of pure action. Mount McGregor was a kind of archetype of American retrospection: recollection performed as heroic deed. Improbably, Grant became the greatest of the rememberers of a war so morally and dramatically fascinating that Americans have returned to it ever since, generation after generation, as if to a text of inexhaustible meaning.

The Civil War was fought to expunge the American original sin (slavery) and to save the dream and the power. It was all of Homer and Shakespeare come to the New World. It was the American discovery of tragedy, and of modern death, proceeding from the jaunty, clumsy toy soldiering of First Bull Run to Sherman's scorched earth and Grant's trench slaughter, which were a moral preview of the twentieth century.

The Rumanian scholar Mircea Eliade made the distinction between a people's "profane time" and its "sacred time." In sacred time, he thought, deeds done in historical time partake of the permanence of myth. In his dying hours on Mount McGregor, Grant labored to transport the Civil War, and himself, into sacred time. The war arrived there intact. Grant, however, has remained in a dusk somewhere between myth and Galena, Illinois.

The Bishop of
Our Possibilities

There is a moment in one of Vladimir Nabokov's novels when the narrator
sees a mirror being unloaded from a van on a street in Berlin. Suddenly
the mirror, by a tilt of grace, becomes "a parallelogram of sky."

A sentence of Ralph Waldo Emerson's is sometimes like that: the mind
held at an unexpected angle . . . a sudden burst of lovely blue light. It is
not a transcendental illumination, exactly. Transcendentalism was a short-
lived American moonshine. Emerson's light is brighter. It glows with an
eerily sweet intelligence and morning energy. Emerson's sentences make
a moral flute music—prose as a form of awakening. They move in a dance
of sensual abstractions, small miracles of rhetoric. He had no genius for
massive literary architecture; he dealt in the lustrous fragments of his
essays, in a succession of quiet flashes.

It is strange that this orphic saint who dined on clouds became a prophet
of the culture's materialism. He was the nation's first international-class
man of letters. He taught much of the nineteenth century how to write.
He gave America a metaphysics; he sought to join the nation's intellect
to its power. Emerson sanctified America's ambitions. Like the nation,
he was, he said, "an endless seeker, with no past at my back." He was
the wonder-rabbi of Concord, Massachusetts, our bishop, the mystic of
our possibilities.

The world's tribe of Emersonians has dwindled, but it is still a moderately robust and sometimes unlikely collection. André Gide enjoyed
Emerson; discovering that is like learning (in the other direction) that the
theologian Paul Tillich had a taste for pornography. Ex-coach Woody
Hayes of Ohio State University is a passionate Emersonian. That makes

more sense. Part of Emerson—only a part—is a bright theology of pep, a half-time transcendentalism. "Emerson," says Hayes, "he's on my starting eleven"—meaning the authors Hayes most regularly rereads. "In fact, he's my No. 1."

Hayes was one of the speakers at Harvard's Sanders Theater in May 1982, as Emersonians observed the hundredth anniversary of Emerson's death. It had been an important year in the Emerson business. In the fall of 1981 Gay Wilson Allen's handsome biography, *Waldo Emerson* (Viking), had arrived. The Harvard University Press issued a volume of extracts from Emerson's journals in June 1982, chosen and edited by Harvard's Emerson scholar Joel Porte. The journals, a lifetime accumulation of notebooks containing much of the raw material from which Emerson fashioned his essays and other writings, are the most interesting of his works: brusque and shadowed and doubting and human in ways that the finished productions are not.

It is a shame that Emerson had to harden into a monument, into mere required reading, or worse, the man superseded by Kurt Vonnegut on the course lists. Too many generations came to regard him as a chill, gnomic bore, the best of American aphorists, no doubt, but also the most relentless ("A foolish consistency is the hobgoblin of little minds," "Traveling is a fool's paradise," ". . . fired the shot heard round the world," and even the sixties' dreamy license, "Do your thing"). His fatally worthy subjects (Self-Reliance, Prudence, Friendship) have oppressed generations of eighth-grade English classes. People should probably be forbidden the use of Emerson until their thirtieth birthday. He gets better as one gets older. Inside the marble, there is a wonderful writer struggling to escape the stone reverence with which he is usually imposed on adolescents.

Yet for a mild ex-Unitarian clairvoyant dead over one hundred years, Emerson is still capable of stirring surprising hostility. In a baccalaureate address to his senior class, Yale University President A. Bartlett Giamatti blamed Emerson for the ugliest tendency of the American character—"a worship of power." Emerson, he said, "freed our politics and our politicians from any sense of restraint by extolling self-generated, unaffiliated power as the best foot to place in the small of the back of the man in front of you." This is Emerson as Uncle Sam in a Nietzsche suit.

Earlier readers had a deeper problem with Emerson. His voice seemed too rarefied, ethereal to the point of disconnection with reality—and in any case demonstrably incomplete. He seemed almost bizarrely and willfully ignorant about the darker side of things. Henry James put his finger

on it with an exquisite condescension: a "ripe unconsciousness of evil
. . . is one of the most beautiful signs by which we know him." The
Candide of Concord.

Emerson was the rhapsodist of beginnings. In the disintegration of Puri-
tanism, he cut loose from the granite Thou Shalt Nots of his forebears,
seven generations of New England clergy. The twentieth century has
apocalyptic fantasies about the end of things. The trajectory of our
thoughts tends to be downward. We are transfixed by Auschwitz and Hiroshima and Cambodia and Bangladesh and lesser barbarisms. The twentieth century has rarely felt transcendental. What does Emerson's optimism
have to say to such a civilization?

Emerson should not be understood too quickly. As William James explained, "Emerson could perceive the full squalor of the individual fact,
but he could also see the transfiguration." Emerson had wonderful lines
about the fallen world: "It seems as if heaven had sent its insane angels
into our world as to an asylum, and here they will break out in their native
music and utter at intervals the words they have heard in heaven; then the
mad fit returns and they mope and wallow like dogs."

Perhaps the twentieth century is merely one of the moping-dog phases. It
may be the sin of pride to claim so much evil and despair for oneself. The
Black Death killed off one-third of Western and Central Europe in the fourteenth century, but in the Emersonian calendar of the perfectible universe,
it was only a temporary epidemic—something that was going around.

Emerson sought to organize the individual soul, not an entire society.
His works were essentially prayers for intelligence and character. He
preached the holiness of the conscious mind. It is a vision of personal
possibility, not a program for the state. Emerson must be held blameless
for the fact that his exaltations on individual get-up-and-go have ended,
in the fullness of time, by producing George Steinbrenner.

One can look for too much in Emerson; he claimed so much for himself: "Of the universal mind each individual man is one more incarnation. . . . A man is a bundle of relations, a knot of roots, whose flower
and fruitage is the world." Emerson was also a bundle and knot of contradictions. He recoiled against the doctrinal chill and constriction of New
England, yet he became a sermon and a prayer. His rhapsodies were
lovely and extremist in the way of a Puritan metaphysician: "I am God
in nature; I am a weed by the wall."

Advertisements
for Oneself

Advertisements
for Oneself

It is an odd and compact art form, and somewhat unnatural. A person feels quite uncomfortable composing a little song of himself for the classifieds. The personal ad is like haiku of self-celebration, a brief solo played on one's own horn. Someone else should be saying these things. It is for others to pile up the extravagant adjectives ("sensitive, warm, witty, vibrant, successful, handsome, accomplished, incredibly beautiful, cerebral, and sultry") while we stand demurely by. But someone has to do it. One competes for attention. One must advertise. One must chum the waters and bait the hook, and go trolling for love and laughter, for caring and sharing, for long walks and quiet talks, for Bach and brie. Nonsmokers only. Photo a must.

There are poetic conventions and clichés and codes in composing a personal ad. One specifies DWF (divorced white female), SBM (single black male), GWM (gay white male) and so on, to describe marital status, race, sex. Readers should understand the euphemisms. "Zaftig" or "Rubenesque," for example, usually means fat. "Unpretentious" is liable to mean boring. "Sensuous" means the party likes sex.

Sometimes the ads are quirkily self-conscious. "Ahem," began one suitor in the *New York Review of Books*. "Decent, soft-spoken sort, sanely silly, philosophish, seeks similar." Then he started to hit his stride: "Central Jersey DM WASP professional, 38, 6′2″, slow hands, student of movies and Marx, gnosis and news, craves womanish companionship . . ."

The sociology of personals has changed in recent years. One reason that people still feel uncomfortable with the form is that during the sixties and early seventies personal ads had a slightly sleazy connotation. They showed up in the back of underground newspapers and sex magazines, the little billboards through which wife swappers and odd sexual specialists communicated. In the past several years, however, personal ads have become a popular and reputable way of shopping for new relationships. The *Chicago Tribune* publishes them. So does the conservative *National Review,* although a note from the publisher advises, *"NR* extends maximum freedom in this column, but *NR's* maximum freedom may be another man's straitjacket. *NR* reserves the right to reject any copy deemed unsuitable." *National Review* would likely have turned down a West Coast entreaty: "Kinky Boy Scout seeks Kinky Girl Scout to practice knots. Your rope or mine?" *National Review's* personals are notably chaste, but so are those in most other magazines. The emphasis is on "traditional values," on "long-term relationships" and "nest building." The sexual revolution has cooled down to a domestic room temperature. The raciest item might call for a woman with "Dolly Parton-like figure." One ad in Los Angeles stated: "Branflake patent holder tired of money and what it can buy seeks intellectual stimulation from big-bosomed brunette. Photo please." The *Village Voice* rejected the language of a man who wanted a woman with a "big ass." A few days later the man returned with an ad saying he sought a "callipygian" woman.

Every week *New York* magazine publishes five or six pages of personals. The *New York Review of Books* publishes column after column of some of the most entertaining personals. Many of them are suffused with a soft-focus romanticism. Firelight plays over the fantasy. Everyone seems amazingly successful. The columns are populated by Ph.D.s. Sometimes one encounters a millionaire. Occasionally a satirical wit breaks the monotony: "I am DWM, wino, no teeth, smell bad, age 40—look 75. Live in good cardboard box in low-traffic alley. You are under 25, tall, sophisticated, beautiful, talented, financially secure, and want more out of life. Come fly with me."

Humor helps, especially in a form that usually gives off a flat glare of one-dimensional optimism. It is hard not to like the "well read, well shaped, well disposed widow, early sixties, not half bad in the dusk with the light behind me." She sought a "companionable, educated, professional man of wit and taste," and she probably deserved him. Her self-effacement is fairly rare in personals. The ads tend sometimes to be a little nervous and needing, and anxiously hyperbolic. Their rhetoric tends to get overheated and may produce unintended effects. A man's hair stands on end a bit when he encounters "Alarmingly articulate, incorrigibly witty, overeducated but extremely attractive NYC woman.'' A female reader of *New York* magazine might enjoy a chuckling little shudder at this: ''I am here! A caring, knowing, daffy, real, tough, vulnerable and handsome brown-eyed psychoanalyst.'' One conjures up the patient on the couch and a Freudian in the shape of Daffy Duck shouting: ''You're desPICable!''

The struggle in composing one's ad is to be distinctive and relentlessly self-confident. What woman could resist the ''rugged rascal with masculine determined sensual viewpoint''? An ad should not overreach, however, like the woman who began: ''WANTED: One Greek god of refined caliber.''

Not all the ads are jaunty or dewy-eyed. One begins: ''Have herpes?'' Some are improbably specialized: ''Fishing Jewish woman over 50 seeks single man to share delights of angling.'' Or: ''Literate snorkeler . . . have room in my life for one warm, secure, funny man.''

Anyone composing a personal ad faces an inherent credibility problem. While we are accustomed to the self-promotions of politicians, say, we sense something bizarre when ordinary people erupt in small rhapsodies of self-celebration that are occasioned by loneliness and longing. One is haunted by almost piteous cries that come with post-office-box number attached: ''Is there anyone out there? Anyone out there for me?''

Composing an ad with oneself as the product is an interesting psychological exercise, and probably good training in self-assertion. Truth will endure a little decorative writing, perhaps. The personals are a form of courtship that is more efficient, and easier on the liver, than sitting in bars night after night, hoping for a lucky encounter. Yet one feels sometimes a slightly disturbed and forlorn vibration in those columns of chirpy pleading. It is inorganic courtship. There is something severed, a lost connection. One may harbor a buried resentment that there are not parents and aunts and churches and cotillions to arrange the meetings in more seemly style.

That, of course, may be mere sentimentalism. Whatever works. Loneliness is the Great Satan. Jane Austen, who knew everything about courtship, would have understood the personals columns perfectly. Her novel *Emma,* in fact, begins, ''Emma Woodhouse, handsome, happy, clever, and rich, with a comfortable home and happy disposition.'' The line might go right into the *New York Review of Books.*

The Shoes of Imelda Marcos

A man's Self is the sum total of all that he can call his.
—William James, 1890

The palace doors came loose on their hinges, and the inventory began tumbling out of the overstuffed world of Ferdinand and Imelda Marcos. It was an impressive accumulation: a billion here, eight-hundred million there; an office tower in Manhattan; a waterfront estate on Long Island; dozens of country houses in the Philippines; and even a second palace in Marcos's home province, Ilocos Norte, which almost no one knew about. One took the spectacle in with a feeling of wonder and disgust, something like one's reaction, as a child, upon learning that Egypt's King Farouk ate six hundred oysters a week.

In the Marcos accounting, a central question—what might be called the Farouk Conundrum—kept arising. The conundrum was prefigured by Farouk's grandfather, Khedive Ismail, a grandee who died in 1895 while trying to guzzle two bottles of champagne in one draft. Khedive Ismail kept a harem of three thousand women. The question posed by Ismail's harem, by Farouk's oysters and by Marcos's billions is this: Why, exactly?

One may focus the question of meditating upon the twenty-seven hundred pairs of shoes that Imelda Marcos left behind in Malacañang Palace. A person's vision may cloud a little as he tries to peer into the shadows of Swiss bank vaults or into the double-bottomed luggage of the Marcos real estate deals. But the image of the fifty-four hundred shoes of Imelda Marcos makes the metaphysics vivid.

Sophie Tucker said, "I have been rich, and I have been poor. Rich is better." Of course it is. But when most people imagine what life would be like after winning the lottery, they do not come up with fifty-four hundred shoes. The methodical analyst switches on his calculator. If

Imelda Marcos changed her shoes three times a day, and never wore the same pair twice, it would take her more than two years and five months to work through her shoe supply—as it existed on the day she fled Manila. Since she undoubtedly would continue to buy new shoes even while trying to do justice to the old supply, it is clear she could never wear all of her shoes.

The parable of Imelda's shoes has something to teach. She could never wear them all. Nor could the Marcos family, one suspects, manage to spend the billions of dollars they plundered from the Philippines. As easily could Khedive Ismail labor through his harem of three thousand women. (It is perhaps just as well that Ismail's champagne overdose spared him the exhaustion of trying to scale that particular Everest.)

Why accumulate so much—twenty-seven hundred pairs of shoes, three thousand women—if there is no use for all of them? How much gold is enough? Only a sane person would think to ask. An Eskimo hunter who kills only the game necessary to feed his family would have been horrified by Theodore Roosevelt, who could not have consumed more than one ten-thousandth of the animals he slaughtered. Roosevelt loved hunting the way that Imelda loves shopping. He loved the kick of the gun and the smell of the powder. He loved the antlers. The same sportive hormones may be active in Imelda. Nature is filled with wild waste, unthinkable redundancies. Why does nature toss off a billion sperm when only one of them is necessary to fertilize a human egg? Imelda's shoes, ecologically baffling, are part of the mystery of life.

Consider her profligacy in another way. What is the purpose of riches? To buy freedom—to purchase choices, immunities from the will of others, or of fate. If Imelda kept a collection of twenty-seven hundred pairs of shoes, it was not because (as some candle-snuffing moralists might think) she should be expected to wear them all, and must be judged a wastrel if she did not, but because the twenty-seven hundred pairs gave her options. Her step no doubt grew lighter in the knowledge of such freedom. Did she display her shoes the way that Jay Gatsby reveled in his wonderful shirts?

Or were the Marcos shoes, like the billions of stolen dollars, merely grotesque? The Russian word *poshlost* suggests the transcendent vulgarity at work in the Marcos spectacle. *Poshlost* is something preposterously overdone but without self-knowledge or irony. It is comic and sad and awful. An eighteenth-century French merchant of great wealth named Beaujean came to the same dead end as Marcos with his Swiss gold and his ruined kidneys. "He owned amazing gardens," the historian Miriam

Beard wrote of Beaujean, "but he was too fat to walk in them. . . . He had countless splendid bedrooms and suffered from insomnia . . . a monstrous, bald, bloated old man in a bed sculptured and painted to resemble a gilded basket of roses."

Children often have delusions of omnipotence, and perhaps adult megalomania derives from that, with a sinister admixture of the child's spirit of play and exhibitionism. As the economist Robert Heilbroner wrote, "Analysis finds . . . that even after the child separates the world outside from the world within, he continues to endow outside things with the magical property of being part of himself. To put it differently, he sees his personality as contagious, shedding something of itself on objects of importance. His possessions are part of his self."

Wretched excess comes in many forms. Theologians distinguish the excess called avarice—the sheer, mean taking and hoarding of things— from the excess called prodigality, which is a messier and more full-blooded fault, a form of generosity, almost, but one that has come unhinged. Ideally, world-class plundering should try to pay its way as entertainment. The Romans had a genius for transforming loot into colossally vulgar display, ostentation on an imperial scale. The Emperor Elagabalus, it is said, ordered his slaves to bring him ten thousand pounds of cobwebs. When they finished the task, Elagabalus observed, "From this, one can understand how great a city is Rome." Louis XIV of France wore a diamond-covered coat that, at the turn of the eighteenth century, was worth a dazzling fourteen million francs: the Sun King got up in the splendors of Liberace. And so on.

The Marcos plundering seems ultimately a cheerless affair, covert though sometimes ostentatious, avaricious though often prodigal. Christ said, "If thou wilt be perfect, go and sell what thou hast, and give to the poor, and thou shalt have treasure in heaven." Marcos did not wish to wait. He turned Christianity upside down. He took nourishment from the mouths of the poor and transformed it into his treasure on earth. Such venality is not a matter of either Freud or metaphysics. It is just a brutal habit, the crocodile reflex of a man too long in power. It is a subdivision of the banality of evil.

Scribble, Scribble, Eh, Mr. Toad?

Toad gave up pen and pencil years ago, when he discovered the Smith-Corona manual portable typewriter. Toad loved his Smith-Corona. He played upon it like a flamboyant pianist. Now he massaged the keyboard tenderly through a quiet phrase, now he banged it operatically, thundering along to the chinging bell at the end of the line, where his left arm would abruptly fire into midair with a flourish and fling home the carriage return.

If Toad ever put pen to paper, it was reluctantly, to scribble in the margin of a college textbook ("Hmmmmm" or "Sez who?" or "Ha!"), or to write a check. Over the years, Toad's handwriting atrophied, until it was almost illegible. Who cared? Sonatas of language, symphonies, flowed from the Smith-Corona.

At length, Toad moved on to an electric model, an IBM Selectric, and grew more rapturous still. Toad said the machine was like a small private printing press: the thoughts shot from his brain through his fingers and directly into flawless print.

Then one winter afternoon, Toad came upon the marvel that changed his life forever. Toad found the word processor. It was to his Selectric as a Ferrari is to a gypsy's cart. Toad now thought that his old writing machines were clattering relics of the Industrial Revolution.

Toad processed words like a demon. His fingers flew across the keys, and the words arrayed themselves on a magic screen before him. Here was a miracle that imitated the very motions of his brain, that teleported paragraphs here and there—no, *there!*—as quickly as a mind flicking through alternatives. Prose with the speed of light, and lighter than air!

Toad could lift ten pounds of verbiage, at a whim, from his first page and transport it to the last, and then (hmmm), back again.

A happy life, until one day, Toad, when riding his bicycle in the park, took a disastrous spill. Left thumb broken, arm turned to fossil in a cast, out of which his fingers twiddled uselessly, Toad faced the future. He tried one-handing his word processor, his hand jerking over the keyboard like a chicken in a barnyard.

It was no use. There is no going back in pleasure. "Bother!" said Toad. He picked up a No. 1 Eberhard Faber pencil. He eyed it with the despair of a suddenly toothless gourmand confronting a life of strained carrots and peas. He found a schoolboy's lined notebook and started to write.

The words came haltingly, in misshapen clusters. Toad's fingers lunged and jabbed and oversteered. When he paused to reread a sentence, he found that he could not decipher it. The language came out Etruscan.

Yet Toad perforce persisted. It had been years since he had formally and respectfully addressed blank paper with only pen or pencil in hand. He felt unarmed, vulnerable. He thought of final exams long years ago— the fields of rustling blue-book pages, the universal low, frantic scratching of pens, the smell of sour collegiate anguish.

Toad drove his pencil onward. Grudgingly, he thought, This is rather interesting. His handwriting, spasmodic at first, began to settle after a time into rhythmic, regular strokes, growing stronger, like an oarsman on a long haul.

Words come differently this way, thought Toad. To write a word is to make a thought an object. A thought flying around like electrons in the atmosphere of the brain suddenly coalesces into an object on the page (or computer screen). But when written in longhand, the word is a differently and more personally styled object than when it is arrayed in linear file, each R like every other R. It is not an art form, God knows, in Toad script, not Japanese calligraphy. Printed (typed) words march in uniform, standardized, cloned shapes done by assembly line. But now, thought Toad, as I write this down in pencil, the words look like ragtag militia, irregulars shambling across the page, out of step, slovenly but distinctive.

Toad reflected. What he saw on the penciled page was himself, all right, not just the content of the words but the physical shape and flow of thought. Some writers do not like to see so much of themselves on the page and prefer to objectify the words through a writing machine. Toad for a moment accused himself of sentimentalizing handwriting, as if it were home-baked bread or hand-cranked ice cream. He accused himself of erecting a cathedral of enthusiasm around his handicap.

At length Toad could see his own changes of mood in the handwriting. He could read haste when he had hurried. He thought that handwriting would make a fine lie-detector test, or a foolproof drunkometer. Handwriting is civilization's casual encephalogram.

Writing in longhand does change one's style, Toad came to believe, a subtle change, of pace, of rhythm. Sentences in longhand seemed to take on some of the sinuosities of script. As he read his pages, Toad considered: The whole toad is captured here. *L'écriture, c'est l'homme* (Handwriting is the man). Or, *L'écriture, c'est le crapaud* (Handwriting is the toad). What collectors pay for is the great writer's manuscript, the relic of his actual touch, like a saint's bone or lock of hair. What will we pay in future years for a great writer's computer printouts? All the evidence of his emendations, his confusions and moods, will have vanished into hyperspace, shot there by the Delete key.

Toad found himself seduced, in love, scribbling away in the transports of a new passion. Toad was always a fanatic, of course, an absolutist. He bought the fanciest fountain pen. His word processor went first into a corner, then into a closet with the old IBM.

Toad thought of Henry James. For decades James wandered Europe and the United States, staying in hotels or in friends' houses. He was completely mobile. He needed only pen and paper to write his usual six hours a day. Then in middle age, he got writer's cramp. He bought a typewriter, and, of course, needed a servant to operate the thing. So now James was more and more confined to his home in Sussex, pacing the room, dictating to the typist and the clacking machine. James became a prisoner of progress.

Toad, liberated, bounded off in the other direction. Light of heart, he took to the open road, encumbered by nothing heavier than a notebook and a pen. Pausing on a hilltop now and then, he wrote long letters to Ratty and Mole, and folded them into the shape of paper airplanes, and sent them sailing off on the breeze.

The Island of
the Lost Autocrats

The Emperor Nero entered his Golden House for the first time. He inspected the statue of himself, one hundred and twenty feet high. He saw the enclosed lake surrounded by buildings that were designed to represent the cities of the empire. He admired the pillared arcade that stretched for a mile, the dining rooms paved with porphyry, the ceilings of gold and fretted ivory inlaid with jewels. "At last," he said, "I am beginning to live like a human being."

Eventually, Nero's armies revolted and the Senate condemned him to be flogged to death with rods. He decided to resign from office by stabbing himself in the throat. At least suicide spared him the fate of some other toppled rulers—the long twilight of exile, the sort of haunted afterlife endured by Napoleon, say, or the Shah of Iran. Exile is not necessarily a fate worse than death, but there is something poignantly ignominious in the spectacle of the once all-powerful turned out in obscure pastures to graze on their memories, their paranoid retrospections.

Napoleon's young aide-de-camp, General Gaspard Gourgaud, left a journal describing the Emperor's last years on St. Helena, a speck of British territory in the South Atlantic. Gourgaud's entries, unintentionally hilarious, record the great man's stupendous banality after he lost the thing that made him interesting—his power. "October 21 [1815]. I walk with the Emperor in the garden, and we discuss women. He maintains that a young man should not run after them. . . . November 5. The Grand Marshal [Montholon] is angry because the Emperor told him he was nothing but a ninny. . . . January 14 [1817]. Dinner, with trivial conversation on the superiority of stout over thin women. . . . January 15. I

fetch the *Imperial Almanac*. The Emperor looks up the ages of his brothers. 'Josephine faked her age.' [He] looks at the names of the ladies of
his court. He is moved. 'Ah! it was a fine empire. I had 83 million human
beings under my government—more than half the population of Europe.'
To hide his emotion, the Emperor sings. . . . January 27. We read *Paradise Lost*. The Emperor wants to buy a cow, but where shall we keep
it?'' The imperial party acquires a cow, but someone turns it loose. ''Feb-
ruary 4. The Emperor is in a very bad humor, and full of the cow inci-
dent. At dinner, the Emperor asks [his coachman] Archambault, 'Did
you let the cow get away? If it is lost, you will pay for it, you blackguard!'
. . . His Majesty, in a very bad humor, retires at 10:30, muttering, 'Mos-
cow! Half a million men!' '' After dinner a few days later, the Emperor
remarks, ''I should enjoy myself very much in the company of people of
my own fortune.''

Exactly. Not every deposed ''strongman'' and dictatorial Alldaddy ends
up as shattered as Lear on the heath. Napoleon was comfortable enough.
He had a girlfriend called Rosebud and spent much of his day soaking in
the tub. But no doubt a peculiar loneliness descends upon the autocrat
condemned to live out his days in one of the upstairs rooms, like a mental
case in the family. He is the Wizard of Oz, bereft of his wonder machine.

At one time, an overthrown Big Boy almost invariably expired along
with his power. Now, in the era of telephone and television (to keep track
of how close the other side is coming) and the helicopter and jet (for rapid
extraction when the front door gives way), there is building an exclusive
international brotherhood of exiled Big Boys with leftover lives to kill.

The membership is scattered. Ferdinand Marcos settles in Hawaii.
''Baby Doc'' Duvalier moves to France for the time being. Uganda's Idi
Amin managed to make himself all but invisible in Saudi Arabia. And so
on. But such men are rarely welcomed, and never feel at home, in the
places where the jet stream has deposited them. They keep out of sight.

Like Napoleon, some of the deposed might enjoy the ''company of
people of my own fortune.'' Instead of shuffling these men around uncomfortably, it may be time to consolidate the arrangements, to establish
a home for them, a sort of Island of the Lost Big Boys, a Club Med for
the undone.

The mayor of Honolulu has suggested settling Marcos on the island off
Oahu that served as a set for the television series *Gilligan's Island*. That
bears exploration. The others could join him. There is something to be
said for Alcatraz, which shut down its penitentiary twenty-three years
ago. It is secure. The decorators responsible for Caesar's Palace might

redo the prison in red-velvet flocking and gilt. Still, the island is small, the night air chilly, and the foghorns mournful. Strongmen from sunnier latitudes might find themselves depressed.

A better choice perhaps would be the Dry Tortugas, just below the Florida Keys. Once a haven for pirates, an old prison island surrounded by shipwrecks, by sharks and barracuda and stingrays and poisonous fantasies of treasure, the place shimmers with the right sunny-sinister atmospherics for the brotherhood.

Bullion extracted from Swiss banks would pay to remake the Dry Tortugas. Pastel villas for the Big Boys. A grand hotel for their rich friends. The bar would offer drinks like ''the Caligula'' or ''Vlad the Impaler.'' Imelda Marcos and Michelle Duvalier could meet by the pool for a ''Lady Macbeth.'' The Big Boys could swagger around and try to seduce one another's wives. Steam baths, massages, the camaraderie of the locker room. They could shoot pigeons and get drunk, and now and then they could pretend to have one of their flunkies taken out and shot. Or, the victim could just vanish, without explanation, without a trace. The good old days.

Would the Big Boys enjoy one another? A sentimentalist likes to think so. They, more than anyone, should be able to appreciate one another in a professional way. But the wise mother knows that only children do not necessarily get along with other only children. Sociopaths have trouble socializing. Could they play together? Would they interact? What statues would adorn the hotel lobby? Who would laugh at whose jokes? Who would be *primus inter pares* among these sullen husks?

The collisions of ego might be wonderful—gridlocking motorcades as they move from villa to casino, colossal bribes to get the best table in the restaurant. St. Helena with a dozen Napoleons on it, huge solipsisms crashing into one another, interpenetrating, great weather balloons of malignant ego drifting in the subtropical breezes.

The dayrooms of mental hospitals are famously filled with Napoleons. The Dry Tortugas might be the same sort of place. If, like Napoleon, the Big Boys consulted *Paradise Lost,* they would find there the words that Satan uttered: ''Which way I fly is Hell; myself am Hell.'' Most dictators are not so self-aware.

Changing the
Gestures of Passion

Humphrey Bogart was a brilliant smoker. He taught generations how to hold a cigarette, how to inhale, how to squint through the smoke. But as a kisser, Bogart set an awful example. His mouth addressed a woman's lips with the quivering nibble of a horse closing in on an apple. Better to study, say, the suave carnality of Cary Grant and Ingrid Bergman in *Notorious*.

Everyone learned how to kiss from the movies. It is difficult to imagine what people did before Edison for instruction in the subject. They blundered through, no doubt, across centuries of bruised lips and chipped teeth, and the clumsy lunges that end with noses banging, or the woman accidentally mummmphing a mouthful of beard.

With the visual aid of moving pictures, however, the lovers of the Western world could dramatically improve their technique. For the first time, it was possible for the masses to study, close up, the romantic style of the great masters. It may not have always been wise to imitate the ideal, of course. Rudolph Valentino, for example, favored a hyperbolic style, arching the woman back into a circumflex and doing semaphor with his eyebrows. He had the technique of a gifted and tormented periodontist. Nor is it always advisable for amateurs to try to reproduce the unforgettable scenes, like the one in which Burt Lancaster and Deborah Kerr tumble in the Hawaiian surf in *From Here to Eternity*. Those who attempt that on Cape Cod arise with abrasions on their shoulders and plankton in their sinuses.

Still, movie kisses have been one of the educational advances of the twentieth century. Even the best scholars had something to learn, although in these matters academics are generally among the last to know. Early in the century, the *Encyclopaedia of Religion and Ethics* published an entry on customs of kissing around the world. The author, an anthropologist named Alfred E. Crawley, expatiated on the nose rubbing of the Maoris and the Sandwich Islanders, on the billing of birds and the antennal play of insects. "The kiss seems to have been unknown in ancient Egypt," the writer noted. "In early Greece and Assyria, it was firmly established." Then, in a gemstone of Victorian scholarship, Crawley remarked, "In abnormal forms [of kissing], some use of the tongue occurs."

The first movie kiss was recorded in a brief 1896 production called *The May Irwin–John C. Rice Kiss,* or simply *The Kiss.* Irwin and Rice, looking overstuffed and upholstered, he sporting a grand mustache, fastened onto one another for long seconds as the reel flickered on. Their kiss suggested not so much the heat of passion as a mishap involving dry ice or Krazy Glue. Still, *The Kiss* passed for erotica. It created a sensation and called down the eloquent wrath of a Chicago publisher named Herbert S. Stone, who wrote, "The spectacle of their prolonged pasturing on each other's lips was hard to bear. . . . Such things call for police interference."

There was none, of course. Romantic kissing was permissible sex, an intimacy that could be accomplished while fully clothed, even when dressed in tuxedo or ballgown. Kissing is, among other things, a subtle and civilized medium of expression. It is a preliminary and surrogate for sex, an enticement that is also provisional. Kissing is a promise that preserves the right of refusal. A kiss is mute, and highly articulate. It involves a brief fusion of two heads, the head being the residence of mind and soul. The mouth is simultaneously the front office of language and of hunger. The kiss is a wordless articulation of desires whose object lies in the future, and somewhat to the south.

What made the screen kiss stimulating in the old days was that the consummation was left to occur in the viewer's imagination. Consider the effect if Rhett Butler had carried Scarlett up the stairs and then the camera had followed them into her bedroom to record the next half-hour. As it was, Vivien Leigh's next-morning smile remains one of the most graphically suggestive moments in the history of movies. Usually, directors were clumsier. In *Picnic,* Kim Novak and William Holden knelt beside the railroad tracks and kissed as a train thundered out of the tunnel. Elsewhere the censorship of the Hays office produced kisses that culminated in horses rearing, waves crashing, flames leaping. Or the camera would cut heavenward through sunlit trees.

In the Hays office days, even married couples had to keep one foot on the floor. After the sexual revolution it became possible for William Hurt, in 1981's *Body Heat,* to kiss his co-star with both hands up her dress. Open-mouthed kissing, the old "French kiss," in the past fifteen years or so became common not only in movies but also in television dramas. Actors did not give the subject much thought until it came out that Rock Hudson had given Linda Evans a passionate kiss on *Dynasty* when he knew he had AIDS. No one in Hollywood talked about anything else. The screen kiss suddenly became a frightening threat. The Screen Actors' Guild sent a letter to seven thousand producers and agents informing them that from now on they must notify actors in advance of any scenes that require openmouthed kissing.

The institution of the movie kiss will probably survive as long as the romantic kiss itself. But actors and actresses are chastened by the knowledge that their business of make-believe can get caught up in fatal realities. The mystery of romance loses something when it is overwhelmed by anxiety about what someone has been doing with himself for the past five years.

But what is the alternative to a movie kiss? In *Sleeper,* Woody Allen had his characters at a futuristic cocktail party pass around a shiny metal sphere that when fondled produced a narcissistic ecstasy. In *Tom Jones,* Tom and the ribald Mrs. Waters consume a memorable dinner that is the moral equivalent, or the immoral equivalent, of a passionate night in bed. Perhaps in screenplays of the future, kisses will be blown on the wind like pheromones. The signals of passion might be changed: an ear might be nibbled, for example, or the nape of a neck nuzzled. Actual kissing may have to be handled by the special-effects department: an artful illusion. Producers may lie around the pool of the Beverly Hills Hotel, smoking cigars, reading Jane Austen and Henry James, looking for a hot love scene.

Invasion of the Body Snatchers

The novelist John le Carré says that he will never write again about George Smiley. Le Carré cannot think of Smiley anymore without seeing Alec Guinness. The actor stole the author's creation, hijacked it into flesh. One remembers that some primitive peoples feared being photographed because they thought the camera would make off with their souls. Mention George Smiley to anyone who knows le Carré's spy novels and his memory will instantly throw onto its screen the image of Alec Guinness. Smiley will not be fat and smudgy looking, as the novelist imagined him. He will be simply, immutably, Guinness, impersonating Smiley. Incarnation of this kind is an interesting negotiation between words and pictures. It is a form of translation.

A one-way form of translation: the filmed flesh, the visible image, seems to have the advantage. Great movie characters do not often beat on the gates of prose, begging to be turned back into words. (Movies get "novelized" sometimes, of course, but novelization is merely a spin-off, like a doll or a T-shirt.) Margaret Mitchell's *Gone With the Wind* sold a million copies in its first seven months. After the movie appeared, Rhett Butler was irreversibly Clark Gable. Scarlett O'Hara was Vivien Leigh. Mitchell's prose withered to the irrelevance of an architect's blueprint after the house is built. Dashiell Hammett created Sam Spade. Humphrey Bogart became Sam Spade. The idea of a character becomes imprisoned in the body of the incarnator, and even the creator cannot liberate the prisoner. The character has acquired features and hair and costume. But something valuable, the subjective suggestiveness that hangs around the edges of words and comes alive only in the reader's imagination, may have died of specificity. Abruptly, the embodied character takes on the limitations of individual flesh.

Sometimes the incarnations compete. In the early film versions, Ian Fleming's James Bond became Sean Connery. Then Bond turned into Roger Moore. Convinced that Bond was Connery, some moviegoers dismissed Moore as an impostor. Charlton Heston, conversely, performed a miracle of dramatic consolidation in the 1950s and '60s. He became Moses, Ben-Hur, Michelangelo, Andrew Jackson, and John the Baptist: everyone this side of God. Heston possessed such brooding *gravitas* that he could plausibly pass for an abstraction, the decalogue with a strong chin.

The translation from one medium to another becomes stranger when one of the mediums is reality itself. If one thinks of George Patton, the image that appears on the mental screen is that of George C. Scott. The officer, real in history, a vivid and powerful coherence, a life proceeding through time toward a death, becomes someone else. The writer Cleveland Amory has reported taking his father, who knew Patton well, to see the movie. When the general's aide, Charles Codman, was introduced on the screen, Amory's father protested, "It isn't Coddie." Amory whispered that it was not meant to be Coddie, it was just an actor playing Coddie. But Amory's father insisted, "If they could get Georgie, they could certainly have got Coddie."

These artistic enactments are forms of mythmaking. They rearrange experience to endow it with drama and significance. The novelist John Gardner once wrote a version of *Beowulf* from the monster Grendel's point of view. In Gardner's telling, a blind harper appears at King Hrothgar's hall and sings, transforming Hrothgar's bloody, sordid career into "ringing phrases, magnificent, golden, and all of them, incredibly, lies. The man had changed the world, had torn up the past by its thick, gnarled roots and had transmuted it, and they who knew the truth, remembered it his way—and so did I."

The mind needs its illusions. One thinks of the story of a mother walking with her child. A stranger exclaims, "What a lovely girl!" The mother replies, "That's nothing, you should see her picture!" Sometimes the actors who play villains in television soap operas have women come up in restaurants and slap them. The dreams become more intense than the moments of conscious vision.

Some artistic incarnations can be dangerous to the incarnator. Eugene O'Neill's father, James, was a talented actor who played the Count of Monte Cristo so many times, and so lucratively, that he ruined himself for anything else. He became the part. The illusion that was his success (the count) became his failure. (And so, in the artistic hall of mirrors, his playwright son reincarnated him in *A Long Day's Journey into Night* in order to destroy him once again.)

In a refinement of the idea, some characters have destroyed themselves precisely by incarnating themselves. Toward the end of his life, Charles Dickens, pressed for money, set off on grueling reading tours in which he became "Dickens," a lecture-hall version of himself. The labor exhausted him and hastened his death. Ernest Hemingway was a splendid man—generous, intelligent, full of curiosity and energy and talent—until sometime in middle age, when he became "Ernest Hemingway," a besotted parody of himself.

Writers who turn themselves into celebrities run such risks. Balzac is said to have formed a theory about the dangers of being photographed, which may have something to do with the hazards of celebrity in general. Everybody is composed of a series of ghostly images superimposed in layers of infinity, the theory said. Since man is not able to create something out of nothing, each photograph must lay hold of, detach, and use up one of the layers of the body on which it was focused. The self is peeled away like an onion.

Ambassador Joseph P. Kennedy set in motion a fascinating drama of incarnations—a tragedy of myth transmittal attempted as dynastic policy. Each of his sons, by turns, was to enact the dream. When Joseph Kennedy, Jr., was killed, then Jack Kennedy became the incarnation. Then Bobby Kennedy. Ultimately, Ted Kennedy took up the burden, by then almost too heavy and bitter to bear.

Sometimes the process of incarnation veers off in metaphysically unexpected directions, translating selves into roadside institutions. Consider this recent exchange:

Child: What was the first movie you ever saw, Daddy?
Father: I don't remember the title, but it starred Roy Rogers.
Child: Why would you want to see a movie about a restaurant?

Why and When and Whether to Confess

It was the most aggressively competitive series of confessions since Jean-Jacques Rousseau. Like a sinner who does not want to miss any bets, Billie Jean King made the rounds of the major churches and synagogues of press and television. She unburdened herself to ABC's Barbara Walters, the one woman in America empowered to hear confessions and grant absolution. She went over the scandal with Rona Barrett. She spent ten hours with an old friend from *People* magazine.

King was bouncing back from public humiliation better than any similarly poleaxed public figure in a long time. She had slipped only briefly at the start of the ridiculous business. When her former secretary Marilyn Barnett filed for "palimony," claiming a long lesbian relationship with King, Billie Jean first responded with a denial.

Then she got very smart, very fast. Her instinct for competitive public relations, as shrewd and sure as her court sense, told her that you win only if you control the game. She knew that the story was shaking loose, and that more denials would only put reporters into a feeding frenzy. She knew that if Barnett had to prove the sapphic connection in court, she could organize a parade of witnesses who would keep the tabloids happy for weeks. So King decided that she herself must manage the stagecraft of her public humiliation. Her parents on one side, her husband, Larry, on the other, wearing an expression of indecipherable calm, she faced a press conference and admitted the lesbian affair; it was, she said, a "mistake." The homosexual rights movement may have curled its lip just then. And feminists, if they thought about it, might worry about the almost cynically unliberated way that Larry later took the rap for his wife's affair, saying that it was his long absences on business that drove her into the arms of another for consolation, like a sulking housewife. Never mind. Billie Jean practiced first-class damage control and won the grace-under-pressure award for the month. She managed to transform an ugly public embarrassment into something else: an affectingly human little drama about Billie Jean King in trouble.

Perhaps her athlete's instincts told King that when the ghastly truth splits open like a suitcase, one's moves must be fast and sure. Public figures rarely have that aplomb: when someone abruptly turns on the light and catches them, they blink in astonishment and guilt or reach their palms out desperately to cover the lens of the minicam.

What is the best strategy to adopt when the undignified or even incriminating truth comes out? Reactions are always a matter of personal style and self-possession. The possibilities range from stonewalling ("Never apologize, never explain," as the British classicist Benjamin Jowett said) to full disclosure. Within that range there are as many subtle variations as there are shades of the truth.

Indifference is an impressive but somewhat risky ploy. Rarely do public figures command the easy Gallic disdain of former French President Valéry Giscard d'Estaing. When *Le Canard Enchaîné* reported that Giscard had accepted 250,000 dollars' worth of diamonds as gifts from the Central African Republic's butcherous Emperor Bokassa, Giscard's reaction was roughly, "So what?" Of course, the French have a tradition of *Non, je ne regrette rien.* Across the channel, the Duke of Wellington once displayed something of that spirit when an old mistress (a Frenchwoman) threatened to publish all kinds of lurid details about his grace. "Publish and be damned!" the Iron Duke responded, or words to that effect. Grover Cleveland ("Ma, Ma, where's my pa?/Gone to the White House—ha ha ha!") also managed a show of imperturbability about an illegitimate child who turned up.

The Fifth Amendment allows citizens to remain silent. But it looks bad. Emanations of a man's guilt, as Freud once put it, "ooze from all his pores." Even the hard, grim stonewall of the Nixon White House eventually crumbled. Richard Nixon, in fact, is a fascinating case study in the psychology of confession. The "Papyrus of Nu" from the eighteenth dynasty of Egypt records what scholars have come to call the negative confessions. Therein the Egyptian advises the gods of all the crimes he has *not* committed during his life ("I have not polluted myself. . . . I have not carried away milk from the mouths of children" and so on) and concludes in an ecstasy of self-exoneration: "I am pure. I am pure."

During the 1952 campaign, when he was running for Vice President, Nixon was accused of having an improper eighteen-thousand-dollar slush fund set up for him by California businessmen. Eisenhower thought seriously of throwing Nixon off the ticket. Nixon responded with the masterfully corny Checkers speech, in which he pharaonically denied wrongdoing and told the nation about his wife's "respectable Republican cloth coat" and his daughters' pet dog. It worked; the country loved it; Ike kept him. Years later, his painful writhings during Watergate were ultimately unavailing, but there was some echo of the Papyrus of Nu in Nixon's "I am not a crook!"

After Chappaquiddick, in 1969, Edward Kennedy practiced what might be called the preemptive deflective confession. The idea was to assume the guilt in one large abstract gulp in order to silence any further specific inquiries. It did not work well for Kennedy. He spent a full week in a fortress of silence while the reassembled talents of Camelot labored over a text for him. Then he went on national television to take the responsibility for a young woman's death unto himself but also, simultaneously, to leave himself in a state of dazed blamelessness. His biggest mistake—all penitents beware—was to soak the speech in a disagreeable self-pity.

But almost everyone is mortal and clumsy when scandal hits him on the blind side. In the past few years an interesting though not always persuasive variation has become popular with U.S. Congressmen: the alcoholic-deflective approach. Actually, it amounts to a plea of temporary insanity. Arkansas's Wilbur Mills began behaving strangely in public with an exotic dancer called the "Argentine Firecracker." When he recovered himself for a moment, he told his constituents it all came from drinking champagne with foreigners. But then he landed with the Firecracker at Washington's Tidal Basin in the middle of the night. Mills got hold of himself, acknowledged to himself and everyone else that he was an alcoholic, and sought treatment.

In some peculiar way, alcohol has become a convenient way to mitigate public embarrassments. Betty Ford, Joan Kennedy, Billy Carter, and others have reported that their unsteady, occasionally weird behavior resulted from drinking. That sort of confession can be exemplary and thus publicly useful. But in others it can also be opportunistic. Maryland's conservative Congressman Robert Bauman pleaded not guilty to making homosexual advances to a sixteen-year-old boy; Bauman, with his stricken wife standing behind him—her eyes glazed with that I-am-not-here-I-am-actually-in-Chicago look—told a press conference that booze made him do it. Then in the formulation of media penance, in which a celebrity hears his own confession before lights and cameras and solemnly grants himself absolution, Bauman announced, "I do not have to elaborate. I have confessed my wrongdoings to my God." If God has the case under advisement, who are we to pursue it?

Often it is not the act itself but the denial, the cover-up, that wrecks a reputation. A suspicion will always linger that if Nixon and his men had not tried to cover up, his presidency would have survived; if only he had got up and confessed *something*. If only he had made what the Catholic Church calls a sincere act of contrition. It was not so much John Profumo's recreation with Christine Keeler that finished him as Britain's State Secretary for War. It was the way he lied about it.

Some people, of course, go to the other extreme and produce detailed confessions even when nobody asked them. The nation surely had no "need to know," as the White House says, but Jimmy Carter confessed to *Playboy* in 1976 that he had felt lust in his heart for women other than his wife. That robust literary charlatan Frank Harris went to the trouble of inventing all kinds of elaborate sexual adventures to confess; with both Carter and Harris, confession shaded into exhibitionism.

For sheer gratuitous detail in confession, for self-revelation that slips across the border into self-abasement, few can compete with former South Carolina Congressman John W. Jenrette, Jr., and his wife Rita. Charged with taking bribes in the Abscam case, Jenrette denied his guilt. But then his life and marriage began to unravel. The Jenrettes went in for full public disclosure—and then some. Rita appeared in a spread of nude photographs for *Playboy*. She revealed how the Jenrettes, the most fun couple in town, had copulated on the steps of the U.S. Capitol one night. It was ultimately sad, a spectacle of self-destruction that seemed almost ceremonial, like a samurai's hara-kiri after a public shame.

In the somewhat sleazy pathology of their case, the Jenrettes forgot the main purpose of confession for public figures: to get the truth out, to have the embarrassment aired and cleared away as soon as possible, and then to begin repairs on one's dignity. Once privacy has been invaded, confession is very often the only means to control the way that the truth emerges, to script and stage-manage it.

But as Roman priests and Viennese psychoanalysts know, confession is also good for the soul. It purifies the conscience, discharges guilt, and enables new beginnings. Psychiatrist Theodor Reik explained the clinical mechanics this way: "To suffer the anxiety of confession and the act of confession, which itself is felt to be painful, is that partial gratification of the need for punishment which we claim for the confession.'' Most confessions are privately made—to friends, priests, bartenders, spouses, psychiatrists. When they are publicly done, the penitent must pay the price of being a temporary entertainment to the world; that is the punishment, the penance of indignity. But all confession is a drama of accounting, a settling of disturbances, a way of making peace. Sometimes, as with Billie Jean King, it implies an odd and sidelong kind of redemption and even a curious assertion of our community with one another.

Last Words

There was a time when the deathbed was a kind of proscenium, from which the personage could issue one last dramatic utterance, full of the compacted significance of his life. Last words were to sound as if all of the individual's earthly time had been sharpened to that point; he could now etch the grand summation. "More light!" the great Goethe of the Enlightenment is said to have cried as he expired. There is some opinion, however, that what he actually said was "Little wife, give me your little paw."

In any case, the genre of great last words died quite a few years ago. There are those who think the last genuinely memorable last words were spoken in 1900, when, according to one version, the dying Oscar Wilde said, "Either that wallpaper goes, or I do."

Others set the date in 1904, when Chekhov on his deathbed declared, "It's a long time since I drank champagne." His coffin then rode to burial in a freight car marked FRESH OYSTERS.

Only now and then does one catch a handsome exit line today. Gary Gilmore, the murderer executed in Utah in 1977, managed a moment of brisk existentialist machismo when he told the warden, "Let's do it." There was a charm, a mist of the fey overlaying the terror, in the official last words that William Saroyan telephoned to the Associated Press before he died in 1981: "Everybody has got to die, but I have always believed an exception would be made in my case. Now what?" The British Actor John Le Mesurier dictated to his wife his own death announcement, which ran in the London *Times*. It said, "John Le Mesurier wishes it to be known that he conked out on November 15. He sadly misses family and friends.''

Last words are a matter of taste, of course, and judgments about them tend to be subjective. A strong though eccentric case might be made for the final utterance of Britain's Lord Chief Justice Gordon Hewart, who died on a spring morning in 1944 with the words ''Damn it! There's that cuckoo again!'' Tallulah Bankhead used a splendid economy of language at her parting in New York City's St. Luke's Hospital in 1968. ''Bourbon,'' she said. The Irish writer Brendan Behan rose to the occasion in 1964 when he turned to the nun who had just wiped his brow and said, ''Ah, bless you, Sister, may all your sons be bishops.'' Some sort of award for sharp terminal repartee should be bestowed (posthumously) upon an uncle of Oliver Wendell Holmes, Jr., John Holmes, who lay dying in his Boston home in 1899. A nurse kept feeling his feet, and explained to someone in the room, ''If his feet are warm, he is alive. . . . Nobody ever died with his feet warm.'' Holmes rose out of his coma long enough to observe, ''John Rogers* did!'' Then he slipped away.

The great last words traditionally included in anthologies have usually been more serious than that, and often sound suspiciously perfect. General Robert E. Lee is said to have gone in 1870 with just the right military-metaphysical command: ''Strike the tent!'' The great eighteenth-century classicist and prig Nicolas Boileau managed a sentence of wonderfully plump self-congratulation: ''It is a consolation to a poet on the point of death that he has never written a line injurious to good morals.''

While such goodbyes are usually retrospective, looking back on the life, they sometimes peer forward. Such lines derive considerable fascination from the fact that they have been spoken at a vantage that is the closest that mortals can come to a glimpse of what lies on the other side. Thomas A. Edison said as he died in 1931, ''It's very beautiful over there.'' (It is also possible, however, that he was referring to the view outside his window.) Voltaire had a mordant premonition. The lamp next to his deathbed flared momentarily, and his last words were ''What? The flames already?''

Last words are supposed to be a drama of truth-telling, of nothing left to hide, nothing more to lose. Why, then, do they so often have that clunk of the bogus about them? Possibly because the majority of them may have been composed by others—keepers of the flame, hagiologists, busybod-

---

*An English Protestant divine burned at the stake for heresy in 1555.

ies. One hears the little sound of a pious fraud. The last breath is put into service to inflate the larger cause one last time, as with a regret that one has only one life to give for one's country. There is a long-running controversy, for example, over whether the younger Pitt, when departing this life, said, "My country! How I love my country!" or "I think I could eat one of Bellamy's pork pies."

As Hamlet says in *his* last words, "the rest is silence." Great terminal summations are a form of theater, really. They demand an audience— someone has to hear them, after all. More than that, they have been traditionally uttered with a high solemnity. Some last words have the irony of inadvertence—as when Civil War General John Sedgwick was heard to say during the battle of Spotsylvania Court House. "Why, they couldn't hit an elephant at this dist—" But premeditated last words—the deathbed equivalent of Neil Armstrong's "One small step for a man, one giant leap for mankind," the canned speech uttered when setting off for other worlds—have a Shakespearean grandiloquence about them.

Last words are not a congenial form of theater anymore. Suitable stages no longer seem to be available for such death scenes, nor is there much inclination to witness them. People tend either to die suddenly, unexpectedly, without the necessary editorial preparation, or to expire in hospitals, under sedation and probably not during visiting hours. The sedative dusk descends hours or days before the last darkness.

Perhaps the demise of great last words has something to do with a decline in the twentieth century of the augustness of death. The departure of a single soul was once an imposing occasion. An age of holocausts is less disposed to hear the individual goodbyes.

Perhaps some entrepreneur will try to revive the genre of last words by enlisting videotape, a newer form of theater. Customers could write their own final script—or choose appropriate last words from the company's handsome selection ("Pick the goodbye that is you"), and then, well before the actual end, videotape their own official death scenes. The trouble is that most people tend to be windy and predictable when asked to say a few words on an important occasion. Maybe the best way to be memorable at the end is to be enigmatic. When in doubt, simply mutter "Rosebud."

Daydreams of What You'd Rather Be

Kierkegaard once confided to his journal that he would have been much happier if he had become a police spy rather than a philosopher. Richard Nixon always wanted to be a sportswriter. If one considers these fantasies together, they seem to have got weirdly crossed. It is Nixon who should have been the police spy. On the other hand, Kierkegaard would probably have made an extraordinarily depressing sportswriter.

We have these half-secret old ambitions—to be something else, to be someone else, to leap out of the interminable self and into another skin, another life. It is usually a brief out-of-body phenomenon, the sort of thing that we think when our gaze drifts away in the middle of a conversation. Goodbye. The imagination floats through a window into the conjectural and finds there a kind of bright blue antiself. The spirit stars itself in a brief hypothesis, an alternative, a private myth. What we imagine at such moments can suggest peculiar truths of character.

One rummages in closets for these revelations. Kierkegaard's fancy about being a police spy is a dark, shiny little item: a melancholic's impulse toward sneaking omnipotence, the intellectual furtively collaborating with state power, committing sins of betrayal in police stations in the middle of the night. It is not far from another intellectual's fantasy: Norman Mailer once proposed that Eugene McCarthy, the dreamboat of the late sixties moderate left, might have made an ideal director of the FBI. McCarthy agreed. But of course, McCarthy had a sardonic genius for doubling back upon his public self and making it vanish. He did magic tricks of self-annihilation. Nixon's imaginary career—wholesome, all-American, unimpeachable—may suggest both a yearning for blamelessness (what could possibly be tainted in his writing about baseball?) and an oblique, preemptive identification with an old enemy: the press.

The daydream of an alternative self is a strange, flitting thing. This wistful speculation often occurs in summer, when a vacation loosens the knot of one's vocational identity. Why, dammit, says the refugee from middle management on his thirteenth day on the lake, why not just stay here all year? Set up as a fishing guide. Open a lodge. We'll take the savings and . . . The soul at odd moments (the third trout, the fourth beer) will make woozy rushes at the pipe dream. Like a gangster who has cooperated with the district attorney, we want a new name and a new career and a new house in a different city—and maybe a new nose from the D.A.'s cosmetic surgeon.

Usually, the impulse passes. The car gets packed and pointed back toward the old reality. The moment dissolves, like one of those instants when one falls irrevocably in love with the face of a stranger through the window as the bus pulls away.

Sometimes, the urge does not vanish. The results are alarming. In June 1982, Ferdinand Waldo Demara, Jr., died. That was his final career change. His obituary listed nearly as many metamorphoses as Ovid did. Demara, ''the Great Impostor,'' spent years of his life being successfully and utterly someone else: a Trappist monk, a doctor of psychology, a dean of philosophy at a small Pennsylvania college, a law student, a surgeon in the Royal Canadian Navy, a deputy warden at a prison in Texas. Demara took the protean itch and amateur's gusto, old American traits, to new frontiers of pathology and fraud.

Usually, it is only from the safety of retrospect and an established self that we entertain ourselves with visions of an alternative life. The daydreams are an amusement, a release from the monotony of what we are, from the life sentence of the mirror. The imagination's pageant of an alternative self is a kind of vacation from one's fate. Kierkegaard did not really mean he should have been a police spy, or Nixon that he should have been a sportswriter. The whole mechanism of daydreams of the antiself usually depends upon the fantasy remaining fantasy. Hell is answered prayers. God help us if we had actually married that girl when we were twenty-one.

In weak, incoherent minds, the yearning antiself rises up and breaks through a wall into actuality. That seems to have happened with John W. Hinckley, Jr., the young man who shot Ronald Reagan. Since no strong self disciplined his vagrant aches and needs, it was his antiself that pulled the trigger. It was his nonentity. The antiself is a monster sometimes, a cancer, a gnawing hypothesis.

All of our lives we are accompanied vaguely by the selves we might be. Man is the only creature that can imagine being someone else. The fantasy of being someone else is the basis of sympathy, of humanity. Daydreams of possibility enlarge the mind. They are also haunting. Around every active mind there always hovers an aura of hypothesis and the subjunctive: almost every conscious intellect is continuously wandering elsewhere in time and space.

The past twenty years have stimulated the antiself. They have encouraged the notion of continuous self-renewal—as if the self were destined to be an endless series of selves. Each one would be better than the last, or at least different, which was the point: a miracle of transformations, dreams popping into reality on fast-forward, life as a hectic multiple exposure.

For some reason, the more frivolous agitations of the collective antiself seem to have calmed down a little. Still, we walk around enveloped in it, like figures in the nimbus of their own ghosts on a television screen. Everything that we are not has a kind of evanescent being within us. We dream, and the dream is much of the definition of the true self. Lena Horne said that she has always imagined herself being a teacher. Norman Vincent Peale says fervently that he wanted to be a salesman—and of course that is, in a sense, what he has always been. Opera Singer Grace Bumbry wants to be a professional race-car driver. Bill Veeck, former owner of the Chicago White Sox, confided the alternate Veeck: a newspaperman. In a "nonfiction short story," Truman Capote wrote that he wanted to be a girl. Andy Warhol confessed without hesitation: "I've always wanted to be an airplane. Nothing more, nothing less. Even when I found out that they could crash, I still wanted to be an airplane."

The antiself has a shadowy, ideal life of its own. It is always blessed (the antiself is the Grecian Urn of our personality) and yet it subtly matures as it runs a course parallel to our actual aging. The Hindu might think that the antiself is a premonition of the soul's next life. Perhaps. But in the last moment of this life, self and antiself may coalesce. It should be their parting duet to mutter together: "On the whole, I'd rather be in Philadelphia."

In Praise of
Older Women

Perhaps it is a sign of cultural maturity; in any case, it is a welcome, and slightly amazing, development. In an almost measurable way, the average age of desirability in American women seems to have risen by a dozen years or more. Women who might have been inclined to sigh ruefully at the inanity of a shampoo ad telling them, "You're not getting older, you're getting better," are starting to believe that it may actually be true. As for men, many of whom are still afflicted by a kind of sandbox nympholepsy—the women desired being a procession of "playmates"—more of them are now inclined to credit the experience of the Hungarian-born writer Stephen Vizinczey. In his 1965 novel, *In Praise of Older Women,* he wrote: "No girl, however intelligent and warmhearted, can possibly know or feel half as much at twenty as she will at thirty-five."

Anyone watching the popular iconography has been able to see the change. In movies, it may have started in *Robin and Marian;* at forty-six, Audrey Hepburn played an exquisite and sexy Marian to Sean Connery's aging Robin Hood. In *An Unmarried Woman,* actress Jill Clayburgh portrayed a wonderful thirty-seven-year-old whose husband leaves her for a much younger woman; a character in the movie accurately remarks that the husband was crazy to make the exchange. After a decade of tending barricades, Jane Fonda emerged as a fascinating actress and a forceful, attractive woman. *Harper's Bazaar,* which ought to know about such matters, published its list of the nation's ten most beautiful women in April of 1978; none were under thirty. It is painful to remember that

Marilyn Monroe killed herself perhaps because, among other things, she could not bear turning thirty-six.

Men did not initiate this interest in women who are old enough to remember Eisenhower and Stevenson, or who still savor the image of Simone Signoret, everywoman's Bogart, in a trenchcoat, dangling a cigarette, in *Room at the Top.* Rather, a series of changes in women themselves—the way they run their lives, the way they see themselves—seems to have caused the response in men. Feminism has had much to do with it, though not always directly. All kinds of eddies and crosscurrents have swirled around the practice and politics of sex in the past ten years. A feminist leader was once playfully asked if there would be sex after women's liberation. "Yes," she replied, "only it will be better." That seems, for many, to have come true. Women, especially those well past the stage of reading Tolkien, seem smarter, funnier, sexier, and more self-sufficient than before.

As the framework of the sexual drama has changed, age has lost its determining relevance. Older women are no longer quite so afraid of becoming involved with younger men. With feminism and exposure to the brittle fragility of so many marriages in the seventies, women of almost all ages have developed a certain independence. In the past, as a matter of sociobiological order, desirable women (especially in youth-worshiping America) tended to be those of the courting age, from seventeen or so to twenty-five or twenty-eight. Because married women were usually considered off limits, the focus of male desire was officially rather narrow. In a film like *All About Eve,* a bitter, bitchy Darwinism could drive the Bette Davis character to despair as she hit forty, looked over her shoulder, and saw her youthful doppelgänger clawing to replace her. Girls reaching twenty-five would start to panic about finding a husband, and many, two or three years later, would marry slobs just to change their sexual prefixes.

An entire cathedral of customs and fashions was constructed around the rites of mating, which, especially for women, carried certain age regulations, or at least probabilities. The edifice has by no means been dismantled, but it is greatly altered. What women wear, for example, has had psychological impact upon how they thought of themselves, and what they believed to be possible. In the past, women after twenty-five started to dress like matrons. But the vivid costume party of the sixties taught women of all ages to wear almost any damn thing they pleased. Fashions are more subdued now, but many women, of all generations, have escaped the typecasting of dress.

• • •

Fashions have changed in part because women's roles are different. Women of thirty or thirty-five or forty or older are apt to be juggling a career and the care of children, often without a husband. They have figured out their lives for themselves. They have style. They are grown-ups, and they don't conceal their ages; if their lives are tougher, they frequently possess a certain centeredness and strength that is unavailable to those much younger, who seem somehow unformed, incomplete, far less interesting—and sometimes unbelievably ignorant. Not long ago, a Radcliffe senior confessed that she did not know what the Holocaust was. Oh my, oh my.

Age and experience do not merely ravage. They can give a high mellow patina to a woman's face and character—or a man's. As the anthropologist Claude Lévi-Strauss wrote: "Age removes the confusion, only possible in youth, between physical and moral characteristics." Women have often thought somewhat older men more interesting company; now men seem to be finding out the same thing about older women. It might be merely neurotic to cultivate a great age disparity on purpose. But Balzac, for example, discovered in Madame de Berny, who was twice as old as he, a supple and sumptuous intelligence that would have been impossible in a woman his own age. (The French have a rich tradition of appreciating older women.)

Physical conditioning has made a difference. Americans, both men and women, are staying in better shape than in the past. Samuel Johnson, who was married to a woman twenty years his senior, once wrote: *For howe'er we boast and strive/Life declines from thirty-five.* But nutrition and jogging shoes have improved since the eighteenth century. Feminism has taught women to enjoy being athletes. In all of this, there are exceptions. A visit to a suburban shopping mall will disclose women who, at only twenty-five, with pink gauze kerchiefs bandaging their plastic curlers, with fat melting down below their Bermuda shorts, disprove the thesis. And many women simply become worse fools as the years pass. It would be silly to sentimentalize.

One factor involved in the attraction of somewhat older women is what might be called the narcissism of the demographic bulge. The postwar baby-boom generation causes distensions and exaggerations in society in whatever epoch it hits. The cry of many of the boom babies in the sixties was "Don't trust anyone over thirty." Now that so many of them have crossed that barrier, into the golden twilight of their thirties, they are apt to glamorize their new estate just as they did their former.

In the sixties, the very fact of youth carried pretenses to ideological meaning—and a certain menace. Today, one thinks (unfairly perhaps) of so many young women more as the merely immature. Their eyes tend to jiggle in blankish faces, to perform small discos of incomprehension. Too often, they seem to be kittens, babysitters. How much better to look across at that frank loveliness and steady gaze that some women acquire, some time after their twenties, when they seem finally to have taken permanent possession of themselves.

Waiting

Waiting is a kind of suspended animation. Time solidifies: a dead weight. The mind reddens a little with anger and then blanks off into a sort of abstraction and fitfully wanders, but presently it comes up red and writhing again, straining to get loose. Waiting casts one's life into a little dungeon of time. It is a way of being controlled, of being rendered immobile and helpless. One can read a book or sing (odd looks from the others) or chat with strangers if the wait is long enough to begin forming a bond of shared experience, as at a snowed-in airport. But people tend to do their waiting stolidly. When the sound system went dead during the campaign debate of 1976, Jerry Ford and Jimmy Carter stood in mute suspension for twenty-seven minutes, looking lost.

To enforce a wait, of course, is to exert power. To wait is to be powerless. Consider one minor, almost subliminal form. The telephone rings. One picks up the receiver and hears a secretary say, "Please hold for Mr. Godot." One sits for perhaps five seconds, the blood pressure just beginning to cook up toward the red line, when Godot comes on the line with a hearty "How are ya?" and business proceeds and the moment passes, Mr. Godot having established that he is (subtly) in control, that his time is more precious than his callee's. (Incidentally, the only effective response to hearing the secretary's "Please hold for . . ." is to hang up without explanation. After two or three times, Mr. Godot himself will place the call, as he should have done at the start.)

But the "please hold" ploy is a mere flicker in the annals of great and horrible waiting. Citizens of the Soviet Union would think it bourgeois decadence to complain about such a trifle. The Soviets have turned waiting into a way of life. The numb wait is their negotiating style: a heavy, frozen, wordless impassivity designed to madden and exhaust the people across the table. To exist in the Soviet Union is to wait. Almost perversely, when Soviet shoppers see a line forming, they simply join in, assuming that some scarce item is about to be offered for sale. A study published by *Pravda* calculates that Soviet citizens waste thirty-seven billion hours a year standing in line to buy food and other basic necessities. To bind an entire people to that kind of life is to do a little of the work of the Gulag in a different style.

Waiting is a form of imprisonment. One is doing time—but why? One is being punished not for an offense of one's own but often for the inefficiencies of those who impose the wait. Hence the peculiar rage that waits engender, the sense of injustice. Aside from boredom and physical discomfort, the subtler misery of waiting is the knowledge that one's most precious resource, time, a fraction of one's life, is being stolen, irrecoverably lost.

Americans have ample miseries of waiting, of course—waits sometimes connected with affluence and leisure. The lines to get a passport in Manhattan in early summer stretch around the block in Rockefeller Center. Travelers wait four and five hours just to get into bureaucracy's front door. A *Washington Post* editorial writer reported that the passengers on her 747, diverted to Hartford, Connecticut, on the return flight from Rome as a result of bad weather in New York City, were forced to sit on a runway for seven hours because no customs inspectors were on hand to process them.

The great American waits are often democratic enough, like traffic jams. Some of the great waits have been collective, tribal—waiting for the release of the American hostages in Iran, for example. But waiting often makes class distinctions. One of the more depressing things about being poor in America is the endless waiting it entails: waiting for medical care at clinics or in emergency rooms, waiting in welfare or unemployment lines. The waiting rooms of the poor are forlorn, but in fact almost all waiting rooms are spiritless and blank-eyed places where it always feels like three in the morning.

One of the inestimable advantages of wealth is the immunity that it can purchase from serious waiting. The rich do not wait in long lines to buy groceries or airplane tickets. The help sees to it. The limousine takes the privileged right out onto the tarmac, their shoes barely grazing the ground.

People wait when they have no choice or when they believe that the wait is justified by the reward—a concert ticket, say. Waiting has its social orderings, its rules and assumptions. Otherwise peaceful citizens explode when someone cuts into a line that has been waiting a long time. It is unjust; suffering is not being fairly distributed. Oddly, behavioral scientists have found that the strongest protests tend to come from the immediate victims, the people directly behind the line jumpers. People farther down the line complain less or not at all, even though they have been equally penalized by losing a place.

Waiting is difficult for children. They have not yet developed an experienced relationship with time and its durations: "Are we there yet, Daddy?" There can be pleasant, tingling waits, of course, full of fantasies, and they are often connected with children: the wait for the child to arrive in the first place, the wait for Christmas, for summer vacation. Children wait more intensely than adults do. Sheer anticipation makes their blood jump in a lovely way.

Waiting can have a delicious quality ("I can't wait to see her." "I can't wait for the party."), and sometimes the waiting is better than the event awaited. At the other extreme, it can shade into terror: when one waits for a child who is late coming home or—most horribly—has vanished. When anyone has disappeared, in fact, or is missing in action, the ordinary stress of waiting is overlaid with an unbearable anguish of speculation: Alive or dead?

Waiting can seem an interval of nonbeing, the black space between events and the outcomes of desires. It makes time maddeningly elastic: it has a way of seeming to compact eternity into a few hours. Yet its brackets ultimately expand to the largest dimensions. One waits for California to drop into the sea or for "next year in Jerusalem" or for the Messiah or for the Apocalypse. All life is a waiting, and perhaps in that sense one should not be too eager for the wait to end. The region that lies on the other side of waiting is eternity.

At the Sound of the Beep

The telephone shattered distance: it is part of nature now. The Atlantic Ocean does not intervene between one's lips in New York City and the ear of a friend in Paris.

The telephone answering machine subverts time: one leaves a surrogate self back in a little box at home, frozen in time, waiting to be roused by a ring: "Hello," one says, disembodied. "This is Carl. I'm sorry I can't come to the phone now, but . . ."

It is not Carl, of course. It is a fragment of Carl, deputized with a brief memory. It is a crystal of Carl, like one in the ice palace of Superman's heritage from Krypton. Carl, at that moment in any case, is elsewhere. Carl has proliferated a little. His flagship self is steaming across town on some business, plowing along through conventional time. His ancillary self, his butler self, the ghost in the machine, is waiting in its little timelessness.

So the Stepford Carl, once activated, will speak. And then the caller will speak, and the caller's words will likewise be frozen in time, and both of those small ancillary selves will lie side by side for a little while in their other dimension. Words can be chilled down like human seed and thus suspended in time until they are ready to come to life.

Answering machines can be very funny. They have their protocols and social comedies. Does one play one's messages when one has just come home with a guest? What intimacies and embarrassments will come flying out of the machine before one leaps for the stop button? "Gee, I wonder who *that* could have been."

The machines can also be a little spooky, metaphysically spooky. There was a tale about the archipelago called Nova Zembla, which was discovered in the sixteenth century, high in the Arctic Circle. A ship's crew was stranded there, frozen in. The air was so cold, the story said, that when the sailors spoke, their words crystallized in midair and remained there. Presently a thaw arrived, and all the words, warmed up, came cascading down in a tremendous, unintelligible din. The owner of an answering machine knows that there may come a moment when the machine, for all its customary obedience, will disgorge, in a weird, surreal monologue, all the messages accumulated over months and months: disjointed voices, greetings and arguments and appointments long dead. And then one might hear a voice one does not recognize: a sort of gypsy croak, a voodoo voice, heavily accented and far away: "Please call. . . . Eeet eees verrrry imporrrtant!" A cold gust goes through the room.

Usually, the machines are more banal than that. They do still make people uncomfortable, although that is passing with familiarity. Their use has become so widespread that callers no longer feel quite so much the instant of stage fright. Still, the tape on the end of the line, expectantly unreeling, silent as a director awaiting the audition, does intimidate. The caller feels ambushed, like one who has suddenly learned he is being bugged. He becomes more . . . responsible for his words. They are not going to vanish into air. They can be replayed again and again, like the videotape of a fumble. The machine subtly puts the caller on the defensive, thus reversing the usual telephone psychology, in which the caller is the aggressor, breaking in upon another's silence.

Answering machines are handsome instruments of privacy. They have conquered the greatest disadvantage of the telephone: the mere ring does not announce the identity of the caller. In picking up the receiver, one must sometimes pay the penalty for satisfying one's curiosity. But the answering machine has solved that. The little butler in the box answers. The caller must declare himself, and the aristocrat in the armchair can then decide whether he will condescend to pick up the phone. In the world of Henry James, the butler announced at the door, "not at home," meaning "not at home to visitors." One placed one's calling card in a silver tray held in the butler's left palm. The answering machine electronically duplicates the ritual. This maddens callers, who suspect that exactly such a game is going on. "Come on, Carl, pick it up, you jerk. I know you're there!" Pause. Long sigh of irritated resignation. Defeated mumble. "Yeah, well, call me later. . . ."

There once was a story at Harvard about a visiting professor who did not have the time to appear at a weekly seminar and so placed a tape recorder and the recorded text of his lecture in the middle of the seminar table. The students could come each week and play the tape and take notes. One day the professor stopped by the seminar room to see how the class was progressing. No one was there. In the middle of the table, he saw his large tape recorder unreeling his lecture. All around the table, before all the chairs, he saw little tape recorders taking it in. An intellectual antiworld: the big surrogate instructing the little surrogates.

Many telephone callers still refuse to converse with the machine. They hang up. That makes the machine owners nervous. So they turn their messages into jokes or performances, minidramas. The most baleful byproduct of answering machines is these awful shtik. The caller hears madrigals playing in the background, romantic Muzak, or cutely chosen rock songs. One endures impressions of Bogart and Cagney and Nixon: "And I promise not to erase the tape. Huh, huh, huh." The humorist Jean Kerr had friends whose message was a jingle: "We shall not sleep, we shall not slumber/unless you leave/your name and number." Anonymous callers left the only appropriate rejoinder: "Burma Shave."

Across the way from comic impersonation is self-abnegation, strict anonymity: the machine answers not with a name but a hard, bleak number—"You have reached 887-5443. . . ." The self is abstracted, washed blank like a bureaucrat. Inspector 324. Either way, the self has a way of skittering off a little.

It might be an entertainment of the Mel Brooks kind to wonder what sort of messages certain historical figures might have left on their machines in the past two thousand years. The examples one thinks of run toward the grotesque—monsters being *gemütlich*. Nero's message would be one of his awful, overripe lyrics, with strummings. Hitler's, a little Wagner, perhaps, in the background (something from *Tristan*) and a creamy, loverboy's voice: "Hello, this is Adolf. I'm not free to talk now, but . . ."

The machines can park words outside time. But there are situations in which that won't do. The governor calls at one minute to midnight. Ring. Click. "Hello, this is Warden Parker. I'm attending an execution at the moment, but if you'll leave your . . ." Or the President of the United States gets on the hot line and reaches the Kremlin's answering machine: ". . . So please just leave your message at the sound of the boom."

Ranting

"While in the parlors of indignation," Saul Bellow wrote, "the right-thinking citizen brings his heart to a boil." Bellow's character Moses Herzog did that. Herzog wrote crank letters to ex-wives, to Dwight Eisenhower, to Adlai Stevenson, to Spinoza. "There is someone inside me. I am in his grip," Herzog confessed. It was as if his mind had been hijacked.

The little terrorist within the skull can overpower the steadiest mind. Everyone rants now and then. More than occasionally, it happens behind the wheel of a car.

Sometimes one commits a rant to paper. That is always a mistake. A rant should be transient. It should blow away like sudden, violent weather.

The U.S. Supreme Court considered one kind of ranting in the case of a North Carolina man who wrote two colorful letters to the President urging him not to appoint a judge named David Smith as U.S. Attorney for North Carolina. Smith sued the man for libel. The letter writer said that the First Amendment surely protected a citizen's right to send an angry letter to Washington. The court said no, a nasty letter to the President or Congress, even if sent in exercise of the constitutional right "to petition the Government for a redress of grievances," is just as much open to a libel suit as, say, a newspaper editorial.

In a way, it seems a shame to inhibit a good ranter. But ranting is not always entertaining. Often it is embarrassing, even shaming. Sometimes, if it issues forth from a politician or religious zealot with ambitions, it becomes sinister. The United States has a fairly rich tradition of ranters, from Thomas Paine to Joseph McCarthy to Spiro Agnew (whose ranting was actually a satire on the form) to Louis Farrakhan. A citizen named Peter Muggins caught the essence of the rant in an intense if repetitious letter to Abraham Lincoln: "God damn your god damned old hellfired god damned soul to hell" and so on.

Ranting is a form of verbal fanaticism, and other cultures often do it better. The Middle East today is to ranting what Elizabethan England was to theater: the cradle of geniuses. Every faction and tribe has its Shakespeare of denunciation, from the Ayatollah on down. Communist bloc countries have bureaucratically institutionalized ranting. The East German government once issued a list of approved terms of abuse for speakers describing the British: "paralytic sycophants, effete betrayers of humanity, carrion-eating servile imitators . . ."

Ranting has many styles, many purposes. Sometimes its only ambition is to vilify. Robert Burns once let fly at a critic in these terms: "Thou eunuch of language; thou butcher . . . thou arch-heretic in pronunciation, thou scape-gallows from the land of syntax." On and on he went.

Ranting can be a sudden spasm of outrage or a cynical manipulation (the wise demagogue practices ranting in front of a mirror). Private citizens rant at public figures to vent feelings of powerlessness (Muggins to Lincoln, for example). Public figures instinctively use the irrational to call up the irrational—the rant to enlist the people's power, a passion to follow the leader. One man's rant is another's eloquence. General George Patton ranted at his troops to get them to fight. Winston Churchill had a genius for the eloquent rant: "We shall fight on the beaches, we shall fight on the landing grounds, we shall fight in the fields and in the streets, we shall fight in the hills; we shall never surrender."

Churchill and Hitler staged a fascinating theater of ranting. Hitler perfectly demonstrated an essential truth: a person, when ranting, is often talking about himself. Thus Hitler, in 1941, speaking of Churchill: "For over five years this man has been chasing around Europe like a madman in search of something he could set on fire."

Ranting sometimes defeats intelligent argument because it possesses the glamour of the prerational, an animal force. Words get fired up. They go on crusade. They storm across the countryside with aggressive and annihilating intent.

The Old Testament contains masterpieces of apocalyptic rhetoric, notably from Amos and Jeremiah: rants to reduce the ungodly to the finest dust. Jonathan Edwards, the eighteenth-century New England Calvinist, was a genius of the punitive theological rant: "The God that holds you over the pit of hell much as one holds a spider or some loathsome insect over the fire abhors you, and is dreadfully provoked."

Ranters are everywhere. The good ranter is the one you agree with. Jesse Jackson rants. The Klan rants. Most of the United Nations rant. John McEnroe rants at linesmen. Phil Donahue rants at housewives. King Lear rants at the cosmos. New York street crazies rant at something that only they can see.

Zealotries spawn rants. Feminism has summoned up some splendid ranting. In the sixties Valerie Solanis wrote, "It is now technically possible to reproduce without the aid of males (or for that matter, females) and to produce only females. We must begin immediately to do so. The male is a biological accident: The Y (male) gene is an incomplete X (female) gene, that is, has an incomplete set of chromosomes. In other words, the male is an incomplete female, a walking abortion, aborted at the gene state. . . ."

Ranting may be a hot wind carrying lies. But sometimes it is a way of marching out the truth in a noisy parade of dudgeon. In ranting, *veritas*—sometimes. What happens in ranting is that the little editor normally on duty in the brain gets shouldered aside. The words come clambering out of their cells, free at last. Japanese businessmen are encouraged to get together with coworkers in the evening. A man gets drunk and delivers a violent tirade against his boss, but nothing will be said of it next morning, or ever. Ranting is permitted as a form of release from the pressures of Japanese business life.

It is the ranting held inside that is most scalding. That is the internal rant, the rant that is never spoken or written down. It is the rant of what-I-should-have-said. It is the magnificently composed and scathing reply that would have left the son of a bitch for dead, had I but said it.

But the internal rant eats the ranter. It degenerates into impotent eloquence. It tears apart the system like hard drugs. Ranting, after all, is a form of theater, just as theater, too often, is a form of ranting. Both require an audience.

Exaggeration

Exaggeration is an intoxication of words. Language temporarily loses its self-control; it veers around the room making drunken passes at reality, biting its ear, whispering hyperbole, even drooling a little: YOUR SEARING, GUT-WRENCHING WORK IS THE LITERARY EVENT OF THE DECADE . . . SPELLBINDING . . . MAGNIFICENT . . . A WASHDAY MIRACLE, WHITER THAN WHITE . . . A NEW STANDARD BY WHICH ALL THOROUGHBRED DRIVING MACHINES WILL BE MEASURED . . . I WILL NEVER LIE TO YOU . . . I AM NOT A CROOK. I WILL BALANCE THE FEDERAL BUDGET . . . WE'LL GET MARRIED AS SOON AS THE DIVORCE COMES THROUGH. . . . Such episodes leave a man feeling like a fool in the morning; they are the effusions of the moment, wild blossoms with a short but extravagant life.

In events of world-class exaggeration, the tongue likes to disconnect itself from the past and race off obliviously astride any passing enthusiasm, like Toad of Toad Hall. A modest example occurred during the trial of Elvis Presley's doctor in Memphis; Elvis was fervently described as a "musical genius." *Genius* is one of the choice words of breathlessness; if Presley was a musical genius, what are we to say of Beethoven? A reviewer in the *New York Times* wrote that "the fecundity of the Beatles is a phenomenon unmatched in the history of popular culture." The information may have sorrowed Homer, Shakespeare, Dickens, Rodgers and Hammerstein, and Cecil B. DeMille.

The sixties (from which the Beatles appropriately sprang) were an era of fine, ripe exaggeration—all of that bright, angry, lulu rhetoric parading in costume across the counterculture and the war zone, en route to Consciousness III. America was "Amerika." The young were "freaks," the police "pigs." A hundred different chemical substances were on hand to perform radical exaggerations in the brain. The eighties seem to be taking a preppier line with reality; certain voices run to understatement now. Still, a great deal of exaggeration has been built into the culture and, of course, the traditional home of exaggeration: politics. Ronald Reagan so far is not doing his part, however; in 1977, Jimmy Carter described the Shah's Iran as "an island of stability." When the Apollo 11 astronauts returned from the moon, Richard Nixon declared, "This is the greatest week in the history of the world since the Creation."

Most excesses do not display the exaggerator's art in its best light: they are merely blurbs and rodomontade. In more complex usage, exaggeration does dynamic and suggestive work: it can be used to frighten or threaten, to reassure (oneself or others), to glorify and debunk, and, above all, to relieve the tedium of life, to entertain. Exaggeration is one of the methods of all myth—from Olympian deities to giants like Paul Bunyan and John Henry, to mythic historical figures—Mao, say, or George Patton. A child exaggerates his parents' powers to the point of myth; heroes and ideals arise from this distortion toward the larger-than-life. All caricature, of course, is based on the artist's method of exaggerating one feature in proportion to the others.

Americans have historically (with a touch of overstatement) regarded themselves as the world's master exaggerators: spinners of tall tales, an abundantly fabulous people, full of Whitman and vinegar. But this is probably mere cultural narcissism. Other people have spent many centuries perfecting their techniques of overstatement. The French, for all their Cartesian precision, have a strangely unstable hyperbolic side; a casual acquaintance who cannot make it to lunch one day will tell you he is "desolate" because of it. Such linguistic inflation can leave people with their vocabularies depleted when hard times come; what is that man to say of his condition if, say, his wife dies?

The Germans have a deep national habit of earnest exaggeration. The Japanese, of course, practice a style of negative exaggeration—self-abnegation so elaborate as to be a kind of overstatement. On Aug. 15, 1945, Emperor Hirohito observed in the imperial announcement of Japan's surrender: "The war situation has developed not necessarily to Japan's advantage." The British exaggerate in the same direction, indulging in what grammarians call meiosis—understatement. It was an American (born in Wales), however, Henry Stanley, who produced the wonderfully meiotic: "Dr. Livingstone, I presume."

Of the world's exaggerators, none surpasses the Arabs, whose language is a symphony of poetical excess. A Cairo gas station attendant greets his coworkers in the morning: "May your day be scented with jasmine." Sometimes the exaggerations that are inherent in Arabic can be dangerous. Saudi Arabia's late King Saud once told a visiting group of Palestinian journalists that "the Arabs must be ready to sacrifice a million lives to regain the sacred soil of Palestine." It was rhetoric, a flourish; Arabs hearing it would no more take it literally than would an American football crowd hearing "rip 'em up, tear 'em up." But the words made headlines all over the world as a statement of bloody Saudi intent.

The great difficulty with all exaggerations is that while most of the audience may understand that excess and embellishment are in the air, and may automatically do a mental calculation discounting the rhetoric, the fact is that different auditors discount at different rates. It is often difficult to know just how much exaggeration is involved, and how much truth. If Iranians pumping their fists in the air describe the United States as the "Great Satan," how much of that is homicidal hostility, how much is merely Persian literary style?

In simplest definition, exaggeration is a form of lying. Is it therefore bad, an instrument of untruth? It depends. Sometimes the artful exaggeration is a way of evoking, of discovering, an essential truth lying below the prosaic surface of things. The very idea of exaggeration presupposes some discoverable, objective reality; the task of the human eye and scientific intelligence, in this classic view, would be to describe that reality as dispassionately and accurately as possible. The world has its being outside the fanciful brain of the exaggerator, a romantic whose business it is to distort reality. Still, in the late twentieth century, where reality is not stable, where it is instead erratic, skittish, apocalyptic, discontinuous, monstrously surprising (the Holocaust, for example, was an event far beyond the vocabularies of exaggeration), then it is hard to know what is an overstatement and what is not.

But distinctions must be made. There are times when exaggerations are highly useful; there are times when they may be fatal. A partial list:

Do not exaggerate: 1) When performing neurosurgery; 2) in writing military dispatches (before the battle); 3) on job applications (if you are clumsy and may get caught); 4) when running the Bureau of the Budget; 5) in marriage.

Exaggeration may be helpful: 1) in lovemaking and courtship; 2) in leading a cavalry charge; 3) when speaking at funerals; 4) when defending a murderer; 5) in military dispatches (after the battle); 6) in political speeches; 7) when writing thank-you notes.

81

The Morals of Gossip

Gossip has always had a terrible reputation. A sin against charity, they said, quoting St. Paul. The odd, vivid term sometimes used for it was backbiting. The word suggested a sudden, predatory leap from behind— as if gossip's hairy maniacal dybbuk landed on the back of the victim's neck and sank its teeth into the spine, killing with vicious little calumnies: venoms and buzzes.

Gossip is rarely that wild. From the morning of the first individual folly of the race, gossip has been the normal nattering background noise of civilization: Molly Goldberg at her kitchen window, Voltaire at the water cooler. To say that gossip has been much condemned is like saying that sex has sometimes been held in low esteem. It is true, but it misses some of the fun of the thing.

Gossip has always been one of the evil pleasures. It is unworthy, nosy, hypocritical, and moralistic, a sort of participatory nastiness. But does it play a heroic moral role hitherto unnoticed? Is gossip merely a swamp that breeds mosquitoes and disease? ("Each man walks with his head in a cloud of poisonous flies," wrote Tennyson.) Or does it have higher functions in the ecosystem?

Large claims have often been made for homely old salacious gossip— the sort of assertions, one might think, that sweating pornographers used to make in court about the "redeeming social value" of their work. All storytelling, hence most of literature from Homer onward, rises from gossip's fertile lowlands. Even the deepest primordial myths are essentially gossip: "Zeus and Hera are fighting again?" What we hear in Tolstoy or Flaubert or Dickens or Proust, wrote novelist Mary McCarthy, "is the voice of a neighbor relating the latest gossip." Literature coalesces out of base gossip, from Suetonius to Boswell's *Journals*.

Oscar Wilde said that all history is gossip. Such gossip, unlike history, tends to evaporate. Gossip is certainly an instrument of power; Lyndon Johnson understood the magic leverage to be gained from intimate personal details, artfully dispensed. He made it a point to know the predilections of friends, the predicaments of enemies. He orchestrated whole symphonies of power upon the Moog of his own ego. Conversely, gossip seems to cherish a democratic, even subversive impulse: it likes to knock down authority a little. That is why royal families make their servants sign oaths not to write (gossip) about what goes on in the private quarters.

In the late twentieth century, technology has immeasurably complicated the business of gossip. Television, radio, the people pages of newspapers and magazines have all conspired to create international class gossip. This macrogossip detaches the usual human taletelling from its local roots. The result is sometimes a resonant emptiness, the feeling of futility that might overcome the soul after watching Bob Hope and Brooke Shields host a television special. Macrogossip tends to be exemplary, cautionary, ceremonial, and merely entertaining—like public hangings.

But microgossip—the myriad back-nipping, back-fence, kitchen-table, men's-room exchanges all over the world, the low animated buzz of dirt-dishing that emanates from the globe—is the kind of gossip that may perform a kind of social mission. Microgossip keeps tumbling in like the surf, a Pepysian lounge act: routines about Sylvia, about to be fired, and Karl, who can't get a divorce, and Dorothy's Valium.

Perhaps most of the world's gossip—both macro and micro—is done for the interest and entertainment of it. At dinner parties in Georgetown and Beverly Hills and East Hampton, the gossip is a combination of dispassionate vivisection and blood sport: reputations are expertly filleted and the small brown pits of egos are spit out decorously into spoons and laid at the edge of the plate.

Gossip goes in for the negative, not the positive. It is no doubt mean-spirited. "If gossip favors, even *enjoys*, dirt (the failings of character)," wrote the critic John Leonard, "it is because we suspect ourselves, and the suspicion is a shrewd one." Yet, oddly, people do not seem to object to being gossiped about as much as they once did. After all, as macrogossip has instructed, any gossip is a form of attention, a sort of evanescent celebrity. Even gossip works to keep away what Saul Bellow called "the wolf of insignificance." Privacy is not the highest priority; on the contrary, a certain emotional exhibitionism has been gaining ground. Of course, it can get out of hand: a man happy enough to be gossiped about as the office philanderer might grow queasy at learning that gossip is calling him a sadomasochist.

If much gossip is retailed merely for the enjoyment of the exchange, the simple human interest in the passing pageant of follies, it also has subtler purposes. Gossip—which concerns people, while rumor concerns events—is usually an instrument with which people unconsciously evaluate moral contexts.

"Did you see that Glen and Carolyn got out of the same cab at work this morning? And Carolyn was wearing the same dress she had on yesterday?" In gossiping about, say, an office adultery, gossipers will weigh and shift and test the morals involved. Gossip is intimate news (perhaps even false news), but it is also a procession of ethical problems. In gossiping, people try to discover their own attitudes toward such behavior—and the reactions of others. It is also a medium of self-disclosure, a way of dramatizing one's own feelings about someone else's behavior, a way of asserting what we think acceptable or unacceptable. In a book called *The Moralities of Everyday Life*, psychologists John Sabini and Maury Silver write that "gossip brings ethics home by introducing abstract morality to the mundane. Moral norms are abstract. To decide whether some particular concrete unanalyzed action is forbidden, tolerated, encouraged, or required, principles must be applied to the case."

If that is so, then gossip (whatever its individual destructiveness, which can be awesome—ask Othello) also serves as a profound daily act of community. In her novel *Happy All the Time,* Laurie Colwin has a character who prefers to call gossip "emotional speculation." Right. Through the great daily bazaar of bitchiness (men can be just as bitchy as women) passes a dense and bewildering parade of follies. They involve sex and money and alcohol and children and jobs and cruelty and treachery: mostly variations on the seven deadly sins. Gossip is a safe way of sorting out this amoral brawl. It is a form of improvisational daydreaming. "Both the virtue and vice of gossip," write Sabini and Silver, "is that one doesn't confront accusers, or demand proof. . . . Gossip is transitional between things merely said, or even half said, and positions taken in the public domain. Gossip is a training ground for both self-clarification and public moral action." Gossip is the layman's mythmaker and moralist, the small, idle interior puppet-theater in which he tries out new plays, new parts for himself.

Snobs

It was not the Bach on the harpsichord that offended, or his way with celestial navigation, or the servants, or the phone calls from Ronald Reagan. No: his worst affront seemed to be the custom chopped-and-stretched chauffeur-driven Cadillac with the partition and the special backseat temperature control. It was not even the fact that William F. Buckley, Jr., rides around in such a car, like a Mafia don in his land yacht, that gave some reviewers eczema. It was the way that he wrote about it, with such a blithe air of entitlement. No right-wing intellectual on the go, Buckley seemed to suggest, should be asked to function without this minimal convenience, for God's sake.

Buckley's book *Overdrive,* a journal of a few days in his ridiculously overachieving life, is a funny and charming exercise. Some critics who object to Buckley's politics, however, were outraged by his life-style, or more accurately by the obvious pleasure with which he described it. It is all right to live that way, but one should have the grace to conceal it, or at least to sound a little guilty about it; Buckley luxuriates in his amenities a bit too much, and one hears in his prose the happy sigh of a man sinking into a hot bath. So his enemies try to dismiss him as Marie Antoinette in a pimpmobile. They portray him as, among other things, a terrible, terminal snob.

To make the accusation is to misunderstand both William F. Buckley, Jr., and the nature of his snobbery. Buckley is an expansive character who is almost indiscriminately democratic in the range of his friends and interests. He glows with intimidating self-assurance. The true snob sometimes has an air of pugnacious, overbearing self-satisfaction, but it is usually mere front. The snob is frequently a grand porch with no mansion attached, a Potemkin affair. The essence of snobbery is not real self-assurance but its opposite, a deep apprehension that the jungles of vulgarity are too close, that they will creep up and reclaim the soul and drag it back down into its native squalor, back to the Velveeta and the double-knits. So the breed dresses for dinner and crooks pinkies and drinks Perrier with lime and practices sneering at all the encroaching riffraff that are really its own terrors of inadequacy. Snobbery is a grasping after little dignities, little validations and reassurances. It is a way of swanking up the self, of giving it some swag and flounce and ormolu. It is a way of asserting what one is not (not like *them*), what one is better than.

There was a period during the sixties and early seventies when snobbery of the classic sort seemed, superficially, at least, in some danger of disappearing into the denim egalitarianism of the time. It never could, of course. It just changed form; and the Revolution, while it lasted, enforced its own snobberies, its own political and even psychic pretensions. Today, snobbery is back in more familiar channels. A generation of high-class magazines (*Connoisseur, Architectural Digest, House and Garden,* for example) flourishes by telling Americans what the right look is. The American ideal of the Common Man seems to have got lost somewhere; the Jacksonian theme was overwhelmed by the postwar good life and all the dreamy addictions of the best brand names. The citizen came to be defined not so much by his political party as by his consumer preferences. It might be instructive to compare the style of the White House under Ronald Reagan with that of, say, Harry Truman. One imagines the snorting contempt with which Truman would have regarded the thousand-dollar cowboy boots and the Adolfo gowns.

Washington, in fact, is a hotbed of snobbery. It is an essentially brainless city that runs, in the shallowest way, on power and influence and office. Access to power is the magic—access to the President, or access to the people who have access to the President, or access to lunch at the White House mess, or to Ed Meese across a crowded room, or to those chunky little cuff links with the presidential seal. But Washington is like other cities: the snobs reveal themselves by the clothes they wear and the clubs they join and the schools they send their children to and the company they keep and the houses they buy and the caterers they call.

The English, who have flirted with Beatles music and the leveling principle, have returned to their ancient heritage of snobbism. They worship their ancestors and buy *The Official Sloan Ranger Handbook* and dream of country houses and old money. They have a look, both wistful and satirical, at the Duke of Bedford's *Book of Snobs,* with its indispensable advice: "A tiara is never worn in a hotel, only at parties arranged in private houses or when royal ladies are present." They think longingly of the right public school, the right regiment, the right club (Whites, if possible, or Boodles, or Pratt's, if you must). They dread the fatal slip, the moment when they might, for example, eat asparagus with knife and fork: *Use your fingers, idiot!*

It is probably more difficult to be a snob now than it once was. The logistical base is gone. If Buckley were one, he would have to be considered one of the last of the great Renaissance snobs, a generalist capable of insufferable expertise on everything from Spanish wines to spinnakers. But the making of such a handsomely knowledgeable, or even pseudo-knowledgeable, character requires family money and leisure of a kind not often available in the late twentieth century. "A child's education," Oliver Wendell Holmes once remarked, "should begin at least one hundred years before he was born." It does not take quite that much marination to make a great snob, since the secret of snobbery is mere plausibility, the appearance of knowledge of breeding. Still, in a busy world it is difficult to find the time and resources to give the laminations and high gloss, the old patina, that used to be the mark of great snobbery.

The true snob is a complex character. He is not merely a status seeker in Vance Packard's sense of the term, or a simple show-off. (Still, touches of artful swank are essential—the polo mallet cast casually onto the back seat of the car, or the real, working buttonholes on jacket sleeves that betray the Savile Row suit.) The authentic snob shows it by his attitude toward his superiors and his inferiors. Gazing upward, he apes and fawns and aspires to a gentility that is not native to him; looking down, he snubs and sniffs and sneers at those who don't share his pretensions.

Snobbery has traditionally been founded on 1) birth; 2) knowledge or pseudoknowledge, or merely self-assured ignorance, all of them amounting to the same thing in snob terms; 3) access to power, status, celebrity; 4) circumstances, such as the place one lives or even the things one does not do, such as watch television.

Anyone who thinks that birth and heritage are an immutable circumstance should send away to one of the genealogy services that will, for a fee, supply one's family tree and family crest. It is astonishing to learn from these services that most of America, back in the mists, springs from ancient royalty.

Snobbery today tends to be fragmented. The snobbery based on knowledge is particularly specialized. A person who is otherwise completely unpretending and unimpressive may do some reading and become, for example, a wine snob: he will swirl and sniff and smell the cork and send bottles back and otherwise make himself obnoxious on that one subject. Another person may take up, say, chocolate, and be able to discourse absurdly for an hour or two on the merits of Krön over Godiva. This kind of snobbery based upon a narrow but thorough trove of expertise is a bit depressing, because it reduces one of the great forms, snobbery, to the status of a mere hobby.

A larger, more interesting kind of snobbery based on knowledge is language snobbery. The tribe of such snobs seems to be increasing, even as they slog through solecisms and wail eloquently that the numbers of those who understand the English language are vanishing like the Mayas or Hittites. Droves of purists can be seen shuddering on every street corner when the word hopefully is misused. Their chairman of the board is NBC-TV's Edwin Newman, their chief executive officer the *New York Times*'s William Safire. One author, the late Jean Stafford, had a sign on her back door threatening "humiliation" to anyone who misused hopefully in her house.

The snobbery of residence and place persists, although the price of housing makes it more complicated to bring off. Years ago, a Boston banker moved his family two blocks over on Beacon Hill, in the wrong direction from Louisburg Square. Mrs. Mark Anthony De Wolfe Howe, trying to be polite, remarked, "Oh yes, people are beginning to live there now, aren't they?"

Today, snobberies of residence and place can sometimes be achieved by the familiar flip into reverse snobbery. By the process of gentrification, certain snobs can pioneer in new territories (sections of Brooklyn, for example) and achieve a certain cachet of simultaneous egalitarianism and chic. Then too, there is what might be called the ostentatious plainstyle. In West Texas, for example, extremely wealthy ranchers, their oil wells serenely pumping dollars out of the range day and night, sometimes live in willfully ordinary ranch houses and get around in pickups.

Being a snob of any kind is sometimes more difficult now. In a society of high discretionary capital and instantaneous communications, the snob and recherché effects tend to be copied and even mass-produced with stunning speed. For generations, much of America's old money walked around wearing beat-up crew-neck sweaters that had been around from St. Mark's or New Haven: the khakis were always a little too short, ending just at the ankles, and there were Top-Siders without socks. And so on.

Then this came to be known as the Preppie Look, and every upstart from the suburbs was marching around looking as if he were home from Princeton for the weekend. So how were the real aristocrats to proclaim themselves? By going punk? Slam-dancing at the Harvard Club? As soon as one finds something to be snobbish about, everyone else has got hold of it, and so the central charm of snobbery, the feeling of being something special, vanishes.

The very nature of capitalism militates against a stable snobbery: the capitalist seeks the widest possible market; quality chases the dollars of the mob, but when the mob buys en masse, the illusion of quality, of specialness, vanishes. With metaphysical complexity, the makers of Lacoste shirts have understood this, and are making Lacoste shirts that have no alligator on them, a spectacular instance of self-supersession. In one stroke, Lacoste has taken snobbery into another dimension.

Snobbery is always preposterous but also sometimes useful. "The use of forks at table," observes the English writer Jasper Griffin, "seemed to our Tudor ancestors the height of affectation, and the first to follow that Italian custom doubtless did so in large part, to impress their neighbors with their sophistication. Evolution itself is a process of rising above one's origins and one's station." The writer Sebastien Chamfort located what is surely the ultimate snob, a nameless French gentleman: "A fanatical social climber, observing that all round the Palace of Versailles it stank of urine, told his tenants and servants to come and make water round his château."

If Slang
Is Not a Sin

The classic slang of the sixties is almost a dead language now. It survives only under the protection of certain purists with long memories, heirs to the medieval tradition of monastic scribes. Their honorary abbot is Phil Donahue.

The sixties-bred clergyman, especially the Episcopalian, is for some reason a wondrous curator of the lingo. He ascends his pulpit. "God doesn't want you on a *guilt trip*," he begins, inspired. "God's not *into* guilt. *Bad vibes!* He knows *where you're coming from.* God says, 'Guilt, that's a *bummer.*' The Lord can be pretty *far out* about these things, you know." He goes into a wild fugue of nostalgia. *"Sock it to me! Outasight! Right on!"*

But slang cannot live forever on the past, no matter how magnificent it may have been. Slang needs to be new. Its life is brief, intense, and slightly disreputable, like adolescence. Soon it either settles down and goes into the family business of the language (like *taxi* and *cello* and *hi*) or, more likely, slips off into oblivion, dead as Oscan and Manx. The evening news should probably broadcast brief obituaries of slang words that have passed on. The practice would prevent people from embarrassing themselves by saying things like *swell* or *super.* *"Groovy,* descendant of *cool* and *hip*, vanished from the language today."

Where is the next generation of slang to come from? Not from Valley Girl, the argot made famous lately by Singer Frank Zappa and his daughter, who is named Moon Unit Zappa. "Val" is really a sort of satire of slang, a goof on language and on the dreamily dumb and self-regarding suburban kids who may actually talk like that. It would come out all wrong if a minister were to compose his sermon in Val. "The Lord is awesome," he would have to begin. "He knows that life can sometimes be, like *grody—grody to the max! Fer shirr!*"

Still, slang has deep resources. The French resist barbaric intrusions into the language of Voltaire and Descartes. But American English has traditionally welcomed any bright word that sailed in, no matter how ragged it may have looked on arrival. That Whitmanesque hospitality has given America the richest slang in the world.

An inventory of American slang now, however, can be somewhat disappointing. Slang today seems to lack the playful energy and defiant self-confidence that can send language darting out to make raffish back-alley metaphorical connections and shrewdly teasing inductive games of synonym.

Examine one fairly new item: *airhead*. It means, of course, a brainless person, someone given to stupid behavior and opinions. But it is a vacuous, dispiriting little effort. The word has no invective force or metaphorical charm. When slang settled for the drearily literal (*airhead* equals empty head), it is too tired to keep up with the good stuff.

Much new slang originates with people who have to be in by eight. Junior high and even grade school are unexpectedly productive sources. Sometimes children simply take ordinary words and hold them up to the light at a slightly different angle, an old trick of slang. The ten-year-old will pronounce something *"excellent"* in the brisk, earnest manner of an Army colonel who has just inspected his regiment. (*Primo* means the same thing.) The movie *E.T.* has contributed *penis breath*, an aggressively weird phrase in perfect harmony with the aggressively weird psyche of the eight-year-old. In Minnesota, they say, *for weird*. *Bogus* is an ordinary, though slightly out-of-the-way word that has been recommissioned as youth slang that means fraudulent or simply second-rate or silly. *Bogus* is a different shading of *lame*. Something that is easy is *cinchy*. Overexcited? One is *blowing a hype*.

The young, as always, use slang as an instrument to define status, to wave to peers and even to discipline reality. A real jerk may be a *nerkey*, a combination of *nerd* and *turkey*. Is something *gnarly*? That may be good or bad. But if it is *mega-gnarly*, that is excellent. One may leave a sorority house at U.C.L.A. to *mow a burger*. Slang has less idealogical content now than it had in the sixties. Still, it sometimes arises, like humor, from apprehension. High school students say, "That English test really *nuked* me." On the other hand, in black neighborhoods of Washington, D.C., if you had a good time at a party, you *dropped the bomb*.

The old fifties frat-house leer is evident in today's collegiate slang. To *get naked* means to have a good time, whether or not sex is involved. (That is a new shortened form of the *get-drunk-and-get-naked-party,* which collegians fantasized about twenty years ago.) At Michigan State University, one who is vomiting is *driving the bus,* a reference to the toilet seat and the wretch's need to hang on to it. *Sckacks* means ugly. A *two-bagger* is a girl who requires exactly that to cover her ugliness. Young women, of course, retaliate. At breakfast in Bates Hall at Wellesley, they wonder, "Why bother with a guy if he doesn't *make your teeth fall out?"* *Time to book* means time to leave, which can also be *time to bail.* None of this is exactly brilliant. Slang is sometimes merely a conspiracy of airheads.

American slang is fed by many tributaries. Cops, as sardonic with language as criminals are, refer to a gunshot wound in the head as a *serious headache.* Drug users have their codes, but they seem to have lost some of their glamour. Certain drugs have a fatality about them that cannot be concealed in jaunty language. The comedian Richard Pryor introduced the outer world to *freebasing,* and John Belushi died after he *speed-balled* (mixed heroin and cocaine). Punk language has made a couple of its disarmingly nasty contributions: *sleaze* (as in, "There was a lot of sleaze at the party," meaning much of the transcendentally rotten) has passed from the homosexual vocabulary into punk, and is headed for mainstream English.

The Pentagon speaks of *the power curve,* meaning the direction in which things are tending. Employees at McDonald's describe their specialized burnout as being *burgered-out.* Homosexuals possess a decadently rich special vocabulary that is on the whole inaccessible to *breeders* (heterosexuals).

Television has developed an elaborate jargon that has possibilities as slang. *Voice-over, segue, intro,* and *out of sync* have been part of the more general language for a long time. Now there is the *out-tro,* the stand-up spiel at the end of a news reporter's segment. A vividly cynical new item of TV news jargon is *bang-bang,* meaning the kind of film coverage that TV reporters must have in order to get their reports from El Salvador or the Middle East onto the evening news.

Black slang may not be quite as strong as it was in the sixties. That may mean either that black slang is less productive than before or that it is more successful at remaining exclusive and secret. Two expressions that have popped up: *serious as a heart attack* and *that's Kool and the Gang.* The second is a reference to a popular musical group and a little flourish added to the ancient *that's cool.*

The richest new territory for slang is computer technology. That is unexpected. Slang is usually thought of as a kind of casual conversation in the street, not as a dialogue between the human brain and a machine. Those who go mountaineering up the interface, however, are developing a wonderfully recondite vocabulary. *Hackers* (computer fanatics) at MIT and Stanford maintain a Hacker's Dictionary to keep their common working language accessible to one another. *Input* and *output* have long since entered the wider language. So have *software* and *hardware*. The human brain in some circles is now referred to as *wetware*. When a computer *goes down,* of course, it *crashes. Menu*, meaning a computer's directory of functions, is turning up now as noun and verb, as in "let me *menu* my schedule and I'll get back to you about lunch."

In the Hacker's Dictionary, one finds *gronk* (a verb that means to become unusable, as in "the monitor *gronked*"), *gweep* (one who spends unusually long periods of time hacking), *cuspy* (anything that is exceptionally good or performs its functions exceptionally well), *dink* (to modify in some small way so as to produce large or catastrophic results), *bagbiter* (equipment or program that fails, usually intermittently) and *deadlock* (a situation wherein two or more processes are unable to proceed because each is waiting for the other to do something. This is the electronic equivalent of *gridlock*, a lovely, virtually perfect word that describes automobile traffic paralyzed both ways through an intersection). The hacker's lexicon is endless and weirdly witty, and inspiring in a peculiar way: the human language is caught there precisely in the act of improvisation as it moves through a strange new country. The mind is making itself at home in the mysteries and possibilities of the machines.

A word, Justice Oliver Wendell Holmes wrote, "is the skin of a living thought." The flesh of slang is a little weaker than usual now. Why? For several reasons. Perhaps slang follows the economy and now finds itself a bit recessed.

Tribes make slang, and the old tribes are dissolving. Slang has always been the decoration and camouflage of nervous subgroups: youth, blacks, homosexuals, minorities, pickpockets, small tribes using language as solidarity against the big tribes. Slang proclaims one's specialness and conceals one's secrets. Perhaps the slang of today seems a bit faded because we still live in an aftermath of the sixties, the great revolt of the tribes. The special-interest slangs generated then were interminably publicized. Like the beads and the Afros and gestures and costumes and theatrical rages, slang became an ingredient of the national mixed-media pageant.

Now, with more depressingly important things to do (earn a living, for example), Americans may feel a sense of cultural lull.

As the University of Cincinnati's William Lasher remarks, "Slang doesn't get written down, so it doesn't endure. If you do write it down, it gets into the language, and stops being slang." In a maniacally open electronic society, the news and entertainment industries sift hungrily through the culture searching for color, anecdote, personality, uniqueness and, of course, slang. All these items instantly become part of the show. Slang is wonderful entertainment. But its half-life is shorter now. Good slang gets commercial in a hurry.

There may be a deeper reason for the relative decline of slang. Standard English is losing prestige and even legitimacy. Therefore, deviations from the "correct" also lose some of their force. Slang forfeits a little of its renegade quality, its outlaw savor. If slang is no longer a kind of sin, it cannot be as much fun as it once was.

American Dreams

The Shuttle

The eye accepted what the mind could not: a sudden burst of white and yellow fire, then white trails streaming up and out from the fireball to form a twisted Y against a pure heaven, and the metal turning to rags, dragging white ribbons into the ocean. A terrible beauty exploded like a primal event of physics—the birth of a universe; the death of a star; a fierce, enigmatic violence out of the blue. The mind recoiled in sheer surprise. Then it filled with horror.

One thought first of the teacher and her children—her own and her students. One wanted to snatch them away from the sight and rescind the thing they had seen. But the moment was irrevocable. Over and over, the bright extinction played on the television screen, almost ghoulishly repeated until it had sunk into the collective memory. And there it will abide, abetted by the weird metaphysics of videotape, which permits the endless repetition of a brute finality.

In this grief, some people rebelled, a little brusquely, and asked whether the nation would be pitched into such mourning if, say, a 747 went down with three-hundred Americans. Chuck Yeager, protohero of the space age, observed, "I don't see any difference, except for the public exposure of the shuttle, between this accident and one involving a military or a commercial airplane."

That had the machismo of matter-of-factness. It is true that the tragedy played itself out to maximum dramatic effect: the shuttle, now boringly routine, lifting off and then annihilating itself in full view of the world. It is true that television pitched itself fervently into what has become its sacramental role in national tragedies—first wounding with its vivid repetitions of the event, then consoling, grieving, reconciling, administering the anchor's unctions. It is true that Christa McAuliffe, a teacher representing all the right things in America, rode as a nonprofessional, an innocent, into space, and her death therefore seemed doubly poignant and unfair.

But the loss of the shuttle was a more profound event that that suggests. It inflicted upon Americans the purest pain that they have collectively felt in years. It was a pain uncontaminated by the anger and hatred and hungering for revenge that come in the aftermath of terrorist killings, for example. It was pain uncomplicated by the divisions, political, racial, moral, that usually beset American tragedies (Vietnam and Watergate, to name two). The shuttle crew, spectacularly democratic (male, female, black, white, Japanese American, Catholic, Jewish, Protestant), was the best of us, Americans thought, doing the best of things Americans do. The mission seemed symbolically immaculate, the farthest reach of a perfectly American ambition to cross frontiers. And it simply vanished in the air.

Reimagining America

In 1835 Alexis de Tocqueville called America *une feuille blanche,* a blank page, upon which history waited to be written. History has been scribbling away ever since. So have generations of traveling writers. It became a sort of religious obligation, like the Muslim hajj, for European journalists, geniuses, and hacks to make their way to the New World and there test their sensibilities upon the peppy and savage Nova Zembla that interrupted Columbus on his way to the Orient.

America has always been a splendid subject—and a fat target. For years in the nineteenth century, visiting writers could not decide whether the Americans were a vigorous new race, the future's masters, or an interesting breed of chimps. English writers were especially bemused. They arrived the way an ex-wife might visit the home of a remarried husband, some years after a messy divorce: the ex-wife, dressed to kill, encases her curiosity in a ladylike frost. She *notices* things brutally, and repeats them when she gets home. Mrs. Frances Trollope reported back to England in 1832 that Americans gorge their food with "voracious rapidity"; they swill, guzzle, spit, and pick their teeth with pocket knives. In Cincinnati, she related, cows are nonchalantly milked at the house door, and pigs enjoy such citizenship that they wander at will, rooting in the street garbage and nuzzling pedestrians with their moist snouts. Americans seldom declined to provide a bounteous native rubery for the satirist to exercise his superciliousness upon.

Foreign interpreters arrived like immigrant waves. One of the earliest, and still the genius of the genre, was Tocqueville. He saw beyond livestock and table manners; he viewed democracy with an eerily clairvoyant eye. Half a century later came Lord Bryce, whose *American Common-wealth* (1888) still runs a respectable second. But the visitors have rarely been that wise or objective. The interpretation of America has always been a species of self-discovery—and self-indulgence. E. M. Forster said that America is like life because "you can usually find in it what you look for." A man did not even have to be there to conjure up the promise and marvel; from dark, medieval Prague, Kafka imagined his *Amerika*. He believed that everyone there always, invariably, was smiling.

America is—or was at one time—sufficiently vast and enigmatic in its newness to accommodate the most extravagant fantasies. The republic of the questing amateur, because it had no prehistory (for white men), none of the cultural grids grooved by the centuries into old lands, yielded itself to an interminable amateurism of interpretation. Americans were a race of Adams rolling west across Eden, blowing the heads off rattlesnakes with their revolvers.

The great American blank page filled up as cargoes of adjectives spilled out upon it: primitive, hostile, desolate, vacant, dazing, Edenic, blessed, obstreperous, eagle-screaming, slave-driving, egalitarian, myth-stained, rapacious, naive, improvisational, hospitable, dangerous, destined, sanc-timonious, shrewd, sentimental, quick, profligate, protean, complacent, oblivious, uncultured, venal, generous, banal, violent, abstracted, inse-cure, guilt-stricken, self-lacerating, tolerant, ultimately indefinable, and sometimes nice: America.

In *Imagining America* (Oxford University Press) English cultural critic Peter Conrad assembled a fascinating collection of English writers' visions of the New World. Conrad tours the works of Charles Dickens and Anthony and Frances Trollope, of that bird of paradise Oscar Wilde and the doomed poet Rupert Brooke, of Rudyard Kipling and Robert Louis Stevenson, of the futuristic H. G. Wells and the primitivist D. H. Lawrence, of W. H. Auden and Christopher Isherwood, and the satirist-turned-California-mystic Aldous Huxley.

Conrad saturated himself in his writers' work more profoundly than in the subject of their meditations. *Imagining America* is subtle, briskly and even dashingly learned, frequently funny (with an odd undercurrent of nastiness, like the smile of a dog about to bite) and, now and then, totally wrong. But Americans, who have always been abnormally sensitive to the opinions of others and simultaneously oblivious to them, might enjoy the bizarrely colored and refracting lenses that Conrad gathered. They might read the book and wonder through what glass they themselves view the nation now. Conrad's exercise is literary, impressionistic, and symbolic rather than sociological or historical. Through his analysis, a succession of Americas unfolds. There is, first, the dispiritingly uncouth barnyard of Mrs. Trollope and Dickens, a place, as Conrad says, without social amenity or historical depth, a land as temporary and makeshift as its shop fronts.

The exquisite Oscar Wilde, in his overcoat of bottle-green otter fur, made his scented way through America in 1882, scattering epigrams and languidly outraging the locals. "Mrs. Trollope had hoped to redeem America by making it well mannered," writes Conrad. "Wilde hoped to redeem it by making it stylish." Wilde lectured the miners at Leadville, Colorado, on the Florentine painters; he hired secretaries to distribute locks of his hair. Aesthetic in a different way, Henry James once viewed Niagara Falls and, like a fastidious critic, pronounced it to be "thought out" and "successfully executed."

Amid the literary swags, Conrad locates a theme that may be the most profound in American history: the story of man subduing a continent of vast distances and danger and, so it seemed, divinely bestowed wealth. H. G. Wells admired the fierce mechanical aspiration of the Americans: "Cerebral technocrats who will inherit the earth."

If Wells saw the future in American technology, the mystagogic D. H. Lawrence drew a distinction between primal America, which appealed to his fancy sense of atavism, and "the mechanical empire of Uncle Samdom." Auden picked up at least a part of the theme. Wrote Conrad: "The economic vice of Europeans, in Auden's view, is avarice, while that of Americans is waste." Nature, vast and promising, exists ultimately to be conquered and transformed into the benisons of the shopping mall. But at the far end of the interpretation, God's plenitude and bounty begin to be exhausted. What then?

Foreign writers have rumbled across America in buckram and paperback trying to conquer it, to understand it. But Americans themselves now seem to have trouble imagining their country. The terms and arrangements of the American enterprise are changing. The entire American proposition has been built upon the premise of ever expanding opportunity, upon a vision of the future as a territory open-ended and always unfolding upon ascendant history. "We are the heirs of all time," said Herman Melville. What happens if the future seems to be closing down, to be darkening?

A stale air of foreclosure has wafted around. It is not that the United

States is broke. But Americans have always needed to know the point of it all; that has been part of their peculiar national "innocence" and residual Puritan sense of themselves as the new elect of God. Without such grace or rationale, without the comfort of their demonstrable virtue and uniqueness, Americans feel themselves sliding toward triviality, and beyond that, toward an abyss that might swallow the whole experiment like a black hole. "Either America is the hope of the world," one dogmatically friendly Frenchman wrote twenty years ago, "or it is nothing."

In August 1943, after a Japanese destroyer rammed his PT-109, John Kennedy wrote to his parents: "For an American, it's got to be awfully easy or awfully tough. When it's in the middle, then there's trouble." Americans have been rattling around fecklessly in the middle, but now are rolling toward the awfully tough.

All of this moral drifting has complicated the way Americans imagine their country. Many of them remain sunnily confident. But the old interpretations, the old American theology, no longer work very well. Americans invented themselves in the first place, and then were interminably reinvented by the rest of the world. Perhaps more than most peoples, they need to possess an idea of themselves, a myth of themselves, an explanation of themselves.

Dreaming of
the Eisenhower Years

Ronald Reagan preaches "a New Beginning," but Americans (in the summer of 1980) trying to envision his Administration sometimes find their minds drifting back to the 1950s. Ike, they tell themselves. Maybe, if he won, Ronald Reagan would turn into a kind of Eisenhower. Or at any rate, maybe the effect would be the same: a long quiescence, an essentially sane and minimalist White House presiding over a "normality" that the nation has not experienced for a generation. Even some voters who are chilled by Reagan's politics and his followers have begun to take wistful consolation in the thought that the future under Reagan might be a kind of doubling back to the simpler past of the fifties: not the most ennobling American era, they admit, but not such a bad one either. Worse things have happened, such as twenty years of assassinations, riots, Vietnam and Watergate, OPEC's extortions and the dollar's humiliation. *Après Ike, le déluge.* Eisenhower's fifties begin to seem an almost golden time.

The Eisenhower-Reagan comparison is an interesting and almost subliminal effect now forming in the American imagination. It has gone largely unexamined. It is an intuition, a form of anticipatory nostalgia. It may also be an exercise in hopeful self-deception.

The psychological mechanics are tricky. For years Dwight Eisenhower's historical reputation bumped along in the lower ranks of American presidencies. One 1962 poll of American historians and political scientists placed him rather degradingly in the spot between Andrew Johnson and Chester A. Arthur: a mediocre and listless ex-soldier summoned from the links. Ike's sarcastic contemporaries liked to joke about "the bland leading the bland,'' about his goofy grin and the stack of Zane Grey westerns on his night table. He was forever playing golf or fishing, or otherwise treating the White House, they said, as a pleasant retirement home. And there was Ike's language, those famously incoherent press conference sentences that used to move across an idea like a dense fog; the technical term for the disorder is anacoluthon, the sentence that careers around several corners and then lands in a ditch, its wheels spinning unintelligibly. Ike's press secretary, James Hagerty, used to edit the transcripts of his press conferences (body and fender work) before letting him be quoted directly.

But the years since Ike yielded to John Kennedy have changed the perspective on Eisenhower's fifties. He has profited by comparison with the Presidents who followed him; Jack Kennedy promised in 1960 to ''get the country moving again,'' but American society came down with motion sickness. Eisenhower's was the last complete presidency that began and ended without tragedy or trauma and disgrace.

The General's reputation in recent years has been revised and rehabilitated, sometimes rather extravagantly. In the Vietnam era, liberals like I. F. Stone and Murray Kempton found a brilliance in Eisenhower previously undetected by intellectuals. He had resisted the best efforts of his advisers to get him to help the French in Indochina in the weeks before Dien Bien Phu. Despite CIA adventuring around the world, despite the American-sponsored coups in Guatemala and Iran, despite that sunbathing Marine exercise on the Lebanese beaches in 1958, despite Foster Dulles's fondness for leaning over the brink, Eisenhower kept the nation out of war. In *Nixon Agonistes,* Garry Wills called Ike ''a political genius.'' Nixon, for his part, recorded in his *Six Crises* that Eisenhower ''was a far more complex and devious man than most people realized, and in the best sense of those words.'' (Those phrases may be the purest elixir of Nixon's thought that was ever bottled.)

Princeton political scientist Fred Greenstein has spent several years establishing the case in a scholarly way. Eisenhower, says Greenstein, was an extraordinarily intelligent, experienced, and sophisticated President who worked hard, but deliberately concealed much of his effort. ''Hidden-hand leadership,'' says Greenstein, permitted Eisenhower to maintain his own dignified aura and personal authority with the nation (a moral authority never even approximately regained by his successors), while actively managing his presidency. Even those garbled answers at press conferences, Greenstein thinks, were a stratagem meant to conceal, soothe, and deflect. Once, when Hagerty advised Ike to refuse to answer any question about the Formosa Straits, the situation being especially tricky then, the President replied: "Don't worry, Jim. If that question comes up, I'll just confuse them."

Today, the comparative rehabilitation of Eisenhower's reputation works in a subtle way to legitimize the idea of a Ronald Reagan presidency. It is as if an anticipatory revisionism on Reagan were already at work. If he now seems somewhat simple and inexperienced and possibly not up to the job, an undercurrent suspicion goes, well, they said that about Ike once, and look what they are saying now. In other words, this impulse instructs voters to mistrust any unfavorable judgment of Reagan now as a hedge against future revisionism. Reagan borrows some shine from Eisenhower's retrospective glow.

But do Eisenhower and Reagan—in temperament, education, experience, talent, knowledge, and techniques of leadership—have much to do with each other? Some of their characteristics are similar—the winning American grin, the air of decent good guy. In both, the voter senses a remarkably steady emotional grip, a self-confidence; both inspire loyalty. In neither have Americans detected those dark glints of paranoia and compulsion that eventually repelled them in some Presidents after Ike.

Both Reagan and Eisenhower have taken a sort of chairman-of-the-board view of the presidency. Like Eisenhower, Reagan would draw heavily upon industry and commerce for his highest appointees. Reagan and Eisenhower share a preference for successful businessmen as friends and advisers (also an enthusiasm of Richard Nixon's). Reagan in Sacramento, like Ike in Washington, favored a nine-to-five workday regularity, delegating responsibilities heavily to Cabinet and staff.

Philosophically, Ike was a pragmatist. "The path to America's future," he declared in 1949, "lies down the middle of the road." He liked to be called a "responsible progressive." Reagan talks a much harder ideological line; he is the fount of Reaganism, after all. But, in Sacramento, Reagan demonstrated a flexibility about raising taxes and welfare payments that went against his own strict dogmas.

The actor, who performed his World War II service making training films in Hollywood, possesses a respect for the military that borders on awe. Eisenhower, after a professional lifetime in uniform, took a more jaundiced view. He knew more about war and arms than his defense secretaries and joint chiefs ever did. He did not hesitate to contradict them. He resisted military spending. He believed in "nuclear sufficiency," not superiority; he knew that nuclear weapons had forever, unalterably, changed his old profession. Eisenhower was not inclined to rattle the saber too much. Ironically, it was the Democrats in 1960 who campaigned blusteringly about the "missile gap," which they said Ike had permitted.

The most profound differences between Reagan and Eisenhower spring from contrasts in their backgrounds and experience. Eisenhower had orchestrated the largest and most complex military operation in history—the retaking of Western Europe. In that job, he functioned as supreme diplomat as well as soldier. Ike's expertise in foreign policy was thorough, practiced, and instinctive. He dealt with men like Churchill on an equal basis. Reagan has worked as an actor and served eight years as Governor of the nation's most populous state. That experience may exceed Jimmy Carter's when *he* arrived in Washington, but it does not stack up well against Eisenhower's.

Perhaps Eisenhower's greatest asset was his credibility with the American people. If they wished to doze off through the fifties, they counted on Ike to wake them when anything important came up. Reagan, for all of his crinkling, swell-guy charm, says things that tend to keep people sitting bolt upright, with sweat on their palms.

But the core of the psychological comparison lies deeper than résumés and managerial techniques. It has to do with symbols, with faith and luck. Whatever his talents, Eisenhower was an extraordinarily lucky man; he seemed to arrive at the White House between great disasters, and he did nothing to hurry new ones along. The present idea of the Eisenhower years, however, is a nostalgic distortion, an unconsciously artful forgetfulness about what the Eisenhower years were really like.

A certain *Happy Days* sentimentality has encouraged the idea that America in the fifties was touchingly innocent, but at the time the nation seemed infinitely more complicated than that, hugely varied, exuberant, and, at this distance, rather strange. The benign nimbus of Eisenhower presided over all of it, and if people snickered at him behind his back, they seemed like adolescents wisecracking about the Old Man, Oedipal maybe, but not completely malicious.

The decade was a manic burst of inventive, occasionally screwball materialism, a wild exfoliation of pastels and plastics, superhighways and suburban tracts. The entire culture seemed to have teenage glands. New, unsettling dimensions suddenly opened; the interstate highway system, the picture window, the grainy little black-and-white universe of television. Gas was cheap, and bright, big-finned Detroit cars with Dynaflow or Hydra-Matic swooshed Americans up and down the landscape in rhapsodies of mobility, well-being, and heedlessness. In 1954, Oklahoma A&M College surveyed its students to ask their greatest fears and problems. The students answered that their greatest worry in the world was finding a parking space.

The decade was in many ways fascinating and often fun. Everyone who lived through the period carries a mental collage of its dense popular culture; one remembers it now with a small smile of disbelief at the ingenious pointlessness of it: Milton Berle and Pinky Lee, *My Little Margie* and *American Bandstand,* Gorgeous George and Johnny Ray, and Elvis televised from the waist up on the *Ed Sullivan Show.* Grace Metalious (*Peyton Place*) and Mickey Spillane were available for mildly salacious excitement; the new tranquilizers (Miltown, Thorazine) saw to the jitters of civilization; Fulton Sheen and Norman Vincent Peale attended to the soul.

The immense energy of the time left many introspective. The virtues of the time were conformity, domesticity, respectability, security, attention to religion. Norman Mailer hated the whole business enough to call the fifties "one of the worst decades in the history of man." And the dark side was dark enough. A thin film of nuclear terror coated the soul. For a time, Joe McCarthy was loose, with all the blackbirds of his paranoia. When Ike federalized the Arkansas National Guard to integrate the schools of Little Rock, the country had an ugly glimpse of things to come. If we think of the fifties now as the last golden age, a period of moral poise, they seemed at the time very different. Archibald MacLeish wrote in 1955: "We have entered the Age of Despondency, with the Age of Desperation just around the corner." Someone is always saying that; it is almost always true.

The Reagan years, should they come to pass, will occur in a different world. The Eisenhower years were postwar boom time; American power dominated the world then, and gasoline cost thirty cents per gallon. But even then Americans were skittish, with a sense of things sliding out of their hands, of an uncontrollable future.

Whoever wins the presidency must restore to some extent a sense of the future's manageability. What Reagan evokes about the fifties is an attitude of militant nostalgia, a will almost to veto the intervening years and start again on earlier premises. Ike and the fifties are symbols of a state of mind. But as Albert Camus wrote in 1940, when the future was perhaps least manageable of all: "We will not win our happiness with symbols. We'll need something more solid."

Excellence

A biography of Admiral Hyman Rickover records a Navy captain's assessment: " 'Look around. Do you see excellence anywhere? In medicine? In law? Religion? Anywhere? We have abandoned excellence. . . . But Rickover was a genius who gave a generation of naval officers the idea that excellence was the standard.' " Only the nuclear submarines ran on time.

"Abandoned" seems a little strong to describe what we have done to excellence. But of course a note of elegy always haunts discussions of excellence and quality. It is human nature to imagine that our present reality is squalid, diminished, an ignominious comedown from better days when household appliances lasted and workers worked, and manners were exquisite and marriages endured, and wars were just, and honor mattered, and you could buy a decent tomato. The lament for vanished standards is an old art form: besieged gentility cringes, indignant and vulnerable, full of memories, before a present that behaves like Stanley Kowalski: crude, loud, upstart, and stupid as a fist.

Americans seem especially wistful about excellence now. After years of change that hurled the cultural furniture around and turned much of it to junk, they are apt to think longingly of excellence. They may watch a film like *Chariots of Fire,* for example, with a nostalgic pang for the simplicity of its moral lines, its portrait of excellence unambiguously pursued.

Is the Navy captain correct? Has a quality called Excellence gone under like Atlantis in an inundation of the third-rate of deluge of plastics, junk food, bad movies, cheap goods, and trashy thought? The question has been asked since well before the decline of Athens; the answer is generally yes—but wait. There is an enduring ecology of excellence in the world. It is a good idea to remember Thomas Merton's question: "How did it ever happen that, when the dregs of the world had collected in Western Europe, when Goth and Frank and Norman and Lombard had mingled with the rot of old Rome to form a patchwork of hybrid races, all of them notable for ferocity, hatred, stupidity, craftiness, lust, and brutality—how did it happen that, from all this, there should come the Gregorian chant, monasteries and cathedrals, the poems of Prudentius, the commentaries and histories of Bede . . . St. Augustine's *City of God*?"

A couple of rules may apply to generalizations about excellence: 1) all recollections of past excellence should be discounted by at least fifty percent; memory has its tricks of perspective; 2) what might be called the Walt Whitman Rule: exuberant democratic energy usually finds its own standards and creates its own excellence, even though the keepers of the old standards may not like the new. A Big Mac may sometimes surpass the concoctions of Julia Child.

Of course, much that was once excellent has fallen into disrepair, or worse. The dollar, for example. New York City. American public education. Cars from Detroit. Standards of civility (which may not have been as civil in the past as we imagine). Public safety. But who said that any excellence is permanent?

Excellence demands standards. It does not usually flourish in the midst of rapid, hectic change. This century's sheer velocity has subverted the principle of excellence; a culture must be able to catch its breath.

In America and elsewhere in the industrial world, the idea of excellence acquired in the past twenty years a sinister and even vaguely fascistic reputation. It was the Best and the Brightest, after all, who brought us Vietnam. For a long time, many of the world's young fell into a dreamy, vacuous inertia, a canned wisdom of the East persuading them that mere being would suffice, was even superior to action. "Let It Be," crooned Paul McCartney. Scientific excellence seemed apocalyptically suspect— the route to pollution and nuclear destruction. Striving became suspect. A leveling contempt for "elitism" helped to divert much of a generation from the ambition to be excellent.

The deepest American dilemma regarding excellence arises from the nation's very success. The United States has been an astonishing phenomenon—excellent among the nations of the world. But as the prophet Amos said, "Woe to them that are at ease in Zion." It is possible to have repose, or to have excellence, but only some decorative hereditary monarchs have managed to simulate both. Success has cost Americans something of their energetic desire. And those Americans not yet successful (the struggling, the underclass) are apt to aim at ease, not excellence: the confusion contaminates character and disables ambition.

The manic overstimulation of American culture also makes excellence rarer. The great intellectual flowering of New England in the nineteenth century (Hawthorne, Emerson, Melville, Thoreau, Longfellow, *et al.*) resulted in part from the very thinness of the New England atmosphere, an under-stimulation that made introspection a sort of cultural resource. America today is so chaotically hyped, its air so thick with kinetic information and alarming images and television and drugs, that the steady gaze required for excellence is nearly impossible. The trendier victims retreat to sealed isolation tanks to float on salt water and try to calm down.

Yet excellence remains. The United States has won 140 Nobel prizes since World War II—although cuts in government research grants will reduce the level of that particular excellence in the years to come. American medicine, biology, and physics lead the world. American politicians (that least excellent breed) may be better educated, more honest and industrious—more excellent—than ever. Vermont maple syrup is excellent. American agriculture is excellent. Ted Hood's sails are excellent. American telephone service is excellent. American professional sports would be excellent if they were not so drenched in greed. Look abroad: the French language is excellent. Some would argue that the entire country of Switzerland is excellent (if somewhat savorless), from its unemployment rate (.3 percent) to its scenery to its national airline.

Americans have historically allowed themselves to become confused by the fact that their practical excellence has been so profitable. But the meaning of excellence (serious excellence, not Big Macs) is essentially metaphysical. Excellent things are constantly destroyed, of course—bombed, defaced, or else misunderstood; a conquering army may some day bivouac in the Sistine Chapel and take target practice at the ceiling. But excellence is essentially invulnerable. It carries the prestige of the infinite with it, an ancestral resemblance to the ideal. It is ecstatic. For an irrevocable moment, it gives the mind what Melville called "topgallant delight."

The Return of Patriotism

The New American patriotism probably started with the Bicentennial. After Vietnam and Watergate, 1976 turned into a vast, star-spangled ceremony of self-forgiveness. Later came certain movies *(Midnight Express* and *The Deer Hunter,* for example) that were fascinating in their allegory: each portrayed American youth abroad, wholesome and handsome and lovable, yet in the grips of foreigners as evil as reptiles. In early 1980, Americans were inclined to think that reality (whether in Tehran or Bogotá) had confirmed the allegory. U.S. citizens are held hostage far from home; the dangerous and primitive outer world does not play by the rules, it seems. The Soviet Union rolls over Afghanistan with no more moral hesitation than an exterminator spraying pesticide.

A complicated impulse has stirred in Americans' thinking about their country and its place in the world. Patriotism has reappeared, along with its scruffy little half brothers, xenophobia and chauvinism. In an odd but exactly appropriate way, the new sentiment was crystallized most purely in Americans' jubilation over the U.S. hockey team's performance in the 1980 Olympics—the Huckleberry Finn American underdogs whipping the Soviet superteam and then going on for the gold medal.

It was just a hockey game, of course; it had no bearing on American foreign policy or prestige or power in the world. And yet it was such a dramatically and symbolically delicious moment that Americans erupted briefly in spontaneous, childlike gladness. The very innocence of the conquest made it sweetly uncomplicated and morally unimpeachable. The nation indulged in small orgies of flag waving and anthem singing. At a Stop & Shop supermarket in Cambridge, Massachusetts, the PA system suddenly blurted that the U.S. hockey team had beaten the Soviets. The store erupted as bags of cookies, paper towels, and anything else handy were tossed into the air with pandemonious cheering. One psychiatrist reported his patients telling him how, for days, tears shot to their eyes when they thought of those American boys.

It would be a mistake to exaggerate the significance of the joyful outburst; in a tough winter for American morale; the 1980 Olympic hockey team victory was a lovely diversion. Still, the moment was connected in some deeper ways to the emergence of a new patriotic impulse in America. It seems to many that the villains have moved overseas again; fewer Americans are transfixed by any evil within. They have the patriotism of outraged innocence (contaminated somewhat by association with the Shah and by the tales of SAVAK tortures). Americans, for so long vaguely depressed by endless quarrels among themselves, now find they are in an unexpected kinship of common interest and travail.

Patriotism has often had a terrible reputation. Samuel Johnson called it "the last refuge of a scoundrel." Tolstoy thundered: "There never has been a combined act of violence by one set of people upon another set of people that has not been perpetrated in the name of patriotism." Patriotism is both indispensable and dangerous, involving always the hazards of the self being ceded to the larger purposes of the fatherland. Hitler had a sinister little instinct for patriotic sentiment. Patriotism, or a debased form of it, raucous with jingo and the bully's knuckles, has led the United States astray from time to time; citizens hounded German Americans during World War I, for example. They did idiotic and ominous things—imagining that Einstein's theory of relativity had Bolshevist origins, and acclaiming the neonativist persecution of immigrants with socialist ideas.

Patriotism has most often gone wrong when people have confused loyalty to the republic with loyalty to one government or another. Political leaders almost invariably seek to legitimize themselves by the *"l'état, c'est moi"* strategy that makes their own interests inseparable from the well-being of the country itself; disloyalty to one becomes disloyalty to the other. Thus the Nixon Administration had it that its critics were unpatriotic. J. Edgar Hoover used the FBI to try to destroy the lives of "unpatriotic" Americans like Martin Luther King, Jr.

The unpredictabilities of the world have supplied Jimmy Carter with a kind of spontaneous American sense of national community. He has not hesitated to exploit the mood in his campaign for reelection. That is perhaps human and inevitable, but also dangerous. The politician who exploits patriotism for political gain, even if he is president, risks discrediting both himself and, more sadly, a love of country that has only recently begun recovering the self-confidence to show itself in public again.

At its truest, American patriotism has a sort of abstraction about it that makes it uniquely difficult and valuable: it is a devotion not to a specific physical place, gene pool, cuisine, or cultural tradition, but to a political and social vision, a promise and the idea of freedom—an idea not much honored elsewhere in the world or in history. At its worst, American patriotism degenerates into a coarse form of national self-congratulation.

Patriotism should have higher ambitions. Columbia University sociologist Amitai Etzioni saw the stirrings as a fitful groping toward some kind of national unity. The most significant symptom he detected was the jump in the proportions of voters casting ballots in the primaries in 1980. Because of Iran and Afghanistan, said Etzioni, "we have what I call a hinge effect. All projections up to that point have to be redone. We largely put behind us the Vietnam complex. This is the turning point in political apathy. We had a decade and a half of retreat from institutions, identity, directions, and commitment. There was a tremendous yearning there, and there still is."

Americans have a friskily self-destructive habit of turning even their best impulses into junk and kitsch; a Beverly Hills hair salon lately had eight models in tank tops and khaki trousers parading around the shop carrying flags and sporting new "military" hair styles. The entrepreneur turns militarism into a profitable fad. Love of country, by such associations, comes to seem vaguely sick and stupid.

It should be possible to love one's country intelligently, without being either a schlockmeister or an incipient Nazi. (Anyone incapable of distinguishing between the Third Reich and the United States is a moral imbecile.) Patriotism seems so easy to discredit that it dies of contempt a few hours after budding. But the real problem is deeper. Americans who would be patriots must try to learn what it is that they have in common, what it is in the republic that is worth cherishing and preserving. Until they know that, their patriotism will have no more content than a bright, loud afternoon parade.

An Elegy for the New Left

Nothing can last in America more than ten years.
—Philip Rahv

In 1967, the New Left was just starting to harvest its biggest crops of the newly radicalized. Draft cards and American flags went up in smoke. The Spring Mobilization to End the War in Vietnam brought together hundreds of thousands of protesters in San Francisco and New York. Dow Chemical's recruiters were driven off campus. Ahead for the movement lay Woodstock, Chicago, Kent State, the Days of Rage . . .

Ten years later, the children's revolution of the sixties came straggling back, startling to recognize in the summer of 1977. As if they had been flash-frozen in 1970, demonstrators at Kent State had been trying to prevent construction of a gym near the spot where four students died. Sometimes the sixties reappear as a waxworks item of nostalgia: four young men each night took the stage of Manhattan's Winter Garden theater to impersonate the Beatles of long ago. Or else a fable of arrogance brought low: those who warned "Never trust anyone over thirty" are now losing their hair. Bob Dylan's wife ("something is happening here but you don't know what it is do you Mister Jones?") divorced him because she said that, among other things, he was a wife beater.

Once, the generation of the New Left and counterculture believed that its youth, like the war in Vietnam, would go on forever. The period seems prime for revisionism and ridicule. But to see that generation contemptuously as merely the screaming, Spock-coddled army of Consciousness III ignores the great changes it helped to cause in American life. Says Tom Hayden, one of the founders of the Students for a Democratic Society, "We ended a war, toppled two presidents, desegregated the South, broke other barriers of discrimination." The energies of the young during the sixties made Americans begin to think about their environment, about the poor, about the purposes of progress.

The problem—and the charm—was that nobody in the sixties planned anything. And so Hayden is left to wonder ruefully: "How could we accomplish so much and have so little at the end?" Part of the answer lies in an epigram of the social theorist Ernest Becker: "A protest without a program is little more than sentimentalism—this is the epitaph of many of the great idealisms." The first generation raised by the pale blue light of the tube grew up on the sweet simplicities of *Leave It to Beaver;* it had an outrageous inclination to think that all of life's injustices could be straightened out in time for the station break.

The young of the sixties were raised to believe that America was a splendidly virtuous country. When they found—through the Bay of Pigs, Selma, the assassinations, Vietnam—that it was something more ambiguous, they rose up in a horror that now seems touching in its spontaneity. They joined in immense numbers—the baby boom's demographic bulge— and without philosophy or program. That was the strength and ultimate weakness of the movement: it arose out of moral outrage and indignation, and grew larger precisely because it was so formless. When the production ran out of moral energy, it collapsed like a small dying star.

Repression did its part, of course; the Black Panthers had much of their leadership wiped out by the police. But there were other reasons. The war ended. Time passed. Metabolisms changed. Manson and Altamont— a California rock festival where a young man was knifed to death—took the innocence out of being a freak. In a post-mortem on the "tired radicals" of the First World War era, author Walter Weyl wrote, "Adolescence is the true day of revolt, the day when obscure forces, as mysterious as growth, push us, trembling out of our narrow lives, into the wide throbbing life beyond self."

The New Left operated in a cavalier—and ultimately fatal—ignorance of the past. It should have known, should have remembered, that the American left has always been its own worst enemy, that, as historian Christopher Lasch wrote, "the history of American radicalism . . . is largely a history of failure. Radicalism in the United States has no great triumphs to record." Lasch may be too disconsolate. Nonetheless, the radical movement of the World War I era broke up in factionalism and failure after the Bolshevik revolution. The so-called Old Left that grew up in the thirties was split into bitter opposing tribes by Stalinism and then McCarthyism. The New Left, though less doctrinaire, also disintegrated into factions, especially after losing the unifying issue of Vietnam.

The kids who made up the New Left and counterculture are men and women now. They did not merely step onto the centrifuge of the sixties and pinwheel themselves out in the direction of Aquarius, to vanish forever. Many simply settled down. Says David Dellinger, sixty-two, an elder statesman of the movement: "A lot of people had been leading emergency lives for a long time. They had put off schooling, babies, their own lives." Whatever their real accomplishments, the New Leftists and their allies during the sixties were engaged in an immense, new kind of theater. It was a cultural spectacle; eventually, both players and audience were obliged to go and look after things at home.

As always, the United States has demonstrated an infuriating (to radicals) talent for absorbing and accommodating even those who began by wanting to tear the whole place down. Smoking marijuana is practically legal; the draft has been abolished.

A number of American corporations are feeling the presence of executives in their thirties who, having been schooled in sixties virtues, want more openness and disclosure in business, more debate before making decisions, more flexibility in personal and professional styles. Says Stephen McLin, thirty, a vice president for the Bank of America (an outfit some radicals kept trying to burn down about seven years ago): "The impact of this generation will be felt. But the time isn't now. It's coming in about four or five years."

It may be a delusion to think that the country is finished with what used to be called Woodstock Nation. Pierre Joseph Proudhon warned about "the fecundity of the unexpected." The present comparative quiet probably will not last. Issues such as nuclear energy, the arms race (the neutron bomb), the environment, the economy, unemployment and the urban underclass all lie in wait. It would of course be difficult for history to duplicate the long, wild hallucination of the sixties. But Rahv's ten-year rule applies to historical pauses as well as upheavals. The cycle will come around again.

Is the Going
Still Good?

A de Havilland Canada Twin Otter set down on the ice at the North Pole.
The ice cracked and the plane began to sink slowly into the slush of the
Arctic Ocean. Everyone clambered out onto safer ice: two crewmen and
seven tourists.

Their package tour had popped in upon a waste of once mystical in-
accessibility, the place that Peary's dog sled struggled to in 1909. The
tourists landed on an abstraction and almost fell through the top of the
world. They sat for a few hours like a family stuck on a freeway with
engine trouble, and then another plane came and drove them back.

A trip to the North Pole may put the question most purely: Why all of
that expensive motion? Why do we travel? To penetrate mysteries? The
earth does not withhold many secrets anymore. Everyone who did not,
for one reason or another, travel to China last year is sure to go this year.
A tour bus runs down nearly every street in the global village. When does
travel degenerate into snobbism or a stunt? Lars-Eric Lindblad, impre-
sario of the edifyingly exotic, takes the vacationing bartender where Dar-
win most remotely went.

The metaphysics of travel has changed. Television turns us all into what
the author Paul Fussell calls "stationary tourists," electronic cosmopo-
lites. The webbing of satellites around the planet, the "remote feeds"
from almost anywhere, give us the illusion that we are world travelers, or
at least that we are all caught in the planetary claustrum and intercon-
nection. National Geographic specials take us farther, more vividly, than
we would have the courage or knowledge to go if we were traveling in
body, not just in mind. The television anchorman Dan Rather turns up in

rag-top native drag in Afghanistan, the surrogate of our culture with his camera crew, intrepid as Sir Richard Burton sneaking into Mecca.

We sometimes sense that we have reached a moment of critical mass when travel is somehow no longer necessary. The terrestrial explorations have been done. Do we really need to wander through one another's cultures, smelling the cooking? Could we just hook up to each other by videophone, perhaps with a sensory attachment, and simply dial Bali or Maui or Angkor Wat? Must the body go there when the mind can almost make it by other means?

If we do bestir ourselves, we ride out to big airports and climb onto big planes that are as amiably de-cultured as Muzak, as white sound. The jumbo jet is the airborne equivalent of the interstate highway—fast and convenient, but a sort of whispering vacuum. One might as well be stuffed into a cartridge and shot through a pneumatic tube, like interoffice mail.

We travel to be in some sense transformed. Travel is process, a transit, a sheer going there as much as an arriving. Travel equals transformation over time. It is everything experienced from start to finish. What happens to travel when it consists of getting onto a plane and eating a tray dinner and having a drink and watching a movie? And then getting off the plane at an airport much like the one we left and riding to a big hotel and finding a room where the toilet seat wears a paper sash FOR YOUR SANITARY PROTECTION? Our amazement at the world curdles into irony.

The standard threnody for grand travel always sounds like that. In his book *Abroad*, Fussell argues that "travel is hardly possible anymore." Once, the traveler embarked upon the world with a sense of spaciousness and mystery. The modern world's adventuring began with the great explorers sailing west from the Renaissance. Next came the age of grand continental travel, and then a highly literary travel culminating in the wanderings of men like Evelyn Waugh and D. H. Lawrence and Robert Byron in the years after the first World War. Travel had a certain Noel Coward élan. Robert Benchley is said to have cabled home from Venice: STREETS FULL OF WATER. ADVISE.

The upper-class English had a genius for travel; they took their imperial self-confidence with them into the world. Some of them, like T. E. Lawrence, wanted to be someone else; like all intelligent travelers, he knew that landscape is an articulate moral category. He found a hard, almost fanatical clarity in Arabia, a purity that transformed the unhappy Englishman into a mystic desert hero. Other Englishmen and Americans, aloof, invulnerable, their servants laboring under steamer trunks and their gazes trained on cathedrals and pyramids, traveled almost as a means of confirming their own moral superiority. They took their baksheesh back in the form of a deeper smugness. In such cases, travel did not broaden, but rather narrowed the mind.

It is a narcissistic fallacy of travel to imagine that one's mere passing through sets up a charmed understanding between traveler and native, or even a bare comprehension. A kind of Heisenberg Principle usually goes to work: the observation of visitors alters the behavior of the observed, sometimes in ugly ways. Theodore Roosevelt, age eleven, recorded a story in his diary of the family's grand tour in 1869. The Roosevelts tossed small pieces of cake to a crowd of Italian beggars: "We made them open their mouths and tossed cake into it." Like chickens, like pigeons in the park.

In any case, says Fussell, the great age of travel is gone. "The explorer seeks the undiscovered, the traveler that which has been discovered by the mind working in history, the tourist what has been discovered by entrepreneurship and prepared for him by the arts of mass publicity."

It is an old argument—true up to a point, but contaminated by a certain elitism and inattention to the present. Tour groups have changed the nature and freedom and spontaneity of travel. But the backpacking young travel with as much energy and expertise as Waugh did, and with much less money. They prowl the world a little outside the law, at risk—dope smugglers sometimes, or else the dreamy, suburbanite youth between ashrams, on the road to Katmandu. The trouble is that these wanderers rarely can write very well, or bother to.

The depressing truth is that travelers tend to be bores. They tend to be waterbugs skittering across the surface of other cultures without learning anything important that they can express. They learn fugitive skills—how to avoid being cheated, how to cross borders. They come back in a daze of wonder. But even today's writers who travel are remarkably good: Paul Theroux *(The Great Railway Bazaar)*, Edward Hoagland *(African Calliope)*, Jonathan Raban *(Old Glory: An American Voyage)*, and the splendidly mordant V. S. Naipaul.

Why do people travel? Judge it first by its trophies. The tourists at the North Pole had cameras. Their slides from the adventure will be more exciting than millions of others to be assembled this season from the Grand Canyon and Peking and Machu Picchu and Nice.

The night sounds of autumn: slide projectors clicking in the dark to punctuate a drone of travelogue. The audience writhes and dozes and works its eyes open and shut like jalousies. Etna will be seen in a bleeding, theatrical sunset. The Acropolis will be out of focus, Dorothy sharp in the foreground. Here is Carl squirting himself with a wineskin at Pamplona. Retired professors (triumphs of evolution) will stand over Galapagos turtles, grinning like Teddy Roosevelt after a kill. In some former slave-driving colony of the Caribbean, Dwayne will lounge by the pool wearing his Club Med drinking beads and a sun-dazed smile.

Restlessness is a human impulse, something in the genes. We need to find out what is in the next valley. The hominid hunter began it, and people over millenniums traveled for conquest and trade, to find new homes.

America was built by sagas of travel, men and women letting go and leaping west into a primitive, dangerous promise. Now one of the more specialized motives for travel is the roots tour, the journey back to Ireland or Italy or Africa to find ancestors and ties. A travel agency in Atlanta is doing good business taking American blacks to Africa to try the old genetic recessional: Americans in their retrospective dream. Religion has always driven travelers, from the Deus volt of the First Crusade to more peaceful pilgrimages to Jerusalem, Mecca, Lourdes, and Rome.

Freud suggested that men travel to escape the oppressions of their families and their fathers. Maybe that is why people leave Vienna. But they travel with more energy to get a tan.

People travel because it teaches them things they could learn no other way. Herodotus got his real education by traveling. Like Odysseus, he saw ''many cities of men.'' Travel showed him the world and how it worked. Travel is an imperialism of the imagination, a process of acquisition: the mind collects cultures and experiences and souvenirs. The children of the industrial age poured south to dream upon the ruins. Motives are always rich and varied: travel means forms of freedom. Japanese men flock to sex tours in Seoul, Bangkok, and Manila (a woman waiting in the lobby of the hotel when you get off the bus from the airport).

Travel, especially if one travels alone, can make the mind peculiarly alive. Meanings flow by like colors, like smells, the fluid nuances of place. Real travel is work and may profit from an edge of danger. It is not for nothing that we travel in groups—remembering, though, the ultimate bad travel experience that involved the group at the Donner Pass.

The final point of travel is individual and indefinable: it makes the neurons glow in a new way. It excites possibilities. People and scenery mean worlds that they cannot mean except when we come to them for the first time as strangers. It is always oneself that one encounters in traveling: other people, of course, other parts of the world, other times carved into stone now overgrown by jungle—but still, always oneself.

Are Children Necessary?

In the suburban world of the American fifties, the family and the child were enveloped in a cherishing mythology. Americans, it was even said, had grown obsessively kiddified; they were child-worshipers who sentimentalized their offspring in a complacent land of Little League and Disney. Toward the end of the Eisenhower years, the literary critic Leslie Fiedler wrote a lively diatribe about the "cult of the child," which he denounced as "this most maudlin of primitivisms."

Today some Americans worry that in the last decade or so the United States has veered to the opposite extreme, that it has developed a distaste for children that sometimes seems almost to approach fear and loathing. If that is true, the United Nations' International Year of the Child came at an ironic time. The premise of the International Year was not so much that the world's children are disliked or unwelcome as that too many of them are undernourished, badly housed, and ill educated. The First World and the Third World have somewhat different perspectives on children.

Those who detect a pervasive, low-grade child-aversion in the United States find it swarming in the air like pollen. They see a nation recoiling from its young like W.C. Fields beset by Baby Leroy. Of the fifty thousand parents who responded to a query by advice columnist Ann Landers several years ago, 70 percent said that, given the choice again, they would not have children; it wasn't worth it. Although a few states have laws forbidding discrimination by landlords against families with children, huge apartment complexes and even entire communities have policies to keep the brats out. A Georgia couple that endorsed a detergent in a TV commercial were assaulted by angry telephone calls and letters denouncing them for having six children. All over the country, school budgets are being killed in tax revolts. That may be more an indication of disastrous inflation and a protest against bad educational systems than a specifically antichild gesture, but such refusals suggest something about a community's priorities.

Specialists in the field now estimate that there are at least two million cases per year of child abuse, not one million as thought earlier. Even granting that the statistic seems inflated because more cases are reported now, experts think that there has been a substantial real increase in the practice. The Supreme Court decision allowing teachers to spank children in school, thinks Yale psychologist Edward Zigler, sets an example for institutional abuse, an offense that is even more widespread than abuse by parents. The business of child pornography flourishes. In Los Angeles the police estimate that 30,000 children, many of them under the age of five, are used each year as objects of pornography. A number of them are actually sold or rented for the purpose by their parents. Perhaps both child abuse and child pornography can be regarded as merely aberrational; some child abuse is actually a bent expression of too *much* caring, and kiddie porn (both the selling of it and the taste for it) may be just a ragged, ugly leftover of the sexual revolution. Still, the profound hostility accumulated in all that child abuse and pornography could be used to wage a medium-sized war.

The much belabored and quite real self-absorption of the seventies implies, by definition, a corollary lack of interest in children. There are many forms of narcissism, of course; one of the lesser arguments of militant non-propagationists has been that children are begotten for the pleasure of watching one's own little clone toddle around. But today having children often seems to have been trivialized to the status of a life-style—and an unacceptable one. The obsession with being young and staying young has led to the phenomenon of almost permanently deferred adulthood. "I know fifty-year-olds who are still kids," says social analyst Michael Novak. "They're in the playground of the world: single, unattached, self-fulfilling, self-centered. People are trying to make little Disney Worlds of detachment for themselves." For such people, parenthood is an intrusion of responsibility, of potential disappointment and, ultimately, of mortality. The kids are a *memento mori*. It can be disturbing, in a narcissistic time, to have about us, yapping and demanding and growing restlessly, the generation that is going to push us off the planet.

In their history, Americans have passed through periods of appalling cruelty and stupidity toward children. To the early Calvinists, a child was a lump of pure depravity. In Massachusetts Bay Colony, it was against the law for children to play. Things were not much better after behavioral psychologists undertook to dictate the treatment of children. Dr. J. B. Watson, an earlier generation's Dr. Spock, insisted in 1928 that children must be treated with cold scientific detachment. "Never hug and kiss them," he advised.

All of that elaborate—and sometimes cruel—attention to the subject of children in the past presupposed one thing: their inevitability. The great changes in attitudes toward children today may revolve around three factors: 1) Whereas children in earlier, rural settings were economically valuable, needed for their labor, today they are a painfully expensive proposition (according to one estimate, the average middle-class family spends $100,000 to raise a child); 2) Children are no longer considered a necessary and inevitable part of marriage; and 3) For reasons of feminism and/or sheer economic need, more women than ever before are working. In fact, of those women who do have children, more than half have jobs outside of the home. These developments have produced a very complicated series of readjustments, the social machine fine-tuning itself in hundreds of subtle ways.

Around the beginning of the seventies came a convulsion of disgust at what some regarded as the tyrannical conventions of the American family. Both the need for population control and the urgency of women's rights impelled various writers to launch polemics against having kids. It was not an anti-child so much as an anti-parent movement. Among the voices raised against the tyrannies of automatic motherhood was that of Betty Rollin, who is now a correspondent for NBC News. "Motherhood is in trouble, and it ought to be," she wrote. "A rude question long overdue: Who needs it?" The feminist Ellen Peck recruited critic John Simon, TV performer Hugh Downs, and others to form the National Organization for Non-Parents ("None is fun"), devoted to the ideology of non-propagation.

Something interesting has happened to a few of the N.O.N. believers. They have grown older and changed their minds. A number of women who in their twenties concentrated on their careers decided in their thirties, as they began to contemplate the impending biological limit of their childbearing years, to have at least one child while there was still time. Says novelist Anne Roiphe *(Up the Sandbox)*: "We're seeing a whole rash of people having babies just in the nick of time. There's a difference between what one says at twenty and what one says at thirty-eight." Roiphe argues that the dogmas against children—or at least, against having children—are undergoing revision. "There has indeed been a swing of thought against children, but it was against this whole idea that one *must* have a family," she says. "Now I think it's probably going to swing back. All the excesses of the women's movement, including that one shouldn't 'look nice' and so on, are all going to be sifted through."

A doctrinal attitude toward children—for or against—is not the prevailing approach of most Americans. Michael Novak suggests that only the "idea elite," the 10 percent of the population in well-educated, upper-income groups whose work centers on education, the professions, communications, or some such—may harbor ideological or even environmental biases against children. That group could not have accounted by itself for the almost uninterrupted decline in the U.S. birthrate in the seventies. It is very likely that the economics of child rearing has had much to do with the trend toward smaller families, which has been encouraged by legal abortions.

Jerome Kagan, a Harvard professor of developmental psychology, doubts that there is a generalized American antipathy toward children. He says, "With the exception of the Japanese, American parents spend more money on books on child rearing, more time at lectures about children than any parents in the world—and it's been growing." Robert Coles, a child psychiatrist best known for his five-volume *Children of Crisis,* thinks that, if anything, children are unwholesomely overvalued by many parents: "They are the only thing the parents believe in. They don't believe in God, or in any kind of transcendence, and so they believe in their children. They are concerned with them almost in a religious way—which I think is unfortunate—as an extension of themselves. That is quite a burden for a child to experience. In that sense, it is not cruelty to children. It is paganism."

Almost no one can discuss children rationally; having children and raising them successfully is an essentially irrational act. It obeys a profound and sometimes self-punishing logic like salmon thrashing upriver to spawn, an impulse encoded in the race's will to go on. All kinds of aversions to and adorations of children occur simultaneously now. The young are battered and cherished, subjected to violent extremes of malnourishment and indulgence. Children are so swaddled in myth and delusion that Marian Wright Edelman, director of the Children's Defense Fund in Washington, argues that Americans should try not to posture about them but instead look hard at statistics: The United States has the fourteenth highest infant mortality rate in the world; ten million U.S. children have no regular source of basic medical care; 600,000 teenagers a year, most of them grotesquely unprepared for the experience, give birth to children.

Yet more American women than ever in history now have a choice about whether or not to give birth and how often. That is the most encouraging part of the new situation of children. Couples who wait to have children will probably be more mature in handling the ordeal of parenthood. Those who do not want children will not so often, as in the past, be forced to endure them. Very gradually, it may become more probable that those children who are born are also wanted.

The nation now seems to be achieving some new psychological equilibrium about families and children. The swoop from the excessively domestic fifties to the fierce social unbucklings of the sixties and early seventies left confusion and wreckage. A lot of menacing nonsense got flashed around and mingled with difficult truths. Generations bared their teeth at one another. Parents discovered, as if for the first time, how much their children could hurt them; some of the apparent aversion to children is a leftover fear of that palpable, demonstrated, maddening power that the young possess. Today, many new parents start with the lowest expectations about having children—everyone has told them how sick the family is—and then awake in astonished delight to find that the experience is (or can be) wonderful. It is possible that the United States, with its long history of elaborate delusions about children, is beginning to grow up on the subject.

What Is the
Point of Working?

When God foreclosed on Eden, he condemned Adam and Eve to go to work. Work has never recovered from that humiliation. From the beginning, the Lord's word said that work was something bad: a punishment, the great stone of mortality and toil laid upon a human spirit that might otherwise soar in the infinite, weightless playfulness of grace.

A perfectly understandable prejudice against work has prevailed ever since. Most work in the life of the world has been hard, but since it was grindingly inevitable, it hardly seemed worth complaining about very much. Work was simply the business of life, as matter-of-fact as sex and breathing. In recent years, however, the ancient discontent has grown elaborately articulate. The worker's usual old bitching has gone to college. Grim tribes of sociologists have reported back from office and factory that most workers find their labor mechanical, boring, imprisoning, stultifying, repetitive, dreary, heartbreaking. In his 1972 book *Working,* Studs Terkel began: "This book, being about work, is, by its very nature, about violence—to the spirit as well as to the body." The historical horrors of industrialization (child labor, squalor, the dark satanic mills) translate into the twentieth century's robotic busywork on the line, tightening the same damned screw on the Camaro's fire-wall assembly, going nuts to the banging, jangling Chaplinesque whirr of modern materialism in labor, bringing forth issue, disgorging itself upon the market.

The lamentations about how awful work is prompt an answering wail from the management side of the chasm: nobody wants to work anymore. As American productivity, once the exuberant engine of national wealth, has dipped to an embarrassingly uncompetitive low, Americans have shaken their heads: the country's old work ethic is dead. About the only good words for it now emanate from Ronald Reagan and certain beer commercials. Those ads are splendidly mythic playlets, romantic idealizations of men in groups who blast through mountains or pour plumingly molten steel in factories, the work all grit and grin. Then they retire to flip around iced cans of sacramental beer and debrief one another in a warm sundown glow of accomplishment. As for Reagan, in his presidential campaign he enshrined work in his rhetorical "community of values," along with family, neighborhood, peace, and freedom. He won by a landslide.

Has the American work ethic really expired? Is some old native eagerness to level wilderness and dig and build and invent now collapsing in decadence?

The idea of work—work as an ethic, an abstraction—arrived rather late in the history of toil. Whatever edifying and pietistic things may have been said about work over the centuries (Kahlil Gibran called work "love made visible," and the Benedictines say, "To work is to pray"), humankind has always tried to avoid it whenever possible. The Greeks thought work was degrading; they kept an underclass to see to the laundry and other details of basic social maintenance. That prejudice against work persisted down the centuries in other aristocracies. It is supposed, however, to be inherently un-American. Edward Kennedy likes to tell the story of how, during his first campaign for the Senate, his opponent said scornfully in a debate: "This man has never worked a day in his life!" Kennedy says that the next morning as he was shaking hands at a factory gate, one worker leaned toward him and confided, "You ain't missed a goddamned thing."

The Protestant work ethic, which sanctified work and turned it into vocation, arrived only a few centuries ago in the formulations of Martin Luther and John Calvin. In that scheme, the worker collaborates with God to do the work of the universe, the great design. One scholar, Leland Ryken of Illinois's Wheaton College, has pointed out that American politicians and corporate leaders who preach about the work ethic do not understand the Puritans' original, crucial linkage between human labor and God's will.

During the nineteenth-century industrialization of America, the idea of work's inherent virtue may have seemed temporarily implausible to generations who labored in the mines and mills and sweatshops. The century's huge machinery of production punished and stunned those who ran it.

And yet for generations of immigrants, work *was* ultimately availing; the numb toil of an illiterate grandfather got the father a foothold and a high school education, and the son wound up in college or even law school. A woman who died in the Triangle Shirtwaist Company fire in lower Manhattan had a niece who made it to the Bronx, and another generation on, the family went to Westchester County. So for millions of Americans, as they labored through the complexities of generations, work worked, and the immigrant work ethic came at last to merge with the Protestant work ethic.

The motive of work was all. To work for mere survival is desperate. To work for a better life for one's children and grandchildren lends the labor a fierce dignity. That dignity, an unconquerably hopeful energy and aspiration—driving, persisting like a life force—is the American quality that many find missing now.

The work ethic is not dead, but it is weaker now. The psychology of work is much changed in America. The acute, painful memory of the Great Depression used to enforce a disciplined and occasionally docile approach to work—in much the way that older citizens in the Soviet Union do not complain about scarce food and overpopulated apartments, because they remember how much more horrible everything was during the war. But the generation of the Depression is retiring and dying off, and today's younger workers, though sometimes laid off and kicked around by recessions and inflation, still do not keep in dark storage that residual memory of Hoovervilles and the Dust Bowl and banks capsizing.

Today elaborate financial cushions—unemployment insurance, union benefits, welfare payments, food stamps, and so on—have made it less catastrophic to be out of a job for a while. Work is still a profoundly respectable thing in America. Most Americans suffer a sense of loss, of diminution, even of worthlessness, if they are thrown out on the street. But the blow seldom carries the life-and-death implications it once had, the sense of personal ruin. Besides, the wild and notorious behavior of the economy takes a certain amount of personal shame out of joblessness; if Ford closes down a plant in New Jersey and throws 3,700 workers into the unemployment lines, the guilt falls less on individuals than on Japanese imports or American car design.

Because today's workers are better educated than those in the past, their expectations are higher. Many younger Americans have rearranged their ideas about what they want to get out of life. While their fathers and grandfathers and great-grandfathers concentrated hard upon plow and drill press and pressure gauge, some younger workers now ask previously unimaginable questions about the point of knocking themselves out. For the first time in the history of the world, masses of people in industrially advanced countries no longer have to focus their minds upon work as the central concern of their existence.

In the formulation of psychologist Abraham Maslow, work functions in a hierarchy of needs: first, work provides food and shelter, basic human maintenance. After that, it can address the need for security and then for friendship and "belongingness." Next, the demands of the ego arise, the need for respect. Finally, men and women assert a larger desire for "self-actualization." That seems a harmless and even worthy enterprise but sometimes degenerates into a vaporously selfish discontent.

Of course in patchwork, pluralistic America, different classes and ethnic groups are perched at different stages in the work hierarchy. The immigrants—legal and illegal—who still flock densely to America are fighting for the foothold that the jogging self-actualizers achieved three generations ago. The zealously ambitious Koreans who run New York City's best vegetable markets, or boat people trying to open a restaurant, or chicanos who struggle to start a small business in the *barrio* are still years away from est and the Sierra Club. Working women, to the extent that they are new at it, now form a powerful source of ambition and energy. Feminism—and financial need—have made them, in effect, a sophisticated-immigrant wave upon the economy.

Having to work to stay alive, to build a future, gives one's exertions a tough moral simplicity. The point of work in that case is so obvious that it need not be discussed. But apart from the sheer necessity of sustaining life, is there some inherent worth in work? Carlyle believed that "all work, even cotton spinning, is noble: work is alone noble." Was he right?

It is seigneurial cant to romanticize work that is truly detestable and destructive to workers. But misery and drudgery are always comparative. Despite the sometimes nostalgic haze around their images, the pre-industrial peasant and the nineteenth-century American farmer did brutish work far harder than the assembly line. The untouchable who sweeps excrement in the streets of Bombay would react with blank incomprehension to the malaise of some seventeen-dollar-an-hour workers on a Chrysler assembly line. The Indian, after all, has passed from "alienation" into a degradation that is almost mystical. In Nicaragua, the average nineteen-year-old peasant has worked longer and harder than most Americans of middle age. Americans prone to restlessness about the spiritual disappointments of work should consult unemployed young men and women in their own ghettos: they know with painful clarity the importance of the personal dignity that a job brings.

Americans often fall into fallacies of misplaced sympathy. Psychologist Maslow, for example, once wrote that he found it difficult "to conceive of feeling proud of myself, self-loving and self-respecting, if I were working, for example, in some chewing-gum factory. . . ." Well, two weeks ago, Warner-Lambert announced that it would close down its gum-manufacturing American Chicle factory in Long Island City, New York; the workers who had spent years there making Dentyne and Chiclets were distraught. "It's a beautiful place to work," one feeder-catcher-packer of chewing gum said sadly. "It's just like home." There is a peculiar arrogance in those who discourse on the brutalizations of work simply because they cannot imagine themselves performing the job. Certainly workers often feel abstracted out, reduced sometimes to dreary robotic functions. But almost everyone commands endlessly subtle systems of adaptation; people can make the work their own and even cherish it against all academic expectations. Such adaptations are often more important than the famous but theoretical alienation from the process and product of labor.

Work is still the complicated and crucial core of most lives, the occupation melded inseparably to the identity; Freud said that the successful psyche is one capable of love and of work. Work is the most thorough and profound organizing principle in American life. If mobility has weakened old blood ties, our coworkers often form our new family, our tribe, our social world; we become almost citizens of our companies, living under the protection of salaries, pensions, and health insurance. Sociologist Robert Schrank believes that people like jobs mainly because they need other people; they need to gossip with them, hang out with them, to schmooze. Says Schrank: "The workplace performs the function of community."

Unless it is dishonest or destructive—the labor of a pimp or a hit man, say—all work is intrinsically honorable in ways that are rarely understood as they once were. Only the fortunate toil in ways that express them directly. There is a Renaissance splendor in Leonardo's effusion: "The works that the eye orders the hands to make are infinite." But most of us labor closer to the ground. Even there, all work expresses the laborer in a deeper sense: all life must be worked at, protected, planted, replanted, fashioned, cooked for, coaxed, diapered, formed, sustained. Work is the way that we tend the world, the way that people connect. It is the most vigorous, vivid sign of life—in individuals and in civilizations.

Downsizing an American Dream

It is not really what we had in mind. It is not the American house we dreamed of, not even the house we grew up in, the house we remember. Sometimes it stands a little too near the freeway, in a raw mat of sodden lawn—a poignant dry-green whiffle of grass with a single sapling in it that gives no more shade than a swizzle stick. The house has the frank, bleak starkness of the cut-rate. Its interiors are minimalist, and grimly candid about it. No woodwork, no extras, no little frills of gentility anymore. No front hall. One bathroom, with the cheapest fixtures, no bathtub. Closets as shallow as medicine chests. Walls like shirt cardboards, walls that will not hold the nail when we move in and try to hang the family pictures.

All of this—the economy model stripped down to an irreducible ascetic tackiness—can be ours for more dollars than our fathers used to earn, total, in ten or fifteen years, for a price that once would have purchased Tara, or at least the six-bedroom Lake Forest spread of a successful cardiologist.

Americans have always cherished an almost ideological longing for a house of their own. Today, the fantasy of the dream house, the little fortress of home, My Blue Heaven, has jolted up against hard economics.

If inflation has not exactly devoured the dream, it has taken a painful bite out of it. Good, even splendid houses are still built; America is not suddenly being driven out into hovels and Hoovervilles. But the number of Americans who can afford first-class housing is dwindling. The traditional budget formula said that a family should spend no more than one-quarter of gross income on housing. If they obey that rule, less than 10 percent of Americans can afford a median-priced house.

Some older or more nimble Americans (especially those lucky enough to have bought a house in, say, the Eisenhower or Johnson or Nixon years) have done handsomely in the housing bazaar. But a lot of Americans have been left out. Some began to suspect that they were operating under some vast cultural misunderstanding. In a way, they were. Owning a house—a home, "the most lyrical of American symbols," Max Lerner once called it—began generations ago as one of the most basic aspirations. It was merely a hope then, not a sure thing. But some time during the suburban idyll of the postwar years, the idea of owning a house came to harden into a kind of entitlement. The baby-boom children of the broad American middle class were especially seduced by the illusion. Until now, through many headlong cultural confusions, they carried with them a barely conscious expectation, a sort of buried genetic code. When they chose to do so, when the babies started arriving, they could transform themselves into Ozzie and Harriet and find houses like the ones their parents owned—or nicer, maybe—and therein comfortably get on with the American dream. Now they scrunch down in a garden-apartment rental somewhere, with the crib in the living room and wolf frisking in the vestibule, and wonder what went wrong.

Americans feel a little foolish about complaining, or they should. The bungalow on the wrong side of the beltway is still no Mongolian yurt, no tar-paper shack in one of Rio's mountainside *favelas*. It is not Soviet housing, with the five-year waiting list for a room of one's own, and couples sometimes stolidly enduring their marriages because there is no other apartment (no other bed, even) to escape to. It is not like the arrangements in dense Hong Kong, as busily transient as an ant colony, or Tokyo, where much middle-class housing looks like the crew's quarters on a submarine.

The barest ticky-tacky American apartment or tract house gives the occupant on whim: hot water, electric lights, air conditioning pretty often, and far more sheltered space than anyone in the world (except for the most imperial and ostentatious) has ever had the luxury of rattling around in. Neolithic villagers periodically burned down their huts to incinerate their vermin; in the South Bronx people burn out their own apartments to obtain the welfare moving allowance, or landlords torch their buildings for the insurance: life among the ruins. Americans who feel sorry for themselves about their housing, middle-class Americans at least, have not explored the alternatives on the down side of civilization. Anyway, ideals of privacy, cleanliness, spaciousness, and a certain domestic dignity are fairly new to the history of housing. It is not so many generations ago that we stopped keeping pigs in the house. At Tolstoy's estate, Yasnaya Polyana, the serfs curled up anywhere in the house that they felt drowsy and went to sleep like cats.

But Americans always claim their dispensation. A dream house has been a vision at the core of American hopes, a tender blend of expectation and nostalgia. It derives its imagery from the historical spaciousness of the land (God's country, after all, his bounteous land grant, the interminable individualist homestead unfolding toward the horizon) and the simultaneous need for shelter that its harshness imposed. A people so socially and geographically mobile used housing as an instrument to proclaim their wherewithal, their substance, their civic presence. They have sometimes nearly impoverished themselves to anchor their identities in their homes. In a 1920 magazine serial called "More Stately Mansions," a social-climbing wife pouts and wheedles her husband: "Dickie, I've simply *got* to have it. . . . A nice house gives a man self-respect and confidence." A house of one's own is refuge, a tangible, physical thing that implies stability in a democracy all liquid and stormily insecure. American history has sometimes been a wild ride: a house traditionally served as the private fortress in which to recover, in which to repel night prowlers and dangerous social change.

The "nation of immigrants" arrived homeless. From the Pilgrims on, they carved their shelter out of wilderness. Lincoln was born in a frontier hovel. Later generations crowded ten to a squalid room in Lower East Side ghettos. Yet Americans operated on a premise of expansion and progress: the private home—more important, more basic, than the automobile, that bright headlong vehicle of the dream—was the outward artifact by which Americans defined themselves. Perhaps some ancient ghost of feudalism, a deep, fundamental fear of dependence and submission, spooked around the edges of the American's pride of ownership: *this place is mine.* The prototype of Mr. Blandings's dream house was Monticello, that cool Palladian vision built by the American prince of the Enlightenment, Thomas Jefferson.

In a way, the American housing crisis is simply a variation of the American car crisis: in years past, both were overbuilt. Now, in housing as in cars, Americans are suffering the discomforts of what Detroit calls "downsizing." The ultimate result could be both better transportation and better shelter.

Housing has always demanded a sacrifice. Certain chiefs of Pacific Northwest tribes once killed slaves and captives and erected their new houses upon the bodies, for luck. Americans may have come by their housing a little too easily in the past two generations. Starting in the Depression, government agencies like the FHA and later the VA set about turning the United States into a nation of home owners. A young family could start off by paying nothing down and take thirty years to pay off the mortgage. The result was an astonishing national domestication. Today two-thirds of Americans own the places where they live. Home ownership helped to stabilize the United States around a vast and settled middle class; property taxes built the system of public education that gave the United States a good deal of its moral ballast.

But the postwar golden age of American housing (all those folks grinning out at the Eisenhower years from their patios, their barbecues) may have overdone the home comforts. It diverted billions that perhaps should have gone into the nation's industrial plant. The Reagan Administration (for all its warm rhetorical embrace of hearth and family) wants to readjust the nation's tax and credit policies to favor business investment over mortgage investment.

After an initial period of bleakness while the adjustments get made, downsizing and cost cutting may make people think more intelligently about the thing, about the house as an artifact, about what can be done with it. Ultimately, optimistically, the way out of the American housing crisis may not be lower inflation but better design and technology.

Too much American housing, of course, is insipid: mass-stamped suburbs as standardized as boxes on supermarket shelves. It may be fatuous to envision new splendors of design in a nation going to condo and cluster. But interesting, occasionally bizarre ideas are turning up. In the Midwest some builders are digging underground houses with skylights and atriums and a thick dome of earth on top that eliminates abrupt temperature changes from season to season. Friends, even strangers, are getting together to buy a house and share it. Under some arrangements, two couples may buy a condominium with two master bedrooms and two master baths and share the kitchen and living room.

Some construction companies now work at what they call retrofitting, building additions to old houses, opening up interiors, reclaiming the old stock. In central cities, much gentrification is going on: the stylish middle class takes over and polishes up the housing of the poor, leaving the poor to look elsewhere for shelter.

Americans still think of a home of their own as a free-standing one-family house (independence, shelter, family, the Little House on the Prairie still, even when the prairie has turned into Iowa City). One author, Jane Davidson, called one-family suburban houses "an oppressive Utopian idea, a spiritual imperative"—the Levittown version of Ibsen's dollhouse. But economics and demographics intrude on the vision. The size of the average American household has shrunk in twenty years from 3.3 to 2.75, a fragmentation that demands more housing units even at a moment when housing is harder than ever to finance.

With shelter so expensive to build and, once built, to heat and cool, designers are continually trying to redefine what goes into a house. No rearrangement of walls and furniture, however, can endow a building with the sort of soul that houses once possessed. It takes a heap of living, etc. Americans, a nation of transients, seldom linger long enough in a condo to give it ghosts. There was a time when houses—some houses—sheltered whole generations in sequence, witnessed them and thus acquired a numinous life of their own, a moral dimension that was once much sentimentalized. It was real enough all the same. Certain American neighborhoods once possessed a similar palpable soul, the neighborhood being the urban apartment dweller's substitute for an ancestral house and grounds. In a sense, it is the soul that Americans yearn after when they think of houses. After an earthquake or tornado, the news always lists the dead, the missing, and the "homeless," the last being itself a kind of wound, a private desolation. We all drive past the house where we grew up and stare at it oddly, with a strange ache, as if to extract some meaning from it that has been irrecoverably lost.

In 1902 the genteel architect-writer Joy Wheeler Dowd wrote: "Every man or woman hopes one day to realize his or her particular dream of home." It did not have to be a Newport "cottage" or the Baths of Diocletian. It was a small internal grandeur that counted, the sense of refuge and privacy, the Marxist's "bourgeois individualism" tricked out with antimacassars and, in the fullness of time, an island in the kitchen. Americans may have overdone some of that a little.

The turtle comes equipped with a carapace. Is there some naturally ordained allotment for human shelter? In 1920 the Russian "sanitary housing norm" decreed that each citizen was entitled to one hundred square feet of living space, an expansive ideal seldom achieved. Americans occupy at least 140 square feet on average; by most of the world's standards, they live like caliphs. The current constriction of their housing may make some Americans claustrophobic, but cross-cultural comparison might also remind them to be grateful for what they have. It might encourage them, as well, to shift their perspectives outward a little, to conceive of themselves less as isolated units, more as communities. It is not the individual hut that has cultural force and meaning, but the village as a whole, the sum of our larger arrangements as a tribe.

Vietnam
Comes Home

Englishmen who fought at Ypres and the Somme carried the *Oxford Book of English Verse* in their haversacks; such literary brigades in the trenches would find their minds chiming with a line of Keats, or William Dunbar's *Timor Mortis Conturbat Me*. The Americans in Vietnam usually packed more kinetic cultural effects. Images given them over the years by movies and television would sometimes unreel in their brains as they moved toward a tree line or a Vietnamese village, and in bizarre synaptic flips between reality and pictures, they would see themselves for an instant as, say, Audie Murphy winning his Congressional Medal of Honor in *To Hell and Back*. One writer called these dislocating fantasies "life-as-movie, war-as-war-movie, war-as-life." The men could ridicule "John Wayne-ing," but the effect was metaphysically spooky. And, of course, it could get you killed.

Much of the American grief in Vietnam was played out in the national imagination by way of movies and television. If the grunts on search-and-destroy in the Central Highlands sometimes kept themselves going with a jolt of John Wayne from *The Sands of Iwo Jima*, the people at home took their war each night live in their living rooms, mainlined by television directly into the bloodstream. Vietnam was so intimately recorded that it became almost unendurably real—yet also impossibly remote. Nine thousand miles away, a dark hallucination. And along with the war on the tube came the rest of the theater of the sixties' riots, assassinations, the antiwar moratoriums, the Yippies' carmagnoles, the circus of the counterculture.

By the late seventies, those eruptions seemed as long ago as the Great

Awakening or the Indian wars. Besides the sheer passage of time, there appeared to be a willful repression of the nation's longest war and its only military defeat. The forgetfulness amounted almost to national amnesia. Two or three years ago, literary agents would tell their writers: "I can sell anything you do, but not about Vietnam." Except for a foolishly frisky little combat comedy called *The Boys in Company C,* Hollywood would not touch the war—unless you count John Wayne's 1968 *Green Berets,* which might as well have been produced by William Westmoreland. As director Arthur Penn *(Bonnie and Clyde)* put it several years ago, "I don't believe the war in Vietnam can be treated in a 'popular film.' We have no capability to confront events of that enormity head-on." It was taboo, a secret, like a spectacular case of madness in the family.

But now the psychological time-lock on Vietnam seems to have expired. Books have been tumbling out of typewriters, laden with confessions, accusations, and revisionist history. American foreign policy, which for much of the seventies has suffered from a post-Vietnam, post-Watergate reticence and drift, has grown somewhat more assertive; there are even signs of a backlash of truculence in some quarters.

Vietnam was thrust into the forefront of most Americans' consciousness in 1979 in a surprising but somehow fitting manner: at the Academy Award presentations witnessed by an estimated seventy million TV viewers in the United States. So it was movies and television again that brought the war back: the technological media of illusion fancifully reconstructing what was in some ways the most illusory experience in the national history.

Ordinarily, the Academy Awards are a nice, long evening's wallow in the junk culture; you send out for Chinese food or pizza, make popcorn, keep score, watch for the awful fashions and the stilted soliloquies of acceptance. But this year, beneath the usual wisecracks and show business sentimentality, there was interesting drama. Jane Fonda, anathematized for years because of her radical politics and trip to Hanoi during the war, won the Best Actress award for her role in *Coming Home,* an antiwar film focused sympathetically on the suffering of wounded American veterans. (Fonda, who is relentless, gave half of her acceptance speech in sign language "because there are fourteen million deaf people in this country." *New York Daily News* critic Rex Reed wrote bitchily that it "looked like an audition for *The Miracle Worker*.'') Jon Voight, who played opposite Fonda as a paraplegic vet, won the Best Actor award.

At the end of the three-hour, twenty-minute ceremonies in Los Angeles's Dorothy Chandler Pavilion, John Wayne himself came on. The old martial role model, looking gaunt but energetic, his stomach and one lung gone to cancer, presented the Oscar for Best Picture of 1978. It went to another Vietnam movie, *The Deer Hunter,* director Michael Cimino's story of young Ukrainian-American steelworkers from Clairton, Pennsylvania, who play pool, drink beer, watch football on TV, get drunk at a wedding, hunt deer, and then go off to fight the war in 1972. It was the fifth Oscar for *The Deer Hunter* that night. The audience could only guess at the complexities of feeling that ricocheted around John Wayne's mind as he handed over the prize.

The Motion Picture Academy in years past has displayed a distaste for political controversy; half a decade ago, a streaker was more acceptable than an Oscar winner with the temerity to rail against the war. But as a headline in the *Los Angeles Herald-Examiner* put it, THE WAR FINALLY WINS. The awards to two films about Vietnam suggested not so much that the academy has gone hotheadedly controversial as that it judged, like the rest of the nation, that Vietnam has receded enough to keep any discussion of it from exploding into a civil war.

The heat is by no means gone, of course. Outside the awards ceremonies, a remnant group of Vietnam Veterans Against the War shouted protests about *The Deer Hunter,* which in style and message is a world away from *Coming Home.* The vets echoed the criticism of many old antiwar activists, who regard Cimino's cartoon treatment of the Vietnamese (played in the movie, incidentally, by Thais) as screaming sadists, much given to atrocity. Fonda called *The Deer Hunter* ''a racist, Pentagon version of the war''—a judgment she reached without having seen the movie. Gloria Emerson, who covered the war for the *New York Times* and wrote a phosphorescently indignant book called *Winners and Losers,* declared last week: ''Cimino has cheapened and degraded and diminished the war as no one else.''

Coming Home has at least the charm of its political clarity; it is a straightforwardly and movingly antiwar movie that is saved from being a mere tract by its rich performances and its compassion for the Americans who fought and suffered in the war. *The Deer Hunter* is more elusive—more forceful, less coherent, more artistically ambitious but also dangerously close to political simplism, historical inaccuracy, and moral kitsch.

The fascinating difference between the two films is that *The Deer Hunter* presents a version of the American experience in Vietnam that is utterly at variance with the view, widely held among intellectuals, of barbarously overarmed Americans, a nation of William Calleys, doing battle against the frail, gentle, long-suffering Vietnamese. Cimino's victims are the rambunctious guys from Clairton, blue-collar heroes who took their wholesome patriotism to Vietnam and there found themselves alone, morally adrift among savage Southeast Asian exotics who are forever forcing them to play Russian roulette. There is no record or recollection, incidentally, that the game was ever played during the American years in Vietnam, although some old hands recall a few episodes in the twenties and thirties.

Cimino's tale may or may not be a bad description of what happened in Vietnam; it depends on one's politics. It is the implication of American innocence that enrages some critics of the film. Partly the difficulty lies in trying to extrapolate a general statement of American performance in Vietnam from the individual American stories that Cimino presents. The director, now working in Montana on a new film about the immigrant voyages west, speaks bitterly of Fonda's charges about his film. His characters, says Cimino, "are trying to support each other. They are not endorsing anything except their common humanity—their common frailty, their need for each other." Although it may be reading the film too much as allegory, the ending, with the survivors back in their shabby Pennsylvania steel town, sitting around a table and softly singing "God Bless America," has the effect of being an absolution, a subtle exoneration of the American role in Vietnam. Cimino might have intended the scene more as an exoneration of the men who were called on to fight there than of the policymakers who sent them. But that is not necessarily the psychological effect upon his audiences. In any case, as Cimino rightly says, "It will take a lot of films to get at Vietnam. It's still very mysterious to us."

Coming Home and *The Deer Hunter* are only the beginning. Francis Ford Coppola's thirty-five-million-dollar *Apocalypse Now,* based on Joseph Conrad's *Heart of Darkness,* translates the tale of savagery and evil from the Congo to Vietnam. There, Marlon Brando, playing the Mr. Kurtz character, is a renegade Army colonel who has taken over a remote province and set up his own war against the Communists. Captain Willard (Martin Sneen) is sent to assassinate the rebellious Kurtz. Coppola gambled his own reputation and the considerable fortune he made from his *Godfather* movies on the film's success.

Television attempted a *Deer Hunter* of its own in 1979: *Friendly Fire,* an ABC made-for-TV movie based on C. D. B. Bryan's 1976 nonfiction book. Carol Burnett and Ned Beatty played an Iowa farm couple who turn against the war when their son is killed by an errant U.S. artillery round in Vietnam. As their anger grows more obsessive, they gradually alienate their lifelong friends and even their own family. In Bryan's book, the process is deeply moving, but the TV version is cluttered with clichés and civics lessons. The best TV show about the American involvement in Asia remains CBS's Korean War sitcom *M*A*S*H*—and *M*A*S*H*, though controversial by old TV standards, is antiwar in a context shorn of politics and anesthetized by the bedside black humor and reassuring personalities of its principals.

Playwright David Rabe's trilogy *The Basic Training of Pavlo Hummel, Sticks and Bones,* and *Streamers,* explored military brutalizations in the Vietnam era. This week in Manhattan actor Michael Moriarty is opening in David Berry's play *G.R. Point,* an equally brutal work about men doing graves registration duty in Vietnam. Its refrain: "The 'Nam hasn't got any heroes. Dead is dumb, and dead in the 'Nam is dumbest of all."

More and more examinations of the war have also been published. The best of the war novels and memoirs, in many ways, is Michael Herr's *Dispatches* (1977). Herr, who spent a year in Vietnam covering the war for *Esquire,* writes prose that resembles some weapon the Pentagon developed especially for Vietnam—hallucinatory, menacing, full of anxiety, death, and a stunning, offhanded sort of accuracy. Herr is a writer with the talent of a smart bomb. Like James Webb in his fairly straightforward 1978 novel *Fields of Fire,* Herr is able to locate the thing inside the soldiers, and himself, that enjoys the appalling charm of war. Writes Herr: "But somewhere all the mythic tricks intersected, from the lowest John Wayne wet dream to the most aggravated soldier-poet fantasy, and where they did I believe that everyone knew everything about everyone else, every one of us there a true volunteer. Not that you didn't hear some overripe bullshit about it: Hearts and Minds, People of the Republic, tumbling dominoes, maintaining the equilibrium of the Dingdong by containing the ever-encroaching Doodah; you could also hear the other, some young soldier speaking in all bloody innocence, saying: 'All that's just a *load,* man. We're here to kill gooks. Period.' "

Philip Caputo's 1977 memoir, *A Rumor of War,* another excellent and painfully earned book, recalls how he was inspired by John Kennedy's "Ask not what your country can do for you . . ." Caputo joined the

Marines: "Having known nothing but security, comfort, and peace, I hungered for danger, challenges, and violence." At the end of his three-year enlistment, Caputo writes, "I came home from the war with the curious feeling that I had grown older than my father, who was then 51. . . . Once I had seen pigs eating napalm-charred corpses—a memorable sight, pigs eating roast people."

There have been other admirable Vietnam books: Tim O'Brien's *Going After Cacciato,* Larry Heinemann's *Close Quarters,* and Frederick Downs's *The Killing Zone.* Josiah Bunting, a novelist (*The Lionheads*) and former Army officer who served in Vietnam and is now president of Virginia's Hampden-Sydney College, points out an anomaly of Vietnam. "The Norman Mailers and William Styrons and all those guys stayed at Harvard for this war. The real literary genius never went." Nonetheless, Bunting expects that "within the next three or five years, there will be a major, successful *Catch-22*–style novel and film about Vietnam. Only then will we be far enough away so as to see behind the grotesque and see how miserably and squalidly funny the whole thing was."

Movies, TV shows, plays, and memoirs will eventually construct a mythic reality around the American experience in Vietnam. World War I's catastrophic trench warfare, which nearly wiped out a generation of England's best and brightest men (France's and Germany's as well), was so utterly new and unfamiliar that a highly literate assemblage spent the next decade, at least, formulating a conception of what it had all been about. Something of the same process is occurring regarding Vietnam.

Meantime, events in Indochina and the labors of revisionist historians and other experts with second thoughts are bringing the tragedy there into a new perspective. The war that was fought so much with symbols in the American mind has now acquired an entirely new set of symbols: the boat people fleeing and drowning, former South Vietnamese soldiers in re-education camps ringed with barbed wire, Pol Pot's murderous regime in Cambodia. When the French were colonizing Indochina in the middle of the nineteenth century, the Vietnamese were just in the process of conquering Cambodia. Now they have invaded again, and have subordinated Laos as well, advancing that much closer to a possible Vietnamese elevation to the status of overlord. Their move against Cambodia spurred the Chinese, who supported Hanoi through the long American war, to invade the northern provinces of Vietnam just after normalizing relations with the United States.

The psychological effect on Americans of all this crisscross *Realpolitik* has been to lift a lot of the moral burden off the American involvement. At the least, it seems less tenable to hold that the United States was guilty of the uniquely satanic imperialism that antiwar critics often saw—and still frequently see—behind American policy. The new conflicts in Southeast Asia add an element of retrospective perplexity to analysis of what the United States was doing there.

New voices of reconsideration are heard. Jean Lacouture, the French journalist and biographer of Ho Chi Minh and long an expert on Vietnam, has now called for "trials" of Communist crimes in Indochina since 1975, when Saigon fell to the North Vietnamese army. Guenter Lewy, a University of Massachusetts political scientist, fired what may be the opening shot of a revisionist view of the war in his 1978 book, *America in Vietnam.* Lewy examines the process of U.S. involvement and concludes that though the performance was unsuccessful, it was legal and not immoral. Leslie Gelb, now the State Department's director of politico-military affairs, makes a persuasive and subtle case in his new book, *The Irony of Vietnam: The System Worked.* Despite his inflammatory (to war critics) title, Gelb's thesis is limited and, as he says, ironic: "American leaders were convinced that they had to prevent the loss of Vietnam to Communism, and until May 1975 they succeeded in doing just that. It can be persuasively argued that the United States fought the war inefficiently with needless costs in lives and resources. As with all wars, this was to be expected. It can be persuasively argued that the war was an out-and-out mistake and that the commitment should not have been made. But the commitment was made and kept for twenty-five years."

In a sense, the formal foreign policy lessons that the United States learned from Vietnam have been easier to absorb than the deeper psychological and personal meanings, which will be years in unfolding. Says Columbia University historian Henry Graff: "America has learned for the first time that not everything it attempts comes off successfully. What we regarded as decency, honor, and pride were not implemented in the world satisfactorily to make others see us as we thought we ought to be seen. That this could have happened to us is what *The Deer Hunter* is really all about."

After Vietnam, John Kennedy's "pay any price, bear any burden, meet any hardship . . ." formula rings like the penny-bright, dangerous rhetoric that it was. The old policy of containment is, of course, long dead, as is the corollary view of a Sino-Soviet Communist monolith probing ever outward. It was precisely the containment-monolith-domino view of geopolitics that led the United States into Vietnam. Says Henry Kissinger: "We've learned two somewhat contradictory things. One, that our resources are limited in relation to the total number of problems that exist in the world. We have to be thoughtful in choosing our involvements. Secondly, if we get involved, we must prevail. There are no awards for losers." Anthony Lake, director of the State Department's policy planning staff, uses more cautious phrasing: "What Vietnam should have taught us is to be very clear-eyed about our interests and the situations we are getting into when we use our military power. It should not have taught us that we should never use our power. We should be very careful about doctrinaire answers or lessons—either that we should have intervened anywhere, any time or—in response to our Vietnam experience—that we should not intervene anywhere any time."

In all, the United States seems to have become more cautious and considered in international politics as a result of Vietnam. Allies, especially in Western Europe, have adopted a somewhat schizophrenic line toward the United States, first condemning its Vietnam War policies as obnoxiously aggressive, now worrying its policies elsewhere are contemptibly weak. Says former Under Secretary of State George Ball: "Rather than snickering at America's alleged impuissance, our allies should rejoice that we have now achieved the maturity they accused us of lacking during our Vietnam adventure."

It is the psychological, moral, and spiritual adjustment that has proved more difficult and problematic. Some, of course, believe Americans are an oblivious people, who have simply cruised on and learned nothing. "We have no national memory," Lillian Hellman once told Gloria Emerson. "Maybe it's a mark of a young and vigorous people. I think we've already forgotten Vietnam." When William Westmoreland, former U.S. commander in Vietnam, appears on campuses these days, he finds "total change. Crowds are larger, open-minded. Now there's very little criticism, and mostly from professors." Of course, the kids Westmoreland is addressing would have been only about eight years old at the time of the Tet offensive. To them, he could almost be talking about Carthage.

Vietnam fragmented America into constituencies that even now identify themselves according to their war grievances. The veteran versus draft resister issue can still stir anger. William Keegan, now twenty-nine, a steel-foundry worker in Churchill, Pennsylvania, served for a year in Vietnam as a medic after being drafted. He says bitterly: "The real heroes seem to be the guys who ran away to Canada to dodge the draft. Where will the country be if we ever face a crisis again? We'll have a heck of a time getting people to fight, and other countries know this.'' But many draft resisters, slipping into their thirties, also sense their communities' distaste, the snarls of veterans from the nation's more straightforward wars. Still, this month brought at least a modest symbol of reconciliation when Robert Garwood, the Marine private who spent the past fourteen years in Vietnam and may be formally charged with collaborating with the enemy, came home to Greensburg, Indiana. His townspeople carefully refrained from passing any judgment on him; they warmly welcomed him back.

One of the heaviest casualties of the Vietnam War was trust in institutions, in experts, in majorities and consensus. That deep-dyed skepticism, born in the great credibility gaps of the war and Watergate, is one of the most profoundly significant effects of Vietnam. Says Dr. Ronald Glasser, a Minneapolis physician who, after his army service, wrote *365 Days,* one of the finest evocations of the war: "The present inflation, Watergate, our lack of belief in expertise, our confusion, all of these things came out of that war. When someone tells me a nuclear power plant has six back-up systems, I'm immediately suspicious.''

To Walter Capps, professor of religious studies at the University of California at Santa Barbara, ''Vietnam means that patriotism can never again be understood in the simple way it was before.'' It was a loss of innocence for a people accustomed to regarding themselves as uniquely virtous—so much so that some of them took to seeing themselves as uniquely evil. As critic Morris Dickstein has written: ''In Vietnam, we lost not only a war and a subcontinent; we also lost our pervasive confidence that American arms and American aims were linked somehow to justice and morality, not merely to the quest for power.''

In an interview not long ago with public television's Bill Moyers, the poet Robert Bly argued that Americans have yet to experience a necessary catharsis: ''We're engaged in a vast forgetting mechanism and from the point of view of psychology, we're refusing to eat our grief, refusing to eat our dark side, we won't absorb it. And therefore what Jung says is really terrifying—if you do not absorb the things you have done in your life, like the murder of the Indians and bringing the blacks in, then you will have to repeat them. As soon as we started to go into Vietnam, it was perfectly clear to me that what was about to happen was that the generals were going to fight the Indian war over again.''

Yet there has been dislocation, loss, and grief. Dr. Harold Visotsky, chairman of the Department of Psychiatry at Northwestern University, speaks of the "loss of youth, damaged lives, loss of the chance to be young—jumping from youth to middle age." Such losses were sustained by a comparatively small part of the population, of course—the poorer, less visible young men who could not escape the draft through college.

Some psychologists believe Vietnam was like a death in the American family; it may demand that the country somehow go through the various stages of mourning: denial, anger, depression, and finally acceptance. "If people don't mourn," says Loyola University psychologist Eugene Kennedy, "they have other problems. Many of our problems now stem from wanting to be quit of Vietnam but not wanting to work through it. We still tend to deny it: we don't want to hear about the lives sacrificed, and who they were—that they were not the boys in college, but that we sacrificed the sacrificeable ones."

Visotsky, a bit grandiosely, calls movies like *Coming Home* and *The Deer Hunter* "Hollywood's version of our Nuremberg trials." But it is much easier for a people to try its defeated enemies than to sit in intelligent judgment on its own defeat. Victory requires only an idiot grin; defeat demands patience and improvisational wit. Americans should not become impatient with the stages of their adjustment to fallibility. It may be that America's most profound moral experience was the Civil War, but as both races understand, the nation has scarcely begun to absorb all of its implications.

The Way
of the World

The Dance of
Negotiation

The negotiating process: our man (George Steinbrenner, let us say) and their man (Leonid Brezhnev, perhaps) approach a dance floor that is covered with a layer of wet cement. The tinny band strikes up a slow, interminable version of *One Hundred Bottles of Beer on the Wall*. Steinbrenner and Brezhnev come together and lock in a sort of oafish sumo embrace. Slogging, they circle the floor, glaring at each other. They mutter into each other's ears: "Not *that* way, you clumsy idiot! *This* way, you capitalist (or Commie) dog!" They wait for something to happen between them: for the music to stop, for the floor to dry under their ankles and hold them forever in place. Or, in one of those rare moments of international grace, for an understanding to blossom. If that occurs, the dancers rush to the lobby, sit down upon straight-backed, gilt chairs and, using seventeen pens each, sign documents that look like the wine list in an elegant restaurant.

Negotiation can be an ungainly and primitive business. Sometimes the dance floor is an entire continent (Europe, for example); the superpowers galumph, they shake the earth underfoot (a premonition of the last dance) and terrify all those who find themselves standing between them. The spectators flap and screech and march. The United States and the Soviet Union have been practicing a saturnine transcontinental nuclear muscle-and-tooth display. It is really a form of negotiation, or a preliminary to it. But the thunder-footed dance (the idiot dares, the music of doom) has left millions of Europeans in a state of nerves and incipient neutralism.

Anyone who watches such bargaining (watches it in a cold sweat) might conclude that civilization is losing its touch for that sort of thing. It is an optical illusion, maybe, but we suspect it was once done with more style. Eighteenth-century diplomatists liked to think of themselves as elegant wits and dissemblers. Henry Kissinger goes in for that kind of ballroom performance (Metternich played by Fred Astaire), but he is temporarily unemployed. Today, in all forms of haggling, from arms-limitation treaties to used-car deals, the art seems to suffer. Despite improvements in some industries, labor and management still spar lumberingly, in brute confrontation, like slow-motion monsters in the Pleistocene. The air-traffic controllers made a bargaining miscalculation that destroyed their union. Through a combination of blind greed and intellectual brownout, the baseball players and owners sacrificed fifty days of their 1981 season. If that was a sort of surly burlesque, the failure of negotiation in Northern Ireland remains a disgusting tragedy; the ancient bargaining there goes on by bomb blast and spectacles of starvation in the Maze.

It is, of course, arrogant, a fallacy of rationalist optimism, to imagine that all differences in the world can be settled by well-meaning conversations. Neville Chamberlain went to Munich entertaining that notion. Not every human conflict is ripe to be settled in the court of reason. Still, certain kinds of tragedy have become intolerable in the world as they never were before: the lushly cataclysmic plot development that history could once absorb (even to the extent of permitting two "world wars") will no longer do. When the world has so armed itself as to make the use of those arms a stroke of global cancellation, then the casual "Let's talk about it" takes on a ticking urgency. *Que será, será* is not an intelligent policy this side of the Last Day.

Even leaving aside the nuclear Caliban, the future will have to be built by elaborately constructive conversations. The Third World's claims upon the First World's wealth, the rising global sense of entitlement, the abrasions of change on a crowded planet—all demand a high order of bargaining intelligence. Social solutions require space and resources. (Go West! Enlarge the pie!) For many disputes and angers and injustices today, there are no solutions, only settlements.

The sort of negotiation that most postwar diplomats practice (the years-long process that has turned Geneva into the world capital of niggling, for example) has a dreary reputation; so does the brute punch and counterpunch of labor bargaining—the two sides staring at one another across the table with reptile's eyes (their bladders nagging, their minds beginning to buzz and fray, the brain cells winking out like campfires). *No Exit,* a purgatory of silence and cultural incomprehension and stolid grievance, waiting for the other side to crack and start giving away points.

Negotiation should have more élan than that. Negotiators ought to be the future's heroes. To make something out of nothing, to fashion possibilities out of dead ends, is to be literally creative. Negotiation is one of the serious arts of the imagination. The deeper resources of wisdom must collaborate with the nimblest reflexes: the gambler's touch, the athlete's timing, the magician's tricks, the gentleman's equilibrium.

Negotiation rarely works if it is a merely mechanical compromise of polar extremes conducted, as the behavioral scientist says, "in a complex mixed-motive ambience of trust and suspicion." The best negotiations are inventive. A feistily savvy book, Herb Cohen's *You Can Negotiate Anything,* manages to convey the impression that all negotiations should even be fun; at the end of each, like the six solved faces of a Rubik's Cube, lies a "win-win" settlement—a mutuality in which both sides profit. Another book, *Getting to Yes,* arrives (a little more rigorously) at the same conclusion. The authors, Roger Fisher and William Ury, are members of the Harvard Negotiation Project, which explores various bargaining issues.

An instinct for improvisational psychology helps. "Ultimately," write Fisher and Ury, "conflict lies not in objective reality but in people's heads." In confrontation (trying to get the child to bed, trying to get the hostages out), the natural impulse may be either to harden one's position or to be soft and conciliatory, to be nice. Both approaches may be wrong. "Change the game," say Fisher and Ury. Do not negotiate positions, but interests, the real goals that lie behind positions. Separate the people negotiating from the problem being negotiated. When ideology is in heat, it will sometimes emit the cry of "nonnegotiable demands"; but that is mostly just an aggressive display of plumage, a preliminary, and even itself a form of negotiation. The secret always is to figure out your opponents, to find out what they really want. Explain what you want, and see if there are alternatives outside the fixed positions, accommodations that would satisfy both sides. Often a rigid position is only a symbol of what one thinks one needs or wants; fixed positions tend to be crude and unreflective. They've had no test of process. Develop deeper alternatives, including fall-back positions to adopt if the negotiation does not work out—this allows one to negotiate with the strength of detachment. There is always power in knowing you can walk away.

Good negotiations demand trapeze work across wide cultural gaps, sometimes even across cultural time. As Saul Bellow wrote: "Some minds

. . . belong to earlier periods of history. Among our contemporaries are Babylonians and Carthaginians or types from the Middle Ages.'' The Shiite ayatollah in Qum was negotiating across several centuries with a president whose working models of reality had to do with nuclear submarines. The oldest American negotiation, the endless business between black and white, may be subverted more than we know by disharmonies of expectation and assumption.

Dirty tactics can often be deflected simply by recognizing them and exposing them in a bemused but unaggressive way: ''I assume that tomorrow we will switch chairs, so you will have the sun in your eyes.'' The secret is to notice them immediately and, if necessary, to make the dirty tricks themselves a subject of negotiation: ''Not bad, not bad,'' you imply, ''but shall we get serious now?'' Also: never forget the power of silence, the massively disconcerting pause that goes on and on and may at last induce an opponent to babble and backtrack nervously.

Cohen supplies a few ''Soviet-style'' ploys of his own; hanging up the phone in midsentence, for example, giving the impression you were cut off and thus gaining a little additional time to think things over. Then there is the ''nibble''; leading your opponent deep into negotiations, so that he has invested much time and effort in them; seeming to make a settlement, then demanding one last concession; a free necktie, for example, to go with a couple of suits. There is a wonderfully grasping vulgarity in the ploy, an effrontery that should be greeted with admiration, at least in a clothing store. Sometimes the nibble can be immense and sinister—like the bite that Hitler took at Munich. In less apocalyptic negotiations, the nibble should generally be greeted with dignified amusement. If conflict is the natural state of the world, then negotiation may be an unnatural medium, one that goes against the centrifugal force of things. On the other hand, almost every human transaction (sex, marriage, politics, for example) and even human traffic with the divine (religion), is a form of negotiation, the everlasting mating dance of the *quid pro quo*. Those engaged in negotiation, even when they are the bitterest of enemies, are held together within a membrane of hope and desire and (presumably) enlightened selfishness.

Negotiations can be merely a smokescreen, of course: like the bargaining that the Japanese were conducting with the United States before Pearl Harbor. Sometimes negotiations are only empty dances of punctilio: at the Peace of Westphalia in 1648, it took the delegates six months to decide in what order they would enter and be seated in the negotiating chamber; the United States and North Vietnam held similarly intricate discussions about the shape of the table in Paris. Negotiations can produce their own tragedies, as Versailles did, as Yalta did. But without negotiation, things tend to fall more quickly of their own weight into patterns of force and submission, autocracy and abjectness. If the future is forever dark and fogbound, negotiation can sometimes fill the landscapes with better shapes and paths than they would otherwise contain.

The Falklands

Watching the war in the Falklands—remote and ominous and obscurely disgusting—we keep telling ourselves that we cannot do that sort of thing anymore. Once we could indulge ourselves. No more. We will find some substitute, a methadone to ease off the habit. We will take up a surrogate for war—a sport, perhaps: planetary killer golf, or perpetual Olympics. We will meditate, to keep our tempers, and chant a sweet Quaker om. We will sublimate the black bats of our rages into butterflies.

We are kidding ourselves. The presence of nuclear weapons in the world has conjured such a fear of war that hope and conscience have promoted a countering fantasy: we half persuade ourselves that we have already given up war. The fight in the Falklands seems all the more strange because it ought to be an atavism, something forsworn. It should not be happening.

The new metaphysics of war makes this configuration: nuclear bombs preside, in a dark, speculative way, over the human imagination of war. Nuclear is to conventional war what the monotheism of the avenging God was to the old amiably human and relatively harmless idolatries of polytheism. The wrath of God becomes the dread mushroom and megadeath and firestorm—totality, cessation. It is not relative, like the old wars, but absolute, the utter blank of extinction. Nuclear war sits in the mind like the lurid medieval vision of hell: horrible—and yet, well, hypothetical.

The world cannot stare too long at an abyss; the abyss stares back, or simply grows boring. We revert to our customary sins. We do our violent business as usual. Fish gotta swim. War is flourishing—between Iran and Iraq, between Israel and the P.L.O., in Cambodia and Afghanistan. Since the bomb fell on Hiroshima, mankind has fought roughly 125 wars (of one sort or another), including the longest one in U.S. history. But all of these collisions fell short of the nuclear. They thereby seemed weirdly permissible: as sins, venial, not mortal. They were not, after all, the utmost we had to deal out in fatality. We did not drop what we might have dropped onto Hanoi. By this reasoning, nonnuclear bloodshed is forbearing and almost virtuous.

If man by some inconceivable grace were to give up war, it would be an evolutionary step almost equivalent to his primordial emergence from the sea. From the start, or at least since he got himself organized, war has been something that man did. War and peace were the rhythm of history, like night and day. Can we have peace without war? Our moral rhetoric today tends to call war "futile" and "pointless." But, historically, almost all societies have seen the point of war; at any rate, they have always waged it. Today, the civilization's sheer annihilating capabilities make war seem a grotesque old habit of the race, with nothing to recommend it. But at one time, war was young and stirring and beautiful—or at least it had that side as well as its awful stricken one, its waste of life, its writhing and refugees. War made the adrenaline run, it gave life drama and meaning. The young went off to it with a Zouave gaiety. In our own time, we have expected our candidates for public office to have a war record. In his Inaugural Address, John Kennedy, skipper of PT-109, called his a generation "tempered by war." Not every soldier, of course, went to battle with George Patton's mystic glee; he wrote his wife in 1944 that "peace is going to be a hell of a letdown."

Not only the killers and cretins among us have loved war. Hegel recommended it. He thought it kept the state from getting stagnant and corrupt. Bacon thought that a just and honorable war was the best "exercise" for a state, like jogging.

War began as a merely improvisational marauding, a restlessness of tooth and claw: Magyars drifting toward new grazing lands, Vikings blowing down on the north wind to their plunder. Since attack justifies defense, almost everyone came rapidly to participate. War, both waged and endured, got to look like the human condition. The merely private or tribal venture (stealing herds, fetching Helen from Troy) burgeoned into dense public spectacles, whole civilizations on the march. The issues came to be territory or wealth or power or security or sometimes something darker and more confused: vast error (World War I), vast ego and evil (World War II).

•　•　•

War is change effected in an atmosphere of violent exemption from all rules, including those made in Geneva. It is not always change for the worse: war in the past has been constructive and necessary sometimes—one reason why it is so morally difficult to know what to do with it now in a nuclear age. The Battle of Salamis saved the Mediterranean for Greek civilization. World War II aligned good against evil more neatly than life has come to expect.

War in the past was sometimes merely an oaf's answer to the deepest questions: What are we for? What do we do with ourselves? War meant motion, drama, change, risk, adventure, challenge, release, danger, intensity, comradeship, travel, and stories to bore people with years later. It meant a nihilistic freedom. Few of us have come equipped with the spiritual resources and moral poise of Archimedes, who chose to remain in Syracuse, imperturbably thinking about mathematics while invading Romans gashed through town. A soldier stabbed Archimedes to death as he drew a geometrical figure in the sand.

A long and somewhat bloodless view might see wars in the past as a necessary, if messy, shaking out of history. Especially since World War I destroyed an entire generation of Western Europe's best men, the West has tended to call war futile, the kind of thing that brown rats do to each other in a locked room. Seeing its horrors, we conceive of it as history gone mad, the reptilian brain taking over, the savage part of us wading through gore wearing ivory-handled pistols: war as a picnic of cannibals. The Icelandic author Halldor Laxness found the murderous fascination of war in the Old Norse texts of Scaldic poetry, the hymns of the "kill spree." The poets were particular about the best light and color for battle: "The hour before daybreak is all right because it lends to the crimson of liquid blood a nice admixture of an azure sky and the silvery gray of the fading moon."

War sometimes serves civilization and freedom. It is a sin and a mystery and an occasional necessity. Sometimes, too, war puts the highest technology at the service of the lowest impulses. It is the sheer technology today that tears loose the wiring of our consciences—the knowledge that in another year or two or three, almost any country with a backyard plutonium kit will be dealing in apocalypse. Despairing, we send our children back to their Atari and Intellivision electronic zapping games: those may be the playing fields of Eton.

The Dynamics of Revolution

Edmund Burke cast an indignant eye across the English Channel at the French Revolution and wrote sarcastically: "Admidst assassination, massacre and confiscation, they are forming plans for the good order of future society." Burke was the prototype of skepticism about certain revolutions. Since the French Terror, history has paraded past too many utopian dramas of transformation that ended by being as totalitarian, as murderous, as the regimes that they swept away—triumphs of hopeful zealotry over experience. Stalin turned the Russian Revolution into a self-devouring machine that crushed its own in the basement of the Lubyanka. Especially because of the Soviet redemptive passion that ended in the Gulag, revolution in this century has lost much of its violent romance. Outsiders have learned not to judge revolutions quickly. They wait for the other boot to drop.

The Iranian uprising has prompted among the industrial powers a complicated wariness, along with the anxiety and attentive respect due to the world's second largest exporter of crude oil. Without the wealth buried in Iran, much of the fascination would vanish. Since most of the world was unprepared for the uprising and ignorant of Iran's internal stresses, it is difficult for outsiders to know what to make of the revolution. Iranians themselves are no longer certain. Nearly everyone who has carefully watched the event agrees on two propositions:

It has been a widely popular uprising, virtually spontaneous, with support in almost every area of Iranian life.

The revolution is far from over. Its ultimate meaning has not yet developed.

All revolutions are unique, for roughly the same reasons that, as Tolstoy said, all unhappy families are unhappy in different ways. In *The Anatomy of Revolution,* the late Crane Brinton, the Harvard historian, attempted to formulate the stages of revolution. First, in Brinton's model, comes the euphoric phase of good feeling, when expectations and perfectionist rhetoric run high. Soon the practical tasks of governing split moderates and radicals. In the second stage, extremists rise and consolidate their power. Next comes the Terror, when the regime desperately tries to accomplish revolutionary goals no matter what the cost in blood. This horror often engenders a Thermidorean reaction (named for *Thermidor,* the month of the French revolutionary calendar in which the reaction occurred), when moderates regain control and the nation begins a period of convalescence. But ahead lies the danger of the fifth stage: the coming of a dictator still fired by some revolutionary zeal, and beyond that, the possibility of a Bourbonism restored.

Brinton was following the classic pattern of European revolutions, which can translate only partially into other times and other cultures. But some events of the Iranian revolution already correspond disconcertingly to the Brinton pattern: the first euphoria of victory dissolving into factionalism, and now some possibility that leftists among the revolutionaries, better organized than the masses who drove out the Shah, may seize power. As in France, the tenure of forbearance may be short; already Qasr prison, emptied of its prisoners of the Pahlavi regime, is filling again, this time populated by the enemies of the revolution.

But historian Walter Laqueur warns against rigid analogies. If anything, says Laqueur, "you should compare Iran not with France, not with Russia, but with the revolutionary movements in Spain beginning in 1808 against Napoleon, where the revolt was carried out by the crowd, by the mass of people." Princeton University political scientist Robert C. Tucker suggests some similarity to the Russian uprising of 1905. Thousands of unarmed striking workers marched on the Czar's Winter Palace at St. Petersburg. Government soldiers fired on the crowd, killing and wounding hundreds. More strikes broke out. Peasant and military groups revolted. Says Tucker: "That may have been the purest case before Iran in the twentieth century of a great, spontaneous, popular, antimonarchical movement spreading across the country. In that case, it failed; the monarchy caught itself, staggered and survived—temporarily."

For every point of historical comparison, Iran offers at least one anomalous or unprecedented detail. The role of mass electronics was rather weird. Ubiquitous transistor radios and cassette tape recorders with messages relayed over telephone lines to some 9,000 mosques all over Iran allowed a seventy-eight-year-old holy man camped in a Paris suburb to direct a revolution 2,600 miles away like a company commander assaulting a hill.

The most interesting and socially entangled factor in the Iranian revolution has been the role of the Muslim religion. The Ayatollah Khomeini's revolution was aimed to a large extent at restoration, a re-establishment of the Islamic spirituality and law that had been, so the faithful believed, desecrated by the Shah's modernizations and the widespread, profound corruption of everyday life. Iranians were caught in an intolerable bind: their daily routines were elaborately oppressed by a stupid, corrupt bureaucracy, and yet everything in Iran (costs, salaries, the pace of change) was moving at ungodly speeds. Eastern European official stolidity was impossibly combined with Western velocity.

Islam proved to be a liberating vehicle, although an ironic one, to Western eyes. There are several layers of paradox in the relationship between religion and revolution. The word *revolution* first entered the English language as a political term around 1600, and implied restoration of the old order. Later revolutions, like the French and the Russian, were explicitly antireligious, anticlerical. And yet revolution is almost always cryptoreligious in its vocabularies, disciplines, and even operating psychologies. Revolution needs martyrs, saints, zealots, and almost always involves a rigorously ascetic ideal. Revolution, like religion, means faith and commitment, righteousness, intolerance, overriding goals, doctrine, and ideology. In the revolutionary paradigm, the old order is corrupt, out of grace, godless, and therefore to be swept aside. Revolutionaries, of course, tend to seek their heaven on earth, here and now. But the contradiction between revolutionary dreams and religious yearning achieved at least a temporary resolution in Khomeini's Iran. Islam, after all, makes no distinction between the church and state, the secular and the sacred.

In a sense, the Iranian revolution was an exercise in internal anticolonialism: a convulsive rejection of foreign influence that had, so a wide variety of Iranians thought, robbed their culture of its Islamic values and its natural wealth. In a psychological way, the revolutionaries were obeying the logic of many anticolonial fighters who, in the formulation of the revolutionary theorist Frantz Fanon, held that the "native" must be transformed into a free man through struggle against his foreign oppressors. In countries like Algeria and Kenya, the struggle was protracted and violent. In Iran, after a point, the army foreshortened the process by choosing not to resist the revolution.

Some outsiders fear the Moslem revivalism in the revolution. But Robert Wesson, a political scientist at the University of California at Santa Barbara, sees it "not so much as medievalism as a rejection of foreign intrusion. They are not reversing modernization, but giving it a sounder basis in Iranian institutions." Wesson detects a parallel between Islam in Iran and Roman Catholicism in Poland. "There, in a country in a sub-revolutionary situation, the Catholic Church is enormously popular because it is the counter to the government—it is the refuge for freedom. It has become the umbrella for all manner of movements."

In the months of the demonstrations that brought down the Shah and then Prime Minister Shahpour Bakhtiar, Islam performed that unifying function. Several different revolutions coalesced then; now they are subdividing again. The century's earlier revolutionary history may explain the components. The revolutions of the twenties and thirties were either rebellions of redemptionists (sometimes fascists, as in Germany and Italy) intent on rescuing old native virtues from alien influences, or of Communists, or of nationalists (in Ireland, for example). Elements of all three have been at work in Iran. But now the contradictions of the types must be sorted out. Laqueur says: "The Iranian revolution does not exist. There exist various groups, each of which says, 'We caused the revolution, we are the legitimate heirs.' "

The resolution may take months or years. After a period of chaos, it becomes easy to imagine, a variation of the Brinton model might start working: a strongman with an armed force imposing law where there is none. When Bakhtiar was named prime minister, the mind immediately said, "Ah, Kerensky." Now there seems a possibility of multiple Kerenskys: Bazargan, perhaps Khomeini himself. In the Iranian turbulence, an ominous recollection about Russia arises: its two revolutions of 1917 were basically bloodless. Then, from 1918 to 1921, the country was torn apart by civil war.

Israel's Moral Nightmare

The photographs are becoming a sort of genre of the late twentieth century: the massacre shots. We see the crumpled litter of bodies, the familiar, companionably mounded flesh reposing on the bare dirt in the sun in a stunned fatal sprawl. The inarticulate carrion aftermath. We have seen them in Vietnam and El Salvador and Uganda and Rhodesia and God knows where. My Lai is the primordial scene of the type. The same evil black bats burst flapping out of the pictures, into the brain, and each time the mind flinches and contracts and sickens and grieves for a moment. And yet, unless the slaughter has some especially lunatic human interest, as Jonestown did, we move on soon enough to other business. All of that death dissolves by and by into a form of abstraction.

Such killing has become a kind of unofficial policy in the world. The statistics of mass murder in the past decade or so (at least 100,000 Hutus killed by Tutsis in Burundi, for example, or the million or three Cambodians dead under Pol Pot) somehow should make the deaths in the Palestinian camps seem less cataclysmic, less imposingly significant. Horrible, of course. But Lebanese Christians and Muslims have been trafficking in such mutual slaughter forever. Their blood feud in the past seven years has taken more than sixty thousand lives.

But the killings in the camps of West Beirut assumed a significance in the moral thinking and rhetoric of the world. Why? Because of the Israelis. In part, they were being judged by the old double standard. But there was more: the Israelis were actually parked there, just outside the camps, with all of their tradition, with all the edifice of Jewish morality. The

Christians blasted away for a night and a day and a night, and the Jews with the guns averted their gaze.

It was unjust that the blame for the atrocity came down upon Israelis alone. The Christian militiamen who actually did the evil work were rarely mentioned. Presumably, that kind of Hobbesian savagery comes so naturally to them that it hardly bears remarking. There was a strange compliment concealed here. The world accused Israel so violently in part because the massacre profoundly violated Israel's own moral standards. Some of the vitriol, too, was just anti-Semitism dressed up to look like righteous indignation.

Nevertheless, for Israel, for Jews around the world, the massacre was a moral nightmare. It penetrated to the deepest questions of the Jewish character and identity, to the core of the Jewish idea.

In his memoirs, Menachem Begin wrote fiercely of the emergence of "the Fighting Jew." For much of Jewish history, through the long centuries of the Diaspora, that phrase was an oxymoron, a kind of contradiction in terms. Israel was the creation of fighting Jews, of course, but at least until the Six-Day War of 1967, Israel was the heroic and democratic underdog struggling for its very existence in the vast and hostile Arab wilderness. For a couple of thousand years, Jewish morality presupposed a kind of victim's righteousness, the special blamelessness of those without great collective power. Now Israel ranks fourth among the military powers of the world. The deepest question framed by the massacre in West Beirut was this: Has Israel yet managed to formulate a morality that squares its worldly power with the individual consciences of its people?

The unthinkable tragedies of Jewish history conspire with the radical vulnerability of Israel to enforce sometimes an aggressive and absolutist approach to life. In a warrior like Ariel Sharon, that morality hardens into a brute logic: the end justifies the means. It is a complicated and dangerous business when the People of the Book become also a People of the Gun.

Menachem Begin refuses to struggle with this dilemma. He still likes to carry the blank check of Jewish history; he finds it useful in the conduct of government and war. "No one," Begin's government repeats with a baleful glare, "will preach to us ethics and respect for human life." Why not? Because of the record, because of pogroms and the six million dead in the Holocaust. There are many centuries in that line. Begin claims that as the Israeli dispensation. That is the moral capital of world Jewry, cataclysmically acquired. Do not presume to discuss suffering and death with a people that has passed through Auschwitz. Yes. On the other hand, the Begin government's statement suggests clearly that 1) it has nothing left to learn on the subject of ethics and respect for human life, which is demonstrably not true, and 2) it is certainly not for the rest of the world, meaning, implicitly, the historical tormentors of Jews, to presume to give moral instruction to the Jewish people. Begin in his combative mode strikes ugly notes. Last week his government even used the dark phrase "blood libel" to dismiss condemnations of the Israeli army's behavior at the camps. The phrase invidiously linked the critics to the medieval anti-Semites who accused Jews of crucifying Christian children and drinking their blood at Passover.

The Jewish conscience is often a splendid moral instrument, one of the most highly developed in the world. The internal anguish in Israel with half the country calling for the resignation of Begin and Sharon, demonstrated that that conscience is obviously in good working order. Israel seemed to plunge abruptly into mortal fallibility, into the ambiguous mess in which most history occurs.

Given the customary alertness of the Jewish conscience, the Israeli behavior in West Beirut is nearly inexplicable. It seems almost impossible to absolve the Israel Defense Forces of something a good deal uglier than incompetence there. In any case, the civilized do not make contracts with beasts and give them guns and send them out to do a little messy surrogate killing. The beasts will eventually come to inhabit the soul of their sponsor.

Begin and his government have squandered Israel's moral capital. His greatest disservice has been to invite and very nearly to legitimize the intense criticism of Israel all over the world. A deep, sharp apprehension has passed through the world's Jewish community: Will Begin make anti-Semitism popular again? Think of Israel's image in the world after Entebbe. Think of it now. Any fair judgment of Israel's long-run morality, however, should follow what might be called the Doctrine of Characteristic Acts. Was the behavior of the Israeli forces at these camps characteristic of Israeli society, of Israeli morals? The Christian militiamen, who do not seem to have read the teachings of Christ, were thoroughly and catastrophically in character. The Israelis were not.

The Hall of Mirrors

The Decline and Fall
of Oratory

Tennessee's Governor Frank Clement, the most distinguished graduate of Mrs. Dockie Shipp Weems's School of Expression in Nashville, rose up before the 1956 Democratic Convention and demonstrated a dying art. His keynote address that night beside the Chicago stockyards was a symphony of rhetorical excess, a masterpiece of alliteration and allusion, an epic of the smite-'em style of oratorical Americana.

"How long, O how long, America!" cried Clement, in a grandiloquent filch from Cicero's first Catiline oration. "How long, O America, shall these things endure?" In Dwight Eisenhower's foreign policy, Clement declaimed, "Foster [Dulles] fiddles, frets, fritters, and flits." Richard Nixon was "the vice-hatchet man slinging slander and spreading half-truths while the top man peers down the green fairways of indifference." To farmers, the gusty Tennessean pleaded: "Come on home. . . . Your lands are studded with the white skulls and crossbones of broken Republican promises."

The Republican Party in those days was not entirely speechless either. Connoisseurs of the genre remember the sublimely fogbound organ tones of Illinois' Everett McKinley Dirksen. In his early career, writes biographer Neil MacNeil, Dirksen "bellowed his speeches in a mongrel mix of grand opera and hog calling." Over the years, he developed a style of infinitely subtle fustian, whose effect can still be remotely approximated by sipping twelve-year-old bourbon, straight, while reading Dickens aloud, in a sort of sepulchral purr. Would he criticize an erring colleague? someone would ask. "I shall invoke upon him every condign imprecation,"

Dirksen would intone, with a quiver of his basset's jowls and the gold-gray ringlets of his hair.

Dirksen's oratory succeeded in part because it functioned simultaneously as a satire upon oratory, in somewhat the way that Mae West has always been a walking satire upon sex. But all of Dirksen's splendor, with his rapscallion rhapsodies and hints of the mountebank, could not conceal a small truth about what lay ahead for the ancient discipline of rhetoric: an art that wanes into self-mockery is dying.

Today, oratory seems in serious, possibly terminal, decline. Americans rummaging in their memories for the last great speech they heard—great in content and delivery—often find that they must fetch back at least to 1963, to Martin Luther King, Jr.'s soaring, preacherly performance during the March on Washington. Some think of John Kennedy's inaugural address; yet as the sixties wore on, the go-anywhere-pay-any-price rhetoric of that bright January day on the New Frontier began to seem not only suspect but even a symptom of the emptiness of eloquence and the woes that fancy talk can lead a country into. Some, with even longer memories, mention Churchill in Fulton, Missouri, in 1946 ("An iron curtain has descended . . .") or F.D.R.'s first inaugural address ("The only thing we have to fear is fear itself").

Eloquence, of course, is a matter of political taste. Conservatives may rank Ronald Reagan's acceptance speech only a little short of Edmund Burke. Liberals might poignantly remember Edward Kennedy's speech to the 1972 Democratic Convention the night that George McGovern was nominated. Neoconservatives with a taste for the mystagogic might wheel out Alexander Solzhenitsyn's "decline of the West" speech at Harvard. But of course that was delivered in Russian, and therefore flowed a little outside the American rhetorical mainstream.

Heroic eloquence has made more difference in the world than Westerners are now comfortable in admitting. That eloquence, like science, can do great evil is a truth this century acquired the hard way. Hitler's ranting persuasions worked enough disastrous black magic to send his audience pouring out of the stadium to conquer the world; Churchill's answering eloquence quite literally, physically, pushed back the Reich. In each case, the spoken words alone, the voice, worked with an eerie, preternatural force. Perhaps in some instinctive recoil from its demonstrated, primitive powers, Westerners today have learned to treat eloquence as either an amiable curio or a mild embarrassment. American TV audiences see eloquence perfectly domesticated and trivialized in an A1 Steak Sauce commercial in which a bowler, feigning slightly lunatic oratorical inspiration, demands: "My friends, what *is* hamburger?" In a culture that increasingly demands technical or bureaucratic solutions, passionate oratory seems a kind of gaudy irrelevance. It also, rather curiously, makes people uncomfortable. Lord Shinwell, a former British Labor Minister, remarks: "If Churchill came down to the Commons today to call for blood, sweat, and tears, many of his listeners would probably titter or look plain embarrassed."

What has happened to eloquence, to the art of speechmaking? The greatest single factor in its decline has been television. The intrusion of TV cameras into almost every significant public meeting in the United States has vastly extended the range of speakers' voices, but also changed the nature of what they are doing. A play performed on the legitimate stage but carried by TV somehow always seems dislocated and obscurely fraudulent. The politician addressing a large rally in a speech that is being televised has two audiences, the one in the hall and the one at home. He works simultaneously in two media, an extraordinarily difficult trick. TV has an intimate and pitiless eye that can make any exuberantly talented stump speaker look like a sweating and psychotic blowhard.

Before his GOP keynote speech in Detroit in July 1980, Congressman Guy Vander Jagt thought that the dual-medium problem was like "having one bullet and having to shoot north and south at the same time." During his long campaign, Ted Kennedy often seemed on television to be bulging and strident, too angry, radiating heat; the same performance in the hall usually seemed to come off rather well. Eventually, Kennedy began injecting into his thundering utterances a little of the self-satirizing gaiety that Dirksen used.

Ronald Reagan, of all the candidates, best understands TV's intimate eye; he neither shouts nor gesticulates. Reagan owes his entire career to his talent for persuasion; his long years on television gave him just the right media reflexes for the age. Jimmy Carter also possesses a shrewdly understated television style. A Carter speech that seems pale and weak in person comes through coaxial cables giving off just the right small personal glow.

The procedures of television news reporting have very nearly dismantled what is left of oratorical integrity. TV news producers have in effect become the editors of American speeches. The ancient disciplines of rhetoric suffer disastrously as they are trimmed to the electronic purpose. A politician's handlers try to schedule an event for some time around 2 or 3 P.M. to sluice neatly into Cronkite. Instead of constructing a speech on the old Ciceronian blueprint (exordium, argument, refutation, peroration, and so on) or even on a less classical pattern (beginning, middle, and end would do) the politician contrives a speaking performance that contains a few key and newsy sentences in oratorical neon to make the networks. As J.F.K. aide William Haddad says, "A lot of writers figure out how they are going to get the part they want onto TV. They think of a news lead and write around it. And if the TV lights don't go on as the speaker is approaching that news lead, he skips a few paragraphs and waits until they are lit to read the key part. This does not make for a coherent, flowing speech." During the 1976 campaign, says political scientist James David Barber, Jimmy Carter made a useful discovery: "He put all his pauses in the middle of his sentences, and as he neared the period, he would speed up and pass it until the middle of the next sentence. He got more TV time because it was pretty hard for TV editors to chop him in mid-sentence."

Because of television's fragmenting procedures, it is hardly worth a politician's time to treat his speeches as works of art. Mark Twain said it took him three weeks to prepare a good impromptu speech, but few speakers rehearse their lines anymore: Vander Jagt, who polished his keynote speech by orating at the squirrels and pine trees near his Luther, Michigan, home, is an exception in his zeal.

Speeches simply no longer pulse as they once did at the center of political and cultural life. Once they were prized as entertainment. Today armies of business leaders, writers, politicians, actors, and other celebrities are riding the lecture circuit, and yet they remain peripheral. Movies, then radio and television over the past several generations, have reduced oratory to the status almost of quaintness.

By beaming important speeches to the whole nation, TV has also ensured that most politicians and their committees of advisers will orchestrate all oratory to offend the least number of voters. William Jennings Bryan, whose 1896 "cross of gold" speech was one of the last to get Americans out of a chair and make them do something (they gave him the Democratic nomination on the spot), once described eloquence as "thought on fire." Today, in an age of single-issue politics, the ambitious are careful to see that they do not get burned. Says NBC-TV's Edwin Newman: "Advertising, public relations, and polling techniques create attitudes that are designed to appeal to a large number of people. These attitudes tend to flatten out a speech.'' Political speeches may soon be written by computers: pretested paragraphs are tried out on people for reactions, then fed into a computer along with the speaker's philosophy, and out comes a speech. Audiences now wince wearily at the cute and canned self-deprecatory jokes that federal bureaucrats invariably tell when they go out of town to give a speech. Sample: "You know, the three lies most often told are 'I'll still love you in the morning,' 'The check is in the mail,' and 'I'm from Washington and I'm here to help you.' " Bureaucrats today invariably fall short of Gladstone, who once kept the House of Commons enthralled for more than three hours with a speech on the 1853 budget.

In America at least, a tradition of high rhetoric has always competed with a sentimental worship of the inarticulate. In 1939's *Mr. Smith Goes to Washington,* the sleekly senatorial Claude Rains attempts to conceal his corruption behind an impressive tapestry of rhetoric. But Jimmy Stewart, barely able to complete a sentence, engagingly stumbling over his words, wins out because his sheer radiant American virtue shines through the manipulative deceits inherent in language. It is possible that Adlai Stevenson lost the presidency twice in part because he spoke a little too well. This theme returned passionately in the countercultural sixties, when inarticulate sincerity seemed the answer to the state's mendacities. Some preached that imperialism, racism, and sexism are deeply embedded in the language—a fact that, if true, would tend to discredit eloquence, to make it futile and wrong from the start.

Somehow, few speakers today make oratory seem the urgent and necessary approach to the world that it once was. Eloquence implies certitude. "Hear, O Israel," said Moses, his voice reverberating with authority well beyond his own. It is not a posture much adopted now when such previously safe topics as the family, progress, and the future become problematic. (Reagan's acceptance speech rejected doubts about progress, the family and the future, which may explain why the speech worked as oratory.) Eloquence implies premeditation in an age that has made a virtue of spontaneity. It implies (at its historical best) a public consciousness of serious issues in an age that in a profound way prefers gossip. "The personality of the orator outweighs the issues," observes John Leopold, professor of classical rhetoric at the University of California at Berkeley. A psychologically intimate age does not trust issues, but rather impulses; a man would say anything, after all, to get elected, but what is his mental weather? What makes the finger near the button twitch?

Rhetoric—"Mere rhetoric"; "Oh, that's just rhetoric!"—is not taught widely anymore. In its Greco-Roman golden age, rhetoric was the key to civilized persuasion, and therefore to society itself. The Greek apparatus of rhetoric is a brilliantly elaborate armamentarium of speechmakers' devices—synecdoche, syllepsis, symploce, and so on. Almost from the beginning, the power of rhetoric troubled even those who were best at wielding it. Wrote Cicero: "I have thought long and often over the problem of whether the power of speaking and the study of eloquence have brought more good or harm to cities."

As Cicero knew, it depends. Rhetoric has started wars and stopped them. The eloquence of Bernard of Clairvaux dispatched tens of thousands on the catastrophic Second Crusade. Mindless oratory has also caused untold brain damage to audiences over the centuries. The outpouring of verbiage continues. As the political season ramshackles through the summer, the landscape is dense with BOMFOG (an acronym used by political reporters to designate one of the late Nelson Rockefeller's favorite oratorical clichés: Brotherhood of Man under the Fatherhood of God). Americans may sometimes wistfully miss a better quality of oratory. They might grow even more wistful if they reflected on the Japanese, who regard eloquence as a potential threat to their stability-through-consensus. *Haragei,* their ultimate form of communication, can only be envied in the week of a convention. It consists of making oneself understood with silence.

Public Vanishing

John Kennedy used to wonder what he would do with himself after he finished his second term in the White House. He would be at "the awkward age" then, he said, "too old to begin a new career and too young to write my memoirs."

After Dallas, Kennedy was translated into a sudden myth, a permanent luminescence. It is a profitless irony that the drama of his death spared him the long, fading afterlife of the ex-powerful.

There is a phenomenon of public vanishing in America that is poignant. It is a compact enactment of the American themes of success and failure. Remember Walter Mondale? All spring and summer and fall of 1984, Mondale was a presence in American life, his words, his cadences, his voice and visage and body English all injected electronically into the nation's consciousness. Then November. Poof. Mondale vanished, like the minute explosion of light on the screen when one turns off an old television set after the national anthem—the little death of a star. Mondale reappeared not long ago, gave a few interviews, then dematerialized again, disappearing into a Washington law firm. He became, in short, a private man, a resident of the same obscurity (almost) that everyone else calls home.

There are certain words that English ought to have but does not. One is a word for the opposite of memory. *Oblivion* is not quite it. *Forgettery?* That swampy region in the southland of the brain where everything we have forgotten now lies, overgrown with kudzu, something like an enormous automobile graveyard.

Americans are usually gentler and more metaphorical than some other peoples in consigning their public figures to forgettery. Joseph Stalin slaughtered a generation or two of Soviet leadership. He dealt out the ultimate obscurity: death. It was part of his theory of management. Sometimes he invited prospective victims to his all-night dinners (about 10 p.m. to dawn) and later had the NKVD take them off to be shot. One ruler in Central Africa is said to have murdered hundreds of his people and sometimes eaten them for supper. And so on.

In America, it is the people who eat the politicians for supper. Public vanishing is a dramatic spectacle usually because it has to do with power and its loss. If a politician gives a speech and there is no one there to hear it, has he made a sound? Ask Harold Stassen. He knows something about the riddle of the tree falling in the empty auditorium.

American presidents are a special case. At the end of his awful term in the White House, Franklin Pierce vanished into obscurity in New Hampshire. "What can the next president do but drink?" he asked. The United States was shuddering into the preliminary convulsions of Civil War, so Pierce may have had a point. In those days, ex-presidents did not enjoy the sort of opulent afterlife that they now have. They did not busy themselves building their official libraries, those temples to a president's selective memories of power. They did not enjoy lifetime Secret Service protection and hundreds of thousands of dollars in government allowances. Ulysses Grant went broke and, dying of throat cancer, spent his last days laboring over his autobiography to make some money for his survivors. By today's rules, King Lear would have spent a happy retirement on the golf course.

Richard Nixon has accomplished one of the most complicated and impressive acts of ex-presidential vanishing. But then Nixon always did possess a kind of genius for finishing himself off and then re-emerging as a "New Nixon." He left the White House in disgrace, strangling on tapes and expletives. He vanished into his seaside house at San Clemente, California. He fell into a sepulchral, or defiant, silence. It was as if he were passing through the stages of mourning (denial, anger, depression, acceptance) for his assassinated self. Then, after five years, he moved east to New York City, published four more books and built a kind of public private career as writer and elder statesman. Nixon is the marathon man of public vanishers, always running hard to outdistance the old disgrace.

One of the most spectacular vanishing acts of modern times was that performed by Nixon's vice president Spiro Agnew. For a time in the first Nixon Administration, Agnew was a prominent American folk hero or villain, the voice of the Silent Majority standing up to the "nattering nabobs of negativism.'' Then the Justice Department closed in on him for accepting $147,500 in bribes in the days when he was Governor of Maryland. Agnew resigned and disappeared from the face of the earth. Now and then he is sighted spiriting through an airport in the Middle East. He makes his living as an international trade consultant and keeps a house at Rancho Mirage, California, near Palm Springs, not far from Gerald Ford's home. Rancho Mirage is one of the world capitals of vanishing. Plains, Georgia, has its more down-home native obscurity.

Sometimes those who are willfully vanished achieve a mysterious, dark entity—a man like Howard Hughes, for example. His biography became a kind of American antimatter.

Television is the principal theater in which the drama of vanishing is enacted. There is a sermon in the cathode-ray tube, a buried subtext about power and fame and celebrity. TV captures life vividly, intimately. But the images are merely electrons in the air. Moment to moment, they vanish. Being, then nothingness. All conscious life is haunted by the prospect of nullity. Public figures and celebrities become intimately familiar, and then they are gone. ''Buffalo Bill's defunct,'' wrote e. e. cummings. Is public vanishing a psychodrama in which we appease our fears of death? In the phenomenon of public vanishing, one sometimes detects the ghost of a childhood terror of abandonment. Or perhaps the converse impulse: a punitive satisfaction at the mighty brought low, vaporized. It is a theme of Shakespearean size. Power and fame are fugitive. Or, to see it in more banal terms, the world has a short attention span.

But turn the glass a little. What the public perceives as a vanishing may in fact be an escape into a better reality. In October 1984 Massachusetts senator Paul Tsongas, 53, one of the bright hopes of the Democratic Party, learned that he had a mild form of cancer. At first, he decided to plow ahead with his re-election campaign. Then he thought better of it. As a friend told him, ''Nobody on his deathbed ever said, 'I wish I had spent more time on my business.' '' Tsongas gave up his political career to spend his time with his family. He vanished to the public in order to materialize for his family. He may have given a deeper reading to a line of W. B. Yeats: ''Man is in love, and loves what vanishes./ What more is there to say?''

The Perils of Celebrity

In his novel *Humboldt's Gift,* Saul Bellow described the onset of fame: "I experienced the high voltage of publicity. It was like picking up a dangerous wire fatal to ordinary folk. It was like the rattlesnakes handled by hillbillies in a state of religious exaltation." Some who grasp those charged serpents will themselves incandesce in celebrity for a little while and then wink out (goodbye, Clifford Irving; goodbye, Nina van Pallandt): defunct flashlights, dead fireflies. Thus they will have obeyed Warhol's Law, first propounded by the monsignor of transience and junk culture: "In the future, everybody will be famous for at least fifteen minutes." But many survive long after the deadline. Their fifteen minutes stretch into years and years, until the public, whose adulation sometimes conceals a hard little rock of vindictiveness, wishes that, after all, the fifteen-minute rule had been observed.

Contrary to Warhol's essentially democratic premise—everybody, but briefly—fame elevates some mortals into realms where their celebrity achieves a life of its own. While a Tiny Tim or a Judith Exner may flare and fade, others acquire a strange permanence—or its illusion, which is of course just as good. They have been transported into another medium where information and images are permanently (or for years, anyway) stored. In the formula of historian Daniel Boorstin, they have "become well known for being well known." A classic of the category is Elizabeth Taylor. Who, outside of her family and friends, would have the slightest interest in her were she not phosphorescent in her sheer famousness?

As Bellow knew, fame can be a state as complicated as serious religion; at any rate, the vocabularies are sometimes interchanged. Terms like "immortal'' get thrown around. The Beatles' boast in 1966 that ''we're more popular than Jesus now'' was a cheeky little blasphemy that accurately located an intersection between Liverpool and Nazareth. In her book *Fame*, Susan Margolis noticed that ''today the gifted as well as the deranged among us are struggling to be famous the way earlier Americans struggled to be saved.''

In the beatitude of fame, certain privileges and immunities exist. The higher orders may, for example, appear through a curtain, unannounced, in the middle of a Johnny Carson show, exciting little whoops of recognition and incredulity in the audience. (Bob Hope may always do that; Don Rickles can get away with it.) The middle orders make the Dean Martin roast, regularly inhabit the ''People'' pages of magazines and newspapers. All enjoy, at least for a time, immunity from the agent's call proposing that they do an American Express commercial: ''Remember me? I used to . . .''

Fame improves some people. Except for certain saints and others with inner resources, there is nothing ennobling about obscurity. Watergate transformed Carl Bernstein from a cigarette-scrounging city-room fixture and superannuated punk into a superb journalist who carries his fame with a self-assured but quizzical grace. Rosalynn Carter has flourished in the public gaze.

Some celebrities from time to time pronounce their lives a living hell. Raquel Welch not long ago complained that sex symbols are vulnerable and tragic figures ''who have a corner on the misery market.'' Louise Lasser (of TV's late *Mary Hartman, Mary Hartman)* declared, ''When you are a celebrity, you are totally a victim.'' There are plenty of cautionary examples to prove them right: Elvis Presley living like a rhinestone troglodyte, Janis Joplin careering around on quarts of Southern Comfort, Freddie Prinze putting a pistol to his head.

But the public is massively unpersuaded when the rich and famous feel sorry for themselves. Celebrity is by definition an exposed life—except for Howard Hughes, who made a public event of his obsessive absence. If Woody Allen is so shy, why is he always turning up where the photographers are? Celebrity involves a sort of hospitable narcissism: ''Say, I'm absolutely wonderful, come have a look.'' Some of course think it peculiar, and even clinically neurotic, to wish to have millions of strangers monitoring one's life. A sometimes awful intimacy is one of the strangest aspects of fame: people turn their lives inside out for our inspection. Paula Prentiss once explained on a talk show that she had had her intra-uterine coil removed so that she could have a baby.

• • •

People arrive at celebrity by various roads. Some are famous because of accomplishment (Jonas Salk, Beverly Sills, Reggie Jackson) or because they possess power and position (the Shah, say, or the Pope). But there exist categories of celebrity quite outside the usual cause-and-effect logic of merit. W. B. Yeats noticed it bitterly in a couplet: "Some think it a matter of course that chance/Should starve good men and bad advance."

It is those who achieve celebrity's bright orbits without much boost from talent or intelligence who fall victim to the public's readiness to be bored, to discard disposable personalities like empty bottles of Champale. When fame ceases to bear any relation to worth or accomplishment, then the whole currency of public recognition is debased. The famous are merely random iridescences on the oil spot, depending less upon intrinsic value than upon the angle at which the light strikes them. After the four millionth exposure to Farrah Fawcett-Majors's teeth or to Billy Carter's wheezing bray, the celebrity consumer's brain begins to click like Madame Defarge's knitting needles, compiling lists. He begins to think that the Warhol fifteen-minute rule might profitably be applied to everybody. Those who have grown tiresome must have their immortality repealed: Sorry pal, your fifteen minutes are long since up. As Dr. Seuss wrote in one of his books for children, "Marvin K. Mooney, I don't care how/ Marvin K. Mooney, will you please GO NOW!"

The fifteen-minute rule of course works by a natural laissez-faire mechanism in many cases. This is the celebrity version of Adam Smith's Invisible Hand at work; it might be called the Invisible Hook. The Hook has thus ushered away in timely fashion the likes of Mark Spitz, Fanne Foxe, Elizabeth Ray, Evel Knievel, Werner Erhard, Roman Polanski, Margaret Trudeau, Sun Myung Moon, Chevy Chase, and the Captain and Tennille—all the spiritual descendants of Pinky Lee.

Then there is a whole category of celebrities who seem in imminent danger of staying too long: people like Margaux Hemingway, Jimmie Walker, Geraldo Rivera, Princess Caroline, Brooke Shields, Ilie Nastase, Anita Bryant, Sylvester Stallone, Susan Ford. The clock has run even longer on Jann Wenner, Erich Segal, Erica Jong, Vanessa Redgrave, David Frost, and Rex Reed.

But finally there ought to be some kind of fifteen-minutes Hall of Fame—a compilation of those who have egregiously overstayed their welcomes in that part of the national imagination that is always sitting under a hair dryer. Some nominees: Barbara Streisand, Sammy Davis, Jr., Richard Burton, Jacqueline Onassis, Cher, Howard Cosell, Hugh Hefner, Muhammad Ali, Barbara Walters, Dean Martin, Norman Mailer, Bob Dylan, Gore Vidal, Truman Capote . . .

But this is Neronian proscription, a culling process that goes on constantly in the minds of talk-show "talent coordinators" and the audience itself, which always enjoys the reassuring drama of yesterday's famous being returned to oblivion. [Ten years later, half the old list is gone, and one would pile on fresh meat.] Celebrities are intellectual fast food. Perhaps we ought to be troubled by the combination of proliferating celebrities and diminishing public attention spans. If Emerson was correct that "every hero becomes a bore at last," then how much more quickly the famous mediocrity must become unendurable. Shelley thought of Ozymandias. Perhaps we ought to find a metaphor for the evanescence of glory in Monty Rock III's image imploding to a sad white dot on the TV screen as his last Johnny Carson show is switched off.

The Politics of
the Box Populi

No one has ever decided what television is really supposed to be *for.* Is the wondrous box meant to entertain? To elevate? To instruct? To anesthetize? The medium, in its sheer unknowable possibilities, seems to arouse extreme reactions: contempt for its banal condition as the ghetto of the sitcom, or else grandiose metaphysical ambitions for a global village. The tube is Caliban and Prospero, cretin and magician. "What makes television so frightening," writes critic Jeff Greenfield, "is that it performs all the functions that used to be scattered among different sources of information and entertainment." Television could, if we let it, electronically consolidate all of our culture—theater, ballet, concerts, newspapers, magazines, and possibly most conversation. It is a medium of eerie and disconcerting power; one college professor conducted a two-year study that asked children aged four to six: "Which do you like better, TV or Daddy?" Forty-four percent of the kids said that they preferred television.

An old question keeps recurring: Who should control so pervasive a force? A Civil Rights Commission report on the role of minorities on television complained that women, blacks, and others, including Hispanics, Pacific Island Americans, American Indians, and even Alaskan natives are underrepresented in or virtually absent from TV dramas. Composed in a spirit of bureaucratic pedantry, the report suggested that the Federal Communications Commission should lean on the networks a bit by formulating rules that would "encourage greater diversity."

The argument is simplest if it turns on TV purely as entertainment, with no intent larger than diversion. On that basis, the laissez-faire system of the ratings possesses absolute logic: the people decide, voting with their channel selectors. What works as diversion will presumably be highest rated and therefore most successful. But there is a fallacy here: a laissez-faire principle of rule by ratings would be admirable if a wide variety of choices existed. Too many network shows are devoted almost entirely to exploring new dimensions of imbecility. That seems an old and boringly elitist criticism of TV, but it acquires fresh force, even urgency, if one sits through a few hours of *Supertrain, The Ropers,* and *The $1.98 Beauty Show.*

Television drama—leaving aside the question of TV news, whose effects are a different phenomenon altogether—becomes more complicated when it is considered as a medium of persuasion, the little electronic proscenium alive with potentially sinister ideological glints. In years past, American TV has been considered a moderately conservative influence. From the suburban complacencies of Ozzie and Harriet through the vanquishing six-gun authority of Sheriff Matt Dillon, TV entertainment seemed an elaborate gloss on the status quo.

A sometime television writer, Ben Stein, claims, on the contrary, to see in TV entertainment an infestation of liberal chic. In *The View from Sunset Boulevard,* Stein argues that, each night in its prime-time sitcom diet, the vast American TV audience receives near lethal doses of liberalism from a small band of some two hundred Hollywood writers and producers, who exercise a preposterously disproportionate influence in TV's almost subliminal channels of opinion making.

The message of this liberal chic, according to Stein, is, among other things, both antibusiness and antimilitary. The thrust of *M*A*S*H,* for example, is that the Army is constantly trying to get as many people killed as possible, to burn down villages, to separate loved ones. Small towns fare badly on the tube, according to Stein. The *Bad Day at Black Rock* syndrome applies: repeated episodes of peaceful, postcard towns in which something terribly evil is afoot.

Despite this interpretation, most programs obey no pat formula. *Battlestar Galactica,* for example, seems to teach a rigorously militaristic sort of watchfulness; the peacemakers tend to be soft fools with good intentions. On the durable detective show *Hawaii Five-O,* the hero McGarrett exhibits some of J. Edgar Hoover's least attractive qualities. Many shows are almost entirely innocent of meaning: What is the political content of *Mork & Mindy?* What can the bizarre *Incredible Hulk* signify except perhaps an adolescent's fantasies of puissance and rage?

In fact, it would be extremely difficult for a Sunset Boulevard conspiracy to retail a coherent party line even if it wished. Says Michael Jay Robinson, a political scientist at Washington's Catholic University: "Programming is really a sausage—created by grinding together the values of the producers, a few dozen formula plots, network perceptions about audience, and the implied guidelines given by the censors, affiliates, FCC and even the National Association of Broadcasters. And, obviously, the ratings." The National PTA exerts a heavy influence against violence. Since kids so often control the dial, the low audience age dictates a certain level of foolishness.

The operating politics of television has an unexpected subtlety. Through the mid- and late seventies, a procession of shows like *All in the Family, Maude, Three's Company,* and *Laverne & Shirley* promoted a progressive, permissive, liberalized attitude toward such previously untouchable subjects as premarital sex and homosexuality. But, as Robinson suggests, a complex crisscross may have occurred: while television may indeed have coaxed Americans to shift leftward in social matters, the nation seems at the same time to have moved a bit to the right politically. These movements aside, it may be that television's greatest consequence has been to impart velocity to ideas and fads. From antiwar protests to disco dancing, such trends tend to start on the coasts and then get transfused with astonishing speed into the life of the heartland between. TV thus serves to obliterate regional and local distinctions, to create national social values.

This powerful national theater does not often rise to its responsibilities. A certain grotesque *Gong Show* brand of schlock-peddling could be forgiven if it were not for the stupefying dimensions of the American TV habit. The average household's TV set runs six hours a day. Although television does useful service in informing and entertaining, its strange power is bound to arouse a great deal of spiritual disquiet. People may expect too much of TV. It will never replace the printed word as an instrument of thought. Its entertainment side may ultimately be rescued from mediocrity by technological diversifications into cable TV, video tape recorders, video disc, and other elaborate equipment. The new technology will bring a greater selection—and thus a wider, though more personal, choice—to the audience. It is possible, of course, that this could mean that a public already besotted with the tube might become even further enslaved by it.

The Art of Weathercasting

Americans have contemplated this *annus mirabilis* of weird weather (1980) with a special fascination. But even when the barometer is less mercurial, they pay almost abnormal attention to the weather's moods and the people who predict them. Americans are weather junkies. They monitor it the way a hypochondriac listens to his own breathing and heartbeat in the middle of the night. Some people, of course, have an urgent need to know: boatmen, farmers, construction workers, streetwalkers. But others whose daily exposure to the hazards of the open air is limited to three minutes between bus stop and office lobby are also curious to the point of vague anxiety about variations in the temperature and the chances of rain.

This enduring preoccupation has, over the years, developed a native American art form, the television weathercast, and its attending priesthood of TV forecasters. It is an odd and specialized calling: not exactly journalism, not exactly meteorology, not exactly soothsaying, not exactly show business, but parts of all four. TV weathercasters have been much mocked for their polyester jocularity, for what seem bizarrely pseudoscientific discourses to explain that it will be cool and windy tomorrow. It is, critics say, the baton twirling of TV news.

The criticism is essentially unfair; people want to know about the weather, and TV forecasters tell them—not just the niggardly name, rank, and serial number of temperature highs and lows but also the larger meteorological events: cold sweeping down from Canada, a warm front out of the Gulf Stream, or the metastasis of a storm from Martinique. It may sometimes sound like a cheerful patter of mumbo jumbo and Celsius conversions, like a lounge comedian who did a semester at MIT, but on the whole, people learn what they want to know. The audience pays weathercasters the compliment of its attention, and advertisers pay the compliment of their dollars. The weather is always among the surest draws on local news.

Still, the mockery of TV weathercasters is probably inevitable. The art form is an original, without ancestors; it is bound now and then to be a sort of satire upon itself. Every night on millions of TV screens, the breezy wizards conjure hieratically with nature: They prophesy. Warm and cold fronts spearhead across their maps like armies. Black clouds and jagged lightning add a Shakespearean flourish to their charts. Their satellites look down like the eye of God, giving the world a dramatic and curiously abstracted view of what is about to happen to it.

Although the elements change as swiftly as the shapes of clouds, the weathercaster's three-to-four-minute performance is, in its discipline, as rigid as a sonnet or a haiku. The ritual begins with the anchorman passing the baton with an oafishly merry transition line like: "Well, buddy, you sure did it to us yesterday, didn't you?" The weatherman casts his eyes downward with a chastened chuckle, accepting responsibility and thereby obscurely associating himself with nature's higher authorities.

Now the forecaster commences the two-part substance of his report: first the present (a satellite photograph, high and low pressure systems indicated, current readings of wind and temperature), then a commercial break, then the second part, the future (tonight, tomorrow morning, and the "long-range forecast," an educated guess on the next four or five days).

Within the formula, a thousand variations flourish. Weathercasters differ about the measure of dignity the occasion calls for. Before Willard Scott moved to NBC's *Today Show,* he became a Washington, D.C., fixture by giving his WRC-TV weathercast in kilts, Robin Hood costumes, or George Washington getups. Audiences in Savannah have had a weather reporter who talked to a seagull; those in Cleveland have enjoyed one who blew hot licks on his trumpet between temperature recitations. Station KDBC-TV in El Paso has a Lhasa Apso named Puffy Little Cloud who gives a forecast by appearing on camera in an outfit appropriate to the weather.

The history of television weathercasting does not exactly encourage reverence. In the beginning, stations just had a staff announcer rip the forecast off the A.P. ticker. Stations with commercial foresight, however, brought in scientists or pseudoscientists to discourse on occluded fronts and thermal inversions. The weather package was born: a short noncontroversial segment of the local news, with almost universal audience interest. In the mid- and late fifties came the era of the weather girl—sex to relieve the tedium of the millibars. The acts ranged from chirpy to sultry. The women, often blond, busty, and breathy, made a warm front sound like a proposition. NBC's Tedi Thurman used to peek from behind a shower curtain to coo: "The temperature in New York is 46, and me, I'm 36-26-36."

Such a history has tended to damage the self-esteem of TV weathercasters. Sometimes they even suspect themselves of fraud. Willard Scott has been heard to say, with an undercurrent of melancholy: "A trained gorilla could do what I do." In fact, even if some of today's forecasters are merely local station Ken dolls rolled out to mouth data gleaned from WE 6-1212, many are knowledgeable meteorologists who provide a valuable public service.

Almost all TV weathercasters rely primarily upon the basic data provided by the National Weather Service. A private service, Accu-Weather, supplies information to more than forty TV stations around the nation. But weathermen, the good ones at least, are somewhat like doctors: several examining the same patient may arrive at different diagnoses. Experience and savvy count—knowing, for example, when a minor geographical shift of a pressure system might make the difference between a drenching rain and a couple of feet of snow.

Are weathercasts really necessary? Not absolutely. But in a nation of highly mobile and widely scattered people, it is both a comfort and a convenience to see the national weather satellite pictures, to watch the migrant storms and bright patches marbling the land, and know just what kind of weather friends and family are under. An intelligent forecast enables people to plan their lives a little, instead of passively awaiting the atmosphere's surprises. Foreknowledge mitigates the tyranny of nature.

Obsessive weather monitoring, in any case, is an old American custom. Thomas Jefferson was mysteriously compulsive about the weather. He kept interminable logs of changes in the temperature. He knew what millions in the weathercasters' audiences may sense: if you know what the weather (a primal force in the world) is up to, you are somehow, obscurely but actually, in control of it.

Goodbye to "Our Mary"

Her genius was always in her reactions to things. Some small outrage would happen by, and Mary, a Bert Lahr born lovely, would do a fine, slow turn, her indignation developing like a Polaroid: "Oh, Mr. Grant!"

The Mary Tyler Moore Show has amounted to only eighty-four hours of viewing time over seven years. In its final episode, new owners take over Mary's mythical WJM-TV in Minneapolis and decide that WJM's local news program is not much good. Everyone has known as much for years, of course; that was one of its charms—the small, endearing air of incompetence, of inadequacy that surrounded the characters. Everyone on the staff except Ted Baxter, the anchorman with the mane of Eric Sevareid and the brain of a hamster, is fired. So ends the *MTM* show. The real Mary Tyler Moore will take some time off and eventually develop a new series.

In many places around the United States, *The Mary Tyler Moore Show* changed the nature of Saturday nights; it even became fashionable to spend them at home. The show turned the situation comedy into something like an art form—a slight art form perhaps, but a highly polished one. *MTM* was the sitcom that was intellectually respectable. The writing, acting, and directing on *MTM* have been the best ever displayed in TV comedy. Owing much to Moore, who always set a tone of perfectionism, the show has been technically superb and beautifully paced. But unlike 90 percent of TV's sitcoms, *MTM* has always transmitted intelligence, along with a rather unique respect for its characters and its audience. The snorting, hooraying Archie Bunker's *All in the Family* has no such charm. Over the years, *MTM* has been rich enough in its talent to spin off Rhoda (Valerie Harper) and Phyllis (Cloris Leachman) into fairly good series of their own.

In its gentle way, the show changed television's image of women. During the pleistocene era of *Ozzie and Harriet* or *Donna Reed*, the women, in skirts curiously bouffant for housework, had to make their witticisms in or near the kitchen, lest the chocolate-chip cookies burn. Mary Tyler Moore, playing Rob Petrie's wife on *The Dick Van Dyke Show* (1961–66), wore tighter dresses but was a thoroughly suburban housewife: Rob went to work, Laura worried about the pet duck catching cold.

TV shows either reflect or strangely caricature their times. In *That Girl* (1966), Marlo Thomas played a single girl in New York City making her career, but always Mom and Dad hovered; her independence was somehow merely *cute*, a phase. In *MTM,* Mary Richards—Moore's character—gave a humanely plausible version of American women—some American women—in the early and mid-seventies. Not many, of course, are as lovely as Mary or as funny. She was single, independent, pursued her career, was interested in men but not in an obsessive, husband-trapping way. Many women in the audience felt happier with themselves because of her.

Mary Richards was always more interesting and complicated than any subliminal politics of sex. With her independence came a rather sweet vulnerability. Mary could not bring herself to call Lou Grant by his first name; a daughterly side of her character would not permit it. Her sexual attraction had a fascinating ambiguity. Her allure never threatened anyone. Women watchers of the show thought of her roughly as a great gal. Men, who usually found her immensely sexy, also felt somehow protective about her. Several years ago, when Mary Richards spent the night with a date, men all over the country were inconsolable; they felt betrayed.

Mary Richards's age (mid-thirties) was also part of her charm—almost a relief after a period when the nation seemed overrun and overwhelmed by the very young. Timing, in fact, may have contributed to *MTM's* popularity. During Watergate and the long ending of the Vietnam War, when the nation was feeling especially baleful, these characters in an out-of-the-way local TV station, with their family feeling, may have suggested that it was possible to deal with the world without being either Patty Hearst or R. D. Laing. They became part of the viewer's family, comfortable to have around.

On *The Mary Tyler Moore Show,* characters developed, changed, sometimes in ways disconcerting to all those schooled in the inevitability of happy endings. Lou Grant (Edward Asner) and his wife Edie (Priscilla Morrill) separated; she felt stultified and wanted to try a different life. Ah well, the faithful said, they will get back together. They did not; they got divorced. In one of the more touching shows, Edie remarried, with Lou attending; afterward, the entire WJM newsroom ended up weeping uncontrollably in a bar as Lou tried to comfort them. In another moving and improbably funny show, Chuckles the Clown, while dressed up as a peanut, was stomped to death by an elephant. Divorce, death, and departure were part of the show's workings; *MTM* possessed at least that much realism.

But the key to *MTM* was its innocence—its almost Kuklapolitan charm, its absence of malice. Inside all the characters—Mary herself, Ted, Lou, Georgette, newswriter Murray Slaughter, happy homemaker Sue Ann Nivens, Rhoda, and Phyllis while they were still there—were children who coped as well as possible with an adult world, but retained a kind of wistfulness. They sniped at one another, but without bloodshed.

Beyond theory, *The Mary Tyler Moore Show* has been good because the writing has usually come in lovely light bursts of very funny lines. Sue Ann, played with genius by Betty White, flashes a domestic smile as if about to explain how to remove coffee stains; she eyes a man in the room and exclaims with sweet enthusiasm, "What a hunk!" Mary's humor was usually reactive; the funny one-liners revolved around her. Often they concerned her war against her own Wasp primness and repression. "I always wash my hair before I go to the hairdresser," she once confessed disconsolately. "Whenever anyone's stomach rumbles, I'm terrified that someone will think it was me."

We'll Always Have *Casablanca*

It's still the same old story. The Lisbon plane always descends like a kid's toy landing on the living-room rug. Stick-figure Nazis with animal faces (Strasser a wolf, his aide a fat little pig in glasses) come strutting off. That night at Rick's they chorus "Die Wacht am Rhein," the stein-swinging bully song that is the Nazis' idea of good time in a nightclub. The defiantly answering "Marseillaise" stirs the soul and raises its Pavlovian goose bumps for the fifteenth time. They still pronounce "exit visa" weirdly: "exit vee-zay."

Casablanca opened in New York in late fall, 1942. At the time, the real Germans were locked around Stalingrad, and the French scuttled their fleet in Toulon Harbor rather than surrender it to the Reich. In Hollywood's version, civilization was dressed in an off-white suit: Victor Laszlo, played by Paul Henreid. Henreid is still alive. So, for that matter, is Ronald Reagan, whom Jack Warner originally wanted for the part of Victor. (All wrong, too American, as wholesome as a quart of milk.) But Humphrey Bogart and Ingrid Bergman and Peter Lorre and Sydney Greenstreet and Claude Rains and Conrad Veidt are all dead. The movie they made has achieved a peculiar state of permanence. It has become something more than a classic. It is practically embedded in the collective American unconscious.

What accounts for the movie's enduring charm? *Casablanca* is, of course, a masterpiece of casting. Not only the leads but the lesser players as well are perfect, each one a small, vivid miracle of type. Fetching up their names is an old game for the trivialist: Sam (Dooley Wilson), the bartender Sascha (Leonid Kinskey), the waiter Carl (S. Z. Sakall), the jilted Yvonne (Madeleine LeBeau), the Bulgarian couple (Joy Page and Helmut Dantine), the pickpocket (Curt Bois), the croupier (Marcel Dalio).

More people know more lines from *Casablanca,* possibly, than from any other movie. They recite the best ones. They splash around in the sentimentality. They sing along in the way that Churchill used to rumble the lines of *Hamlet* from his seat in the audience at the Old Vic. They stooge around: imagine Howard Cosell in the part of Rick Blaine and recite the lines in Cosellian cadence: "Of all the gin joints in all the towns in all the world, she walks into mine."

The movie is a procession of perfect moments. Its dialogue is an exquisite fusion of the hard-boiled and a shameless, high-cholesterol sentimentality. The lines inspire a laughing, capitulating kind of affection. One cherishes them: "What waters? We're in the desert." . . . "I was misinformed." . . . "Was that cannonfire? Or was it my heart pounding?" . . . "Kiss me! Kiss me as though it were the last time!" . . . "Play it, Sam. Play 'As Time Goes By.' " . . . "I saved my first drink to have with you." . . . "Round up the usual suspects." . . . "We'll always have Paris." It has inspired bits of business: Sydney Greenstreet bowing graciously to Ingrid Bergman in the Blue Parrot and then with brutal abstraction swatting a fly, which for the instant becomes the moral equivalent of any refugee in *Casablanca.* Or the all-time triumphant moment of literal-minded symbol-banging exposition: Claude Rains dropping the bottle of Vichy water into a wastebasket and giving it a kick, the charming collaborator virtuous at last.

Casablanca is, among other things, a fable of citizenship and idealism, the duties of the private self in the dangerous public world. It is a thoroughly escapist myth about getting politically involved. Perhaps today the escapism overwhelms the idea of commitment. Local TV stations run *Casablanca* on election nights, so that Americans can avoid watching news reports about their democracy in action.

One can concoct mock-academic theories about *Casablanca.* One can lay the sweet thing down on a stainless-steel lab table and dissect it with instruments Freudian or anthropological. A doctoral thesis might be written on the astonishing consumption of alcohol and cigarettes in the movie. At that rate, everyone would have died of cirrhosis and lung cancer by V-E day.

Another paper might examine *Casablanca* as the ultimate rationalization of, and sublimation of, adultery. One woman, two men. Woman has affair with man not her husband. But wait: it's all right, she thought the husband was dead. And these are desperate times, good and evil are clashing everywhere. A woman can get confused.

It is *poshlost,* as the Russians say, an overheated lunge toward the profound, to think of *Casablanca* in terms of deeper allegory. Still, it is hard to resist delving for Jungian archetypes, primal transactions of the kind that lurk in, say, the Oedipus story (''Here's looking at you, Mom!''). Much of *Casablanca*'s constituency is collegiate anyway. Generations of Harvard students have wandered out of the Brattle Theater in a state of sappy exaltation. The movie's audience is too large to be described as a cult, but the religious vibration in that word may be oddly right.

Semioticians, who study the significance of signs and symbols, have discussed *Casablanca* as a myth of sacrifice. One can have fun with that. Consider it this way: America is the Promised Land, the place of safety and redemption. Rick Blaine has been cast out of America, for some original sin that is as obscure as the one that cost Adam and Eve their Eden. Rick flees to Europe, which is the fallen world where Evil (the Nazis, Satan) is loose. He meets and beds the widow of Idealism. Idealism (meaning Victor) is dead, or thought dead, but it rises from the grave. Rick, losing Ilsa, falls obliviously into despair and selfishness: ''I stick my neck out for nobody.'' He becomes an idiot in the original Greek sense of the word, meaning someone indifferent to his duties as a citizen.

Rick's Café Americain is the state of the stateless. Rick sets himself up as a kind of chieftain or caliph in his isolated, autonomous, amoral fiefdom, where he rules absolutely. Victor and Rick are splintered aspects, it may be, of the same man. Ultimately, the ego rises above mere selfish despair and selfish desire. It is reborn in sacrifice and community: ''It doesn't take much to see that the problems of three little people don't amount to a hill o' beans in this crazy world.'' Idealism and its bride ascend into heaven on the Lisbon plane; Rick goes off in the fog with Louis, men without women, to do mortal work in this world for the higher cause.

About *Casablanca* there clings a quality of lovely, urgent innocence. Those who cherish the movie may be nostalgic for moral clarity, for a war in which good and evil were obvious and choices tenable. They may be nostalgic for a long-lost connection between the private conscience and the public world. *Casablanca* was released three years before the real moment of the fall of the modern world: 1945. That year, the side of good dropped nuclear bombs on cities full of civilians, and the world discovered Auschwitz. We have not yet developed the myths with which to explain such matters.

Metaphysics

God and Science

Sometime after the Enlightenment, science and religion came to a gentleman's agreement. Science was for the real world: machines, manufactured things, medicines, guns, moon rockets. Religion was for everything else, the immeasurable: morals, sacraments, poetry, insanity, death, and some residual forms of politics and statesmanship. Religion became, in both senses of the word, immaterial. Science and religion were apples and oranges. So the pact said: render unto apples the things that are Caesar's, and unto oranges the things that are God's. Just as the Maya kept two calendars, one profane and one priestly, so Western science and religion fell into two different conceptions of the universe, two different vocabularies.

This hostile distinction between religion and science has softened in the last third of the twentieth century. Both religion and science have become self-consciously aware of their excesses, even of their capacity for evil. Now they find themselves jostled into a strange metaphysical intimacy. Perhaps the most extraordinary sign of that intimacy is what appears to be an agreement between religion and science about certain facts concerning the creation of the universe. It is the equivalent of the Montagues and Capulets collaborating on a baby shower.

According to the Book of Genesis, the universe began in a single, flashing act of creation; the divine intellect willed all into being, *ex nihilo*. It is not surprising that scientists have generally stayed clear of the question of ultimate authorship, of the final "uncaused cause." In years past, in fact, they held to the Aristotelian idea of a universe that was "ungenerated and indestructible,'' with an infinite past and an infinite future. This was known as the Steady State theory.

That absolute expanse might be difficult, even unbearable, to contemplate, like an infinite snowfield of time, but the conception at least carried with it the serenity of the eternal. In recent decades, however, the Steady State model of the universe has yielded in the scientific mind to an even more difficult idea, full of cosmic violence. Most astronomers now accept the theory that the universe had an instant of creation, that it came to be in a vast fireball explosion fifteen or twenty billion years ago. The shrapnel created by that explosion is still flying outward from the focus of the blast. One of the fragments is the galaxy we call the Milky Way—one of whose hundreds of billions of stars is the earth's sun, with its tiny orbiting grains of planets. The so-called Big Bang theory makes some astronomers acutely uncomfortable, even while it ignites in many religious minds a small thrill of confirmation. The Big Bang theory sounds very much like the story that the Old Testament has been telling all along.

Science arrived at the Big Bang theory through its disinterested process of hypothesis and verification—and, sometimes, happy accident. In 1913, astronomer Vesto Melvin Slipher of the Lowell Observatory in Flagstaff, Arizona, discovered galaxies that were receding from the earth at extraordinarily high speeds, up to two million miles per hour. In 1929, the American astronomer Edwin Hubble developed Slipher's findings to formulate his law of an expanding universe, which presupposes a single primordial explosion. Meantime, Albert Einstein, without benefit of observation, concocted his general theory of relativity, which overthrew Newton and contained in its apparatus the idea of the expanding universe. The Steady State idea still held many astronomers, however, until 1965, when two scientists at Bell Telephone Laboratories, Arno Penzias and Robert Wilson, using sophisticated electronic equipment, picked up the noise made by background radiation coming from all parts of the sky. What they were hearing, as it turned out, were the reverberations left over from the first explosion, the hissing echoes of creation. In the past dozen years, most astronomers have come around to operating on the assumption that there was indeed a big bang.

The Big Bang theory has subversive possibilities. At any rate, in a century of Einstein's relativity, of Heisenberg's uncertainty principle (the very act of observing nature disturbs and alters it), of the enigmatic black holes (''Of the God who was painted as a glittering eye, there is nothing now left but a black socket,'' wrote the German romantic Jean Paul), science is not the cool Palladian temple of rationality that it was in the Enlightenment. It begins to seem more like Prospero's island as experienced by Caliban. Some astronomers even talk of leftover starlight from a future universe, its time flowing in the opposite direction from ours. Agnosticism can be shaken by many puzzles besides the creation. Almost as mysterious are the circumstances that led, billions of years ago, to the creation of the first molecule that could reproduce itself. That step made possible the development of all the forms of life that spread over the earth. Why did it occur just then?

A religious enthusiasm for the apparent convergence of science and theology in the Big Bang cosmology is understandable. Since the Enlightenment, the scriptural versions of creation or of other "events," like the fall of man or the miracles of Jesus Christ, have suffered the condescension of science; they were regarded as mere myth, superstition. Now the faithful are tempted to believe that science has performed a laborious validation of at least one biblical "myth": that of creation.

But has any such confirmation occurred? Robert Jastrow, director of NASA's Goddard Institute for Space Studies, has published a small and curious book called *God and the Astronomers,* in which he suggests that the Bible was right after all, and that people of his own kind, scientists and agnostics, by his description, now find themselves confounded. Jastrow blows phantom kisses across the chasm between science and religion, seeming almost wistful to make a connection. Biblical fundamentalists may be happier with Jastrow's books than are his fellow scientists. He writes operatically: "For the scientist who has lived by his faith in the power of reason, the story ends like a bad dream. He has scaled the mountains of ignorance; he is about to conquer the highest peak; as he pulls himself over the final rock, he is greeted by a band of theologians who have been sitting there for centuries."

Isaac Asimov, the prodigious popularizer of science, reacts hotly to the Jastrow book. "Science and religion proceed by different methods," he says. "Science works by persuasive reason. Outside of science, the method is intuitional, which is not very persuasive. In science, it is possible to say we were wrong, based on data." Science is provisional; it progresses from one hypothesis to another, always testing, rejecting the ideas that do not work, that are contradicted by new evidence. "Faith," said St. Augustine, "is to believe, on the word of God, what we do not see." Faith defies proof; science demands it. If new information should require modification of the Big Bang theory, that modification could be accomplished without the entire temple of knowledge collapsing. Observes Harvard University historian-astronomer Owen Gingerich: "Genesis is not a book of science. It is accidental if some things agree in detail. I believe the heavens declare the glory of God only to people who've made a religious commitment."

A number of theologians concur that the apparent convergence of religious and scientific versions of the creation is a coincidence from which no profound meaning can be extracted. "If the last evidence for God occurred twenty billion years ago," asks Methodist W. Paul Jones of Missouri's St. Paul School of Theology, "do we not at best have the palest of deisms?" Jesuit philosopher Bernard Lonergan goes further: "Science has nothing to say about creation, because that's going outside the empirical. The whole idea of empirical science is that you have data. Theologians have no data on God." There comes a point, somewhere short of God, at which all computers have no data either. With the Big Bang theory says Jastrow, "science has proved that the world came into being as a result of forces that seem forever beyond the power of scientific description. This bothers science because it clashes with scientific religion—the religion of cause and effect, the belief that every effect has a cause. Now we find that the biggest effect of all, the birth of the universe, violates this article of faith."

Some scientists matter-of-factly dismiss the problem of creation. Says Harvey Tananbaum, an X-ray astronomer at the Harvard-Smithsonian Astrophysical Laboratory: "That first instant of creation is not relevant as long as we do not have the laws to begin to understand it. It is a question for philosophers and religionists, not for scientists." Adds Geoffrey Burbidge, director of Kitt Peak National Observatory: "Principles and concepts cannot be measured. A question like 'Who imposed the order?' is metaphysical." Still, virtually everyone—both scientists and laymen—is taken by the sheer unthinkable opacity of the creation and what preceded it. Says Jastrow: "The question of what came before the Big Bang is the most interesting question of all."

One immense problem is that the primordial fireball destroyed all the evidence; the temperature of the universe in the first seconds of its existence was many trillion degrees. The blast obliterated all that went before. The universe was shrouded in a dense fog of radiation, which only cleared after one million years, leaving the transparent spangled space we see in the night sky now. The first million years are as concealed from us as God's face. There are many forms of knowing: science, experience, intuition, faith. Science proceeds on the theory that there is method in all mysteries, and that it is discoverable. It obeys, reasonably, what is called the "first law of wingwalking": "Never leave hold of what you've got until you've got hold of something else." Faith, by definition, is a leap. It must await its verification in another world.

If it has done nothing else, however, the new coincidence of scientific and theological versions of creation seems to have opened up a conversation that has been neglected for centuries. Roman Catholic theologian Hans Küng detects the beginning of a new period, which he calls "pro-existence," of mutual assistance between theologians and natural scientists. People capable of genetic engineering and nuclear fission obviously require all the spiritual and ethical guidance they can get. As for theologians, the interchange between physics and metaphysics will inevitably enlarge their ideas and give them a more complex grounding in the physically observed universe. The theory of the Big Bang is surely not the last idea of creation that will be conceived. It does suggest that there remain immense territories of mystery that both the theologian and the scientist should approach with becoming awe.

They're Playing Ur-Song

The crowd at the Grammy Awards in March 1983 looked as if it had just flown in from one of the moons of Saturn: glittering, snorting the intergalactic dust. Touches of the high crass mingled with a sort of metaphysical flash. Stevie Wonder, for example, wore a cumulously quilted white satin tuxedo whose upswept lapels formed great angel wings. The costume had the curious effect of making him look like a Puritan headstone.

The American popular-music industry was having its annual pageant. The program was about to end. Joan Baez walked onstage unannounced. As if she were lost in time, Baez driftingly began to sing Bob Dylan's anthem: "How many roads must a man walk down,/Before you call him a man . . ./The answer, my friend, is blowin' in the wind,/The answer is blowin' in the wind."

At that instant, a television audience of millions, including much of the baby boom that is now losing its hair, went time-traveling with Baez. Some felt twenty again. Some felt a thousand years old. They swooped back, daydreaming. Tears shot to their eyes. She was playing their song.

It is a fascinating, if familiar, process. When songs have that magic in them, they take on strange powers of recall. Commenting on a Noel Coward song, a character in Coward's *Private Lives* remarks: "Extraordinary how potent cheap music is." Songs eerily consolidate the memory, making obscure chemical connections in the brain. They conjure up moments out of time. They reconstitute things long gone, to the point that smells and images and a precise forgotten ache of the heart return hauntingly for a moment. The dramatization that occurs in the mind is intimate and utterly private. One has only to hear a snatch of Simon and Garfunkel's "Mrs. Robinson" ("Where have you gone, Joe DiMaggio?/A nation turns its lonely eyes to you,/Woo woo woo") to be again in a rental car chasing Robert Kennedy's whistle-stop primary campaign across northern Indiana in May of 1968. And other memories cascade down on that.

The conjuring song, in turn, becomes a signature, an act of self-definition. "Blowin' in the Wind," of course, was only one of a thousand defining anthems of the sixties.

Traditionally, it is couples, not generations, that have their songs. Rick and Ilsa would put themselves in a trance by getting Sam to sing "As Time Goes By" in *Casablanca*. Sometimes we have more than one special song, or a different song for a different mate or a different archaeological layer of our lives.

Among the Tuvinian people of the Soviet Union, an individual can sing two melodies simultaneously. That has wonderful possibilities. Might one cross in the Tuvinian mind two simultaneous numbers, like, say, Bing Crosby's "Mississippi Mud" ("It's a treat to beat your feet . . .") with "Rock the Casbah" by the Clash? Would the Tuvinian stay sane if that happened?

A couple's "our song" presupposes an enduring and developing relationship of which the melody will be the theme. Every year on their anniversary, House Speaker Tip O'Neill sings "I'll Be with You in Apple Blossom Time" to his wife of forty-one years, Mildred Anne. It is more difficult to develop a privately meaningful song if you plan to part company in the morning.

There may be an "our song" for a cause ("We Shall Overcome"), for a college ("Bulldog, bulldog, bow wow wow, Eli Yale!"), for a specific event, like the release of the hostages ("Tie a Yellow Ribbon Round the Ole Oak Tree), and even for an era ("Brother, Can You Spare a Dime?"). Nations have them. But "The Star-Spangled Banner" has never quite become "our song" in the way that the "Marseillaise" utterly and unquestionably belongs to the French. Politicians have their "our songs." John Kennedy may have thought of his Administration in terms of the words and music of *Camelot*. But it is said that once, during a reception at the White House, he heard "Hail to the Chief" and muttered to Jackie, "They're playing our song."

The choice may sometimes be perverse. Abraham Lincoln rather liked "Dixie." Someone decided that poor Franklin Roosevelt loved "Home on the Range," so he was condemned to sit through the tune scores of times.

Music is a form of spiritual carbon dating. If one came of age in 1938, then Artie Shaw's version of "Begin the Beguine" might be the signature he went by, the sound that would date his soul like the exact ring on a redwood. A few years earlier, it might have been Hoagy Carmichael doing "Stardust."

One can never quite imagine people younger than oneself having a plausibly magical song of their own. It is a trick of age and generational perspective. Parents believe that the songs their children cherish, far from amassing rich emotional associations, are merely destroying brain cells. The workings of special songs are necessarily subjective, and they promote a kind of hubris. Still, even allowing for that effect, it is sometimes hard to imagine what private anthems will arise from, say, punk or new wave music. Are there couples now that will for years grow mistily tender when they hear a ditty by Meat Loaf?

But a romantic fallacy may be hidden in such prejudices. What the music stirs in the mind need not be mere sentimentality. The evocative magic worked by songs is essentially mysterious. It doubtless has something to do with the organization of the brain. The musical faculty resides chiefly in the right hemisphere, along with the emotions, the nonlogical, intuitive powers of the mind. Music cohabits in the brain with myth. Says Howard Gardner, a research psychologist at Harvard: "Music mirrors the structure and the range of our emotions. It has the same kind of flow as our emotional life." What is the sound of the right brain singing?

We organize time and myth with music; we mark our lives by it. The death by assassination of John Lennon was an event that mingled music and myth and completed the relationship between the two. Music, as the anthropologist Claude Lévi-Strauss once said, "unites the contrary attributes of being both intelligible and untranslatable."

Music is the way that our memories sing to us across time. The loveliest quality of music involves its modulation upon the theme of time. Songs, playing in the mind, become the subtlest shuttles across years.

But sometimes the music is a weapon, and sometimes it is a trap. For centuries, Celts have given themselves battlefield nerve with bagpipes, making the "our song" of the regiment, the tribe, stirring up the blood. The pipes have their wild rhetoric. It may both stiffen and imprison the spirit. Sometimes people cannot escape from their songs. The Irish gift for the instant ballad that glorifies this afternoon's martyr will ruin a human heart and turn children into killers, the heroes of tomorrow's pub songs.

In the past, some scholars have pursued the idea that there is a universal "our song": the *Ur*-song that is said to run through the imagination of every child in the world, an eerie universal croon. Actually, it need not be eerie. For all we know, the *Ur*-song may turn out to sound like the opening bars of Perry Como doing "Hot Diggity."

The Temptations
of Revenge

"Life being what it is," said Baudelaire, "one thinks of revenge." Americans found themselves thinking about it a little more than usual when they watched Iranians in 1980 displaying charred American bodies in front of the Tehran embassy that the dead had been sent to liberate. They thought of it again when Moussavi Garmoudi, the Iranian president's "cultural affairs adviser," appeared before cameramen, reached into a box, and brought out a burned human foot (American), which he laid on a table before them.

Such scenes open a little trap door at the base of the brain. From that ancient root cellar they summon up dark, flapping fantasies of revenge. During the six-month imprisonment of their hostages, Americans have on the whole reacted with a surprising forbearance toward the Iranians. But beneath the surface they have marinated in an atavistic cross-cultural rage. Their anger has been ripened by the long spectacle of their nation's ineffectuality and the humiliation of the failed rescue raid, by the nightly TV pageant of Iranian mobs pumping their fists in the air and screaming death threats in Farsi, and by the image of Sadegh Ghotbzadeh's cretinous smirk. Dark impulses that normally stay below, like Ahab's harpooners, begin to straggle up on deck.

If aggression is the most basic and dangerous of human impulses, revenge gains a step on it by being premeditated. The urge for lurid, annihilating retaliation—vindication, satisfaction, the no-good bastard's head upon a plate—fetches far back to a shrouded moment when the spontaneous animal reflex of self-protection turned to a savage brooding. The human mind, newly intelligent, began to dream of the barbarously fitting ways in which it would get even. Emanating from hurt and the pain of failure and unfairness, the fantasy of revenge became, it may be, even stronger than the imperative of sex.

The gods of man's myths were elaborately, even bizarrely, vengeful. In the *Inferno,* Dante's deity was satanically inventive in making the vengeance fit the crime. The best tragic theater (*Hamlet,* for example) and some of the worst has been built around the deep urge to settle someone's hash. In an orgy of horrific finality and emotional overstatement, Medea murders her two sons and hurls their corpses at Jason. That, God knows, ought to teach him.

History has been just as imaginative as theater and myth. The South American Tupinamba tribe would take a prisoner of war, make him consort with a woman of their tribe, then allow the woman to bear a child so that they could increase the tragedy by slaughtering both the prisoner and his baby. Sometimes in New Zealand, when a chieftain was killed during a war between two tribes, hostilities were broken off while the body of the leader was chopped up by his opponents, roasted and devoured. Among the southern Slavs a mother has been known to lay her infant son down in the cradle to sleep upon the bloodstained shirt of his murdered father. The child was raised to avenge; it became his vocation.

Under the protocols of the blood feud, one act of revenge begot another, so that violence originating in some forgotten crime or slight could reverberate for generations. Eventually the old brutal arrangement was superseded by the laws of the state, which undertook to end the free-lance savageries of personal revenge by meting out justice uncomplicated by private passion. When the state assumed the responsibility for punishing an offense, the matter, in theory, ended there.

Revenge detonates a little explosion of doom for the sake of personal—and usually rather temporary—satisfaction. But some say the practice of vengeance has its salutary, cleansing effect. Better for the circulation, they say, to liberate that maniacal little Nietzsche doll that jumps up and down inside all of us than to let him tear apart his cage.

Furthermore, revenge has its practical uses. The Mafia, first tutored in the exquisitely touchy finishing schools of Sicily, practices revenge as a matter of dispassionate business; the man who ordered the hit sends a horseshoe of flowers. Athletes have some instinct for keeping retaliatory accounts as a practical matter. Reggie Jackson, playing for the New York Yankees in 1979, was brushed back by two pitches by Mike Caldwell of the Milwaukee Brewers. Jackson went out and throttled him. Strictly business, Jackson explained later. If he had let the pitcher get away with it twice, he would have subtly lost respect and a competitive edge on the field.

Is there a practical counterpart in relations among nations? At the end of World War II the United States wisely declined to exact vengeance upon Japan and Germany, but instead helped to rebuild them, turning them at last, ironically, into the real economic victors of war. In the nuclear era, revenge may be too hairy a form of redress and self-gratification to be endured. Yet a cautionary super-revenge, in the latent form of a cataclysmic threat, is the governing principle of the nuclear age. Revenge, of course, sometimes achieves an air of respectability, of *Realpolitik,* if it is called retaliation or, even more innocently, response—as in "nuclear response." The global balance of power is maintained by a threat of revenge that is designed by its sheer unthinkable horror to forestall the first blow.

Revenge is especially dangerous when it lumbers around shaggily between two cultures—like those of Iran and the United States—that profoundly misunderstand each other, that in some ways inhabit different centuries. The Iranians consider that they are exacting revenge for the years of America's association with the Shah. Thus grievances and countergrievances accumulate in some evolutionary rhythm, the way that grazing animals over the millennia developed better teeth and, simultaneously, nutritional plants evolved harder thorns.

Revenge has its undeniable satisfactions. It is a primal scream that shatters glass. But revenge is not an intelligent basis for a foreign policy. This century has already fulfilled its quota of smoke and rage and survivors, gray with bomb dust, staggering around in the rubble, seeking what is left of the dead they loved.

The Importance of
Being Lucky

The satirically pious story tells how a soldier's breast-pocket Bible stopped the bullet en route to his heart. Ronald Reagan had no Bible in his jacket outside the Washington Hilton in April of 1981, but some of the world idly suspected that he may have been otherwise armored—that in some obscure way he may have been protected by his own remarkable luck.

Something in Reagan has always been lucky; it has been part of his attraction, his charm, the nimbus around him. Reagan's luck has a distinctly American shine; his grin proclaims it, the confident expectation of the happy ending. That may be why the nation was drawn to him. Reagan's vehicle on the journey from Dixon, Illinois, to Hollywood to the White House ran on persistence and self-knowledge, all right, but it was also propelled by a breezy admixture of the luck that the country was born with.

So, when an assassin tried to terminate Reagan's progress, his luck seemed to hold again: if the gunman's arm had been jostled even a hair, if the angle of the slug's deflection off the President's seventh rib had been minutely sharper, if the devastator bullet had not been a dud . . . Of course, one can argue it the other way: if the assassin's arm had been jostled, he might have missed Reagan entirely.

When one embarks on elaborate multiple fantasies of ifs, he enters abstract forests of luck and chance, of contingency and probability, where each speculative path opens onto a thousand new possibilities. Usually the mind penetrates only a few steps, looks nervously over its shoulder, then bolts back to the hard terrain of actuality. Luck is, by definition, mysterious, a force that may really be the clunkingly erratic, everyday version of the divine mind. Luck is God in a scatterbrained and even amoral mood, with his sense of justice out of commission. Or, agnostically, luck is the collision of the random with human biography; naturally, human intelligence resents and resists the inexplicable random, and so attributes it to imps, dybbuks, wood sprites, gods of the volcano—all the subdeities of jinx.

Invisible, otherwise undetectable, luck can be known only by its works. It is the strange, unknowable force that deposited Lana Turner in a Schwab's pharmacy fifty-three years ago, that placed a football in Franco Harris's hands ("the immaculate reception") at the end of the Pittsburgh-Oakland championship game in 1972, that put Carl Bernstein in the newsroom of the *Washington Post* a few hours after the police found a strange collection of characters at the Watergate. (Actually, Watergate was a regular soap opera of the fortuitous: if one of the burglars had not stupidly left tape over the latch of a rear door, the night watchman might never have discovered the caper and Congress might never have investigated and the White House tape system might never have been revealed and Richard Nixon might never have resigned.) Luck was the invisible hand that prompted Skylab to scatter its debris over Western Australia, not rush-hour Manhattan. Even transcendently foresighted NASA might admit that the space shuttle's flawless flight in 1981 involved some luck. The luck of the universe (by one new theory) once banged an immense asteroid into the earth, raising a dust cloud so dense that it blocked off the sunlight, ruined the planet's food chain, and thereby brought on the extinction of the dinosaurs—an event that profoundly redirected evolution. It is arguable (at least agnostically for a moment) that life itself—the lightning in the sugar cube, the huge fortuities of weather and climate and chemistry, of amino acids and proteins and oxygen—emanates from sheer cosmic luck.

To call it Divine Providence would do just as well. The religious mind, with a more orderly or merely fatalistic sense of the universe, tends to ascribe to Providence (however mysterious its intentions) events that the more worldly credit to luck, good or bad. People who believe in luck aren't particularly rationalist either, however, since scientific rationalism has as much trouble dealing with luck as theology does. Luck is a weird, pagan, primitive business. Or else, in modern dress, it is a frigidly heartless existentialism. In any case, whatever its occasionally whimsical moments, luck has a philosophically terrifying core.

The world has adopted two different strategies toward luck. Much of the planet for most of its history has tried to woo and conjure and appease it, longingly courting the force to draw near, to descend from the void of the random for an instant and shower fortune on some lucky head. To ward off luck's malevolent side, the infection of a curse, the evil eye, populations have danced and chanted and worked with charms. To predict its whims, they have studied omens, birds' flights, goats' entrails; they have consulted gypsies and star charts.

More "advanced" societies have forgotten the demonic language of superstition and luck, which they are inclined to call "dumb" or "blind." They often have no better explanation than primitives do for luck's strange intercessions, but they generally adopt a strategy both passive and fatalistic, a stoical mixture of rationalism and resignation to luck's works. Today it is mainly gamblers who stay on intimate and dangerous terms with luck and try to tame and possess it. Here and there, state lotteries have tried to bureaucratize luck—a dreary business and a contradiction in terms.

Generally, luck is something that happens to individuals. If a society or a century is considered as a whole, the random individual events that are set down to luck or fortune form more coherent overall patterns; large historical forces become discernible. But entire societies should not mock luck either. The classic Mayan civilization disappeared so strangely, so precipitously, that some massive stroke of bad luck must have been at work—a sudden plague, say, a viral riot.

Of all civilizations, America seemed the luckiest. With its vast Edenic spaces and immense natural wealth, with its extraordinary freedom from the stultifications of caste and poverty, the place seemed born in luck. Or so it appeared to the white Europeans who settled the continent, if not to the Indians they violently displaced or the Africans they imported in slave ships to work the plantations. Americans eventually made the mistake of describing their national luck as their "manifest destiny." In any case, America became the place where the world came to get lucky. Americans believed in the splendidly transforming powers of luck in their land. Men born in poverty made fortunes. They struck oil and gold. Hard work went into it, of course, but for a long time Americans were drunk on the luck of their sheer possibility. Foreigners bemused by America have often thought that too much good luck deprived Americans of a sense of the tragic. In the past fifteen years or so, Americans have been riding a bad streak. It is possible they responded to Reagan because his smile reminded them of a time when America was lucky.

Whatever the motions of free will and necessity, Herman Melville wrote, "chance has the last featuring blow at events." Luck may be simply another name for the odd, unexpected notes in the huge symphony of things, of circumstance and coincidence, chemistry and character, diet and disease, weather and timing, the vastly subtle totality of being. But whatever the agnostics say, luck is not completely blind, or completely wild either. Within limits, it can be domesticated—although it will always be part wolf and may unexpectedly turn mad and eat the children one afternoon.

As Hector Berlioz said, "The luck of having talent is not enough: one must also have a talent for luck." Genius, in fact, may be defined as the ability to control luck. A turbulent gambler like Dostoyevsky was not overcome by the hectic fortunes of his experience, but turned them into his art. Outside the genius class, however, there is such a thing as a predisposition to good luck; it might be said on the evidence up to now that Reagan has it, while Ted Kennedy does not.

Baseball's Branch Rickey once offered a serviceable definition: "Luck is the residue of design." To be sure, luck obeys the laws of a spooky kind of antiphysics, but it responds to risk and reflexes. To some extent, it is true that people make their own luck. Given a lucky chance at the story, Carl Bernstein and Bob Woodward ran hard. Good luck must have room to occur. It can be encouraged, even though its exact mechanics remain perverse and mysterious. For its part, bad luck is so eventually inevitable that it is almost a sin to be surprised by it.

"The older I grow," philosopher Sidney Hook wrote a few years ago, "the more impressed I am with the role of luck or chance in life." The world's distribution of wealth, he pointed out, depends almost as much on luck as on energy, foresight and skill. It is only the luck of the world if one is born in the country club district of Kansas City instead of the Sahel or Bangladesh. It is the sad luck of things for a Colorado oil millionaire if his youngest child, by mishaps of the psyche, turns out to harbor some fetid, lovesick ambition to kill the President.

Surely the ultimate purpose of luck, if there is one at all, is to offer such a spectacle that men and women, besides being vastly entertained, come to recognize their common vulnerability to luck's weird and endlessly inventive impulses. Hook thinks that chastening drama might make people more charitable toward one another. Well—if we are lucky. But perhaps luck, good and bad, also has a deeper physiological purpose, programmed into the human animal in the first dawn of his intelligence: to keep the adrenaline flowing, maybe, and the brain alert to the world's epic of apprehension, terror, greed, and hope. Perhaps luck is the way that life puts history into bas-relief, and differentiates moments, and people: the way that the universe punctuates time.

A Time for
Every Season

The outfield starts to vanish in a thickening whiteness. The umpire gets morally confused. He stands with palms upraised, like a supplicant priest, and stares at the fat crystals falling onto his hands. At last, he calls the game, in wonder and disgust.

A snowstorm in mid-April is a kind of outrage. It is a minor perversion of nature. It makes hairline fractures in the order of things. The earth has schedules. We grow offended when it does not run on time, when our expectations are unseasonably violated.

The weather was weird in the spring of 1983: violent, Shakespearean. It might have been worse, of course. In the *annus mirabilis* of 1811, the air was dense with portents: a comet in the northern sky, an eclipse of the sun. The Eastern United States was broiled by ungodly heat and swept by tornadoes and hurricanes. Multitudes of squirrels, in the tens of thousands, were seen migrating south across Kentucky. In 1816 Connecticut had a blizzard on June 6. On the Fourth of July that year, the highest temperature recorded in Savannah, Georgia, was forty-six degrees Fahrenheit. The prevailing opinion, for a little while, was that the universe had gone crazy.

Nature has mood swings. But people are probably no longer as temperamental about them as they once were, as barnyard animals are. Ridiculous as it seems, the seasons usually occur now at a certain distance. They have some interest, like landscapes glimpsed out a train window. But they are also a little raw and messy.

In fact, it may be a question whether human beings really want seasons at all. Civilization's ambition for centuries has been to mitigate them, even to abolish them. The seasons in many developed latitudes are rough and unpredictable. Man wanted to subdue them, domesticate them. The logic of progress has been to lift humanity out of the yearly cycles and into a higher trajectory. Progress was designed to be an ascendant journey, linear and always brightening, not a mere pointless circular plod around the calendar.

Farmers need seasons. In a lovely, squat little verse to the month of March, A. E. Housman wrote: "So braver notes the storm-cock sings/To start the rusted wheel of things,/And brutes in field and brutes in pen/ Leap that the world goes round again."

Industry and business can proceed in a fluorescent seasonlessness. Human ingenuity has given centuries to the goal of ensuring that the human body might move around at an even sixty-eight-degrees all year. Air conditioning is one of the serious accomplishments of the twentieth century. It produced the Sunbelt. The enclosed suburban shopping mall prefigures those cities of the future that will be entirely domed, like a pheasant under glass. No seasonal variations need be endured.

The preacher of Ecclesiastes gave the list of sublime inevitabilities: "To every thing there is a season, and a time to every purpose under heaven." There was once a cultural geographer named Ellsworth Huntington who suggested—ethnocentrically, his critics later said—that people who lived without seasons could never develop character. So much for the *mañana* cultures. So much, in fact, for San Diego. Such cultures had no Darwinian need for foresight, Huntington thought, no drive to store up nuts for winter. They did not feel that stirring of energy and anticipation and pragmatic dread when the first chill came on, making them think responsibly, in the future tense. Bad weather makes people miserable, and busy. Provide, provide.

The seasons were once the central organizing principle of things. Mankind learned the mysteries, even the tragedies, of limited duration. All of Egyptian civilization coalesced around the annual flooding of the Nile. In the developed countries now, the internal variations of the year begin to have a merely recreational or sentimental interest. They tend to be, at best, decorative and, at worst, inconvenient. It is true that in Minnesota, winter remains a convicted killer. It is also true that things occur in a Southern spring, in north Alabama or Tennessee or the Shenandoah Valley, that go beyond the merely picturesque: a time-lapse film of blossoms opening, that sweet, rich awakening, a sensuous slow motion of nature.

The seasons began by breaking down time into usable units: a time to plow, a time to sow, a time to reap. Distinctly, intensely different periods of the year calibrated time and made it manageable. They enforced disciplines. Now, people often create their own units of usable time without such explicit reference to the external seasons. There are the business seasons and the school seasons. There are model years for cars and fiscal years for budgets. Those man-made schedules are wheels within the abiding great wheel, less noticed now, of the calendar.

People can fragment the year. They can escape it. They can arc not only out of a place but out of a time. They fly in a couple of hours from one season to another: from Chicago's December, say, to Florida's moral equivalent of high summer. Then they fly back into the wan, smudged month that they left, and they are tan. In deep winter, they are exotics walking among all those gray faces at lunchtime like Queequeg on the streets of Nantucket.

But insulation from the seasons is sometimes disorienting. There is reassurance in those felt variations. Those who are seasonless are adrift in time. It is difficult to get one's bearings in time if one stays too long on Oahu. The seasonless also feel less the sacramental uses of the different times. The seasons are the framework of archetypes, and profane time acquires its deeper meanings as it passes through the frame. Each year, after all, recapitulates the process of a life: birth, youth, maturity, old age and, in deep winter, death. Then the rebirth, when the seasons enact most literally nature's drama of redemption, and life pushes its green shoots out of death.

Hard Questions

What Does an
Oath Mean?

In the wistful inner ear, one imagines a soft transcontinental buzz, the sound of thirteen thousand consciences alert and intricately working. "Well," says each troubled voice, "I'd like to strike. I think we have plenty of reason to strike—wages, hours, job strain. But I signed an oath when I took the job. It would be dishonorable to strike. We have to find some other way."

Just hearing things, of course—like listening for waves in a seashell. It did not occur to the air-traffic controllers in 1981 to deliver that sort of archaic soliloquy, haunted by scruples. Most of them judged, briskly enough, that their desire for a thirty-two-hour week and a minimum of $30,462 per year superseded the oath to which they once put their signatures.

For a moment the issue of the violated oath did not come clear. It was deflected a little by a legal question: Don't all workers have a right to strike? Yes, said the American Civil Liberties Union. Not if they are government employees, said a 1947 law and the Reagan Administration. The strikers chose the ACLU's view of things.

But beyond transient legalities, the strike opened the door upon a more primitive question: What is the worth (moral, financial, mystical) of a person's oath? What do we mean when we promise, when we vow, when we pledge our word? Whatever their union's legal case may be, the controllers did take an oath; was that not a binding deed? Many Americans found themselves distantly disturbed that what was once a matter of some human solemnity should be brushed aside as if it were merely a technical detail. The social edifice shuddered slightly; down in the basement, a dusty little taboo fell off a shelf and shattered.

All societies are held together by an immensely intricate webbing of mutual obligation (and perhaps by an equal and opposite network of betrayal). The system starts with nods and smiles and wordless understandings; it elaborates itself interminably through certain assumptions, casual promises, oral agreements, laborious plans, written contracts, and formal vows, and ends finally in that thunderous atavism, the solemn oath: the promise with a jolt of the sacred in it, the upraised hand, the divinity standing by to witness.

With such access to the absolute, the oath has always been promiscuously and even dangerously overemployed. It works efficiently enough as a device to keep court witnesses and public officials moderately honest; there, the sworn word is directly connected to deeds and penalties (perjury charges or impeachment). Ronald Reagan had no trouble making such a connection for the air-traffic controllers. But the dictatorial and the insecure have always been fond of the oath as a way to enforce orthodoxy, to lay down a prior restraint upon people's opinions. During the 1950s the loyalty oath turned into a destructively pervasive American genre, with a legion of earnest patriots afoot, like the ghost in *Hamlet,* crying, "Swear!"

In the first torchlight of the primeval, oaths worked by the magic of the words themselves; later, they glowed with the power of the gods, who were invented to officiate at melodramas. Oaths should be sparingly used and specifically targeted. Their imposing solemnity can shade without warning into the preposterous, into peeled grapes on pledge night, a witch doctoring oogly-boogly like the oath that Tom Sawyer's gang swore in the cave.

One reason why oathing gets overdone is that it is so inherently dramatic, even a form of fanaticism, a way of connecting (spuriously sometimes) to the absolute. Knights, crusaders, saints, and opera singers are forever swearing: it is a lovely plot device. Ahab swears his vengeance on the whale. In *Don Giovanni,* Ottavio vows to avenge the Commendatore by raising his fruity tenor to Donna Anna: *"Lo giuro, lo giuro/lo giuro agli occhi tuoi/lo giuro al nostro amor"* (I swear it, I swear it/I swear it by your eyes/I swear it by our love). Was there ever a prettier oath? It is a form of hero's brag. That may explain why politicians are so reckless with hyperbolic promise. (Douglas MacArthur: "I shall return," a wonderful item of mythic public relations.) Like the ancient kings of Mexico, they like to swear that they will cause the sun to rise, the rain to fall, the crops to grow. Spiro Agnew once told the American people: "I have often been accused of putting my foot in my mouth, but I will never put my hand in your pockets." Jimmy Carter kept fixing America with his china-blue eyes and swearing: "I will never lie to you"—a daredevil approach to his profession.

Oaths have their sinister uses. They can turn into weapons to coerce and restrict. The solemn oath, of course, is not a bad way to lie. The Mafia enforces silence with an oath, and the blood oath over the centuries has killed more people than a medieval plague. But, in a free society, the oath has a crucial ceremonial function. The Hippocratic Oath reminds new doctors of their obligation, of the human context of their calling. An immigrant knows that the oath of citizenship is spiritually, almost physically, nourishing. His oath is a symbolic drama of community.

But the oath is not faring very well now. Americans, a mobile and litigious people, nimble through the loopholes, do not like to be mired down in too many promises. Getting stuck in an old promise looks more and more like a sucker's game: both morals and interest rates change too fast. Baseball players renegotiate their contracts all the time.

The idea that morality is merely subjective has been subversive. Americans claim exemption under what might be called the Doctrine of Discontinuous Selves: if people are forever "growing" and "going through changes," then the man who swore the oath, say, three years ago, is not the same one now called upon to live up to it. This discontinuous series of new selves, emotionally different selves, scatters the mind. It makes for a short moral attention span.

An anti-institutional bias has also been hard on oaths. So has that low-grade chronic ache (inflation, partly, and the erosion of dreams) that tells Americans so often that their society has not fulfilled its end of the social contract. Americans do not find themselves harmonizing much on Robert Frost's lonely, manly lines: "But I have promises to keep/And miles to go before I sleep/And miles to go before I sleep."

But promises, contracts, and oaths are the acts of will and intelligence and anticipation that make a society coherent, that hold it together. If they cannot be trusted, then the whole structure begins to wobble. If the air-traffic controllers do not care to recite Frost, they might consider William Murray, Britain's solicitor general in the eighteenth century: "No country can subsist a twelvemonth where an oath is not thought binding, for the want of it must necessarily dissolve society."

Abortion and
the Unfairness of Life

"Life is unfair," John Kennedy observed at a press conference one day in 1962. The thought had a certain stoic grace about it: its truth was brutally confirmed the following year in Dallas. Life *is* unfair. Kennedy was talking about citizens' military obligations, about the restive Army reservists who were being held on active duty even after the Berlin crisis had subsided. In 1977 Jimmy Carter brought up the unfairness doctrine to explain his policy on abortion. Somehow the dictum came out this time with a mean-spirited edge, like something from the lips of Dickens's Mr. Podsnap.

Abortion, of course, is a painful issue that has given rise to few ennobling ideas. Anyone who comes to an easy decision on the subject is probably a moral idiot. In 1973, the Supreme Court declared it legal to terminate a pregnancy in the first three months, or up to six months in some circumstances. About a million legal abortions are now (in August 1977) performed every year in the United States—a third of them paid for with Medicaid funds. But in July 1977 the Supreme Court decided, by a vote of six to three, that the states and localities are free, if they wish, to deny Medicaid money for abortions. Both houses of Congress have made their contribution by passing provisions that forbid federal Medicaid payments for abortions, although the measures differ in severity.

In other words, abortions are fine for the women who, on the whole, have the least pressing need for them: women at least well enough off to buy their own way out of their fecundity. The women (often young girls) who cannot raise the money must presumably either bear their unwanted children—thus bringing many thousands of new customers to welfare—or find some way to kill the fetus more cheaply. Such methods have had the result of sometimes disposing of the mother as well.

When he was asked at a press conference about the logic of this, then President Carter took up John Kennedy's line. "Well," said Carter, "as you know, there are many things in life that are not fair, that wealthy people can afford and poor people can't." Anatole France in the last century appraised that kind of elegant fatalism: "The law in its majestic equality forbids the rich as well as the poor to sleep under bridges."

Certainly a principal purpose of human government must be to mitigate the unfairness that seems to be an integral part of human life—or, at the very least, not to compound it. The judicial system is meant to mediate, to knock the chaos of human behavior into a manageable pattern. The goal of fairness underlies American education, which has been regarded, sometimes more hopefully than accurately, as the way to give everyone an equal chance. Medicaid was meant to provide fairness in health care, so that if a poor man needs an eight-hundred-dollar appendectomy or a fifteen-thousand-dollar coronary bypass, he will, in theory, receive something like the same treatment as a character who arrives at the hospital by *grossen* Mercedes.

Some people believe, of course, that government has gone entirely too far in trying to make life fairer. The formula of best government equaling least government has vanished into the vast bureaucratic software that produces welfare, food stamps, and unemployment benefits. But if government is indeed, for better or worse, promoting the health, education and welfare of the American people, why should federal help for those who seek abortions be excluded?

One answer is that abortion is morally wrong—even, some say, a blithely conducted form of infanticide. There are painfully compelling reasons to oppose abortion; philosophers and theologians have done so for many centuries. The Hippocratic Oath includes a stricture against aiding an abortion. (Many medical schools now use a rephrased version of the oath to circumvent the abortion issue.) The procedure involves the destruction of a form of human life—life *in utero,* but life nonetheless. By the sixth week, almost all of the human organs are in place; by the eighth, brain-wave activity can be detected. The right-to-life lobby displays pictures of those tiny hands and feet, those grisly fetuses pickled in jars; but bad taste does not disable their argument.

The other reality is just as disturbing. Without legal and affordable abortion, many lives in progress are hopelessly ruined; the unwanted children very often grow up unloved, battered, conscienceless, trapped, and criminal. A whole new virus of misery breeds in the accidental zygotes.

Both technically and morally, the most difficult problem is to decide at what precise instant life occurs. Is it in the actual conceptive collision of sperm and egg? Is it only when the fetus "quickens," at five months or so? The Supreme Court in 1973 simply said that abortion in the early stages of pregnancy should be a medical, not a criminal matter; it was best left to the judgment of the woman and her physician. Given the violence of warring moralities in the abortion debate, the law was unreasonably strained. The statutes forbidding abortion were a kind of Volstead Act, so widely (and often dangerously) violated as to be worse than useless. The court was therefore wise to send the question back to the privacy of individual consciences. The many who believe abortion morally wrong should honor their convictions. But the dilemma is too difficult to permit anti-abortionists to impose their beliefs, no matter how deeply held, upon people who disagree.

What then of public financing for abortions? Should citizens have to pay for an operation they find morally repugnant? A few years ago, stores sold a nihilistically spirited black box: when one pushed a button on its side, the box whirred and opened, a hand appeared from under a lid— and turned the box off. The Supreme Court's decision—and Carter's attitude toward it—has something of the same self-canceling effect. The court made abortion legal; now it has rescinded an important advantage of that legality by making it hard for the poor to obtain abortions. On narrow constitutional grounds, the court does have a point; states and communities should have the right to decide how to spend their tax money. But the refusal to spend it creates a new configuration marked by inconsistency and hypocrisy.

Carter did not contribute much with his reflections on how unfair the human condition is. Everyone knows that life is unfair. It is also, as Thomas Hobbes pointed out, "solitary, poor, nasty, brutish and short." Life's unfairness is so self-evident in, say, slums, or institutions for the retarded and insane, or in any cancer ward, that it needs no sad-but-true sighings from the White House. To be sure, Carter did have other reasons; he fears, for one thing, that abortion may become merely belated contraception. Certainly, responsible people should take greater care to practice contraception in the first place. And surely it is too casual to say, as psychiatrist Thomas Szasz has said, that abortion "should be available [in the first two or three months] in the same way as, say, an operation for the beautification of a nose." Besides, pregnancy is not a disease, except in a metaphorical sense, for those whose lives are blighted by it.

So Carter is correct in suggesting that abortion involves unique moral questions outside the simple rationale for Medicaid payments. Still, the ultimate morality or immorality of it need not be decided in order to judge the principle of fairness. The undoubted risks of making abortion too easily available are outweighed by the risks of making it too difficult or impossible to obtain. Since the only intelligent argument to be made for abortion is that it is a social necessity, fairness and logic dictate that it must be available especially to those who, wanting it, cannot afford it. To say that abortion, while legal, is immoral but that only the poor shall be saved from this immorality by a fastidious government is not only unfair but absurd.

The Powers of
Racial Example

The ghost of Tiresias told Ulysses to carry an oar upon his shoulder and
walk inland until he met a traveler who did not know what an oar was.
Thus Ulysses, exhausted by the sea, would recognize that he was safely
home.

Some day, possibly, the American racial odyssey will end, and racial
hatred, like the oar, will be an item of bafflement and curiosity: What
was the point of all that, anyway? Why was it so fierce, so enduring?

The nation in 1984 has taken a few steps on the inland march. Some
of them were merely tokens of motion, but considered together, they
amount at least to an interesting procession of symbols. The first black
American astronaut went into space. Blacks now are the mayors of four
of the largest American cities: Los Angeles, Chicago, Philadelphia, and
Detroit. Congress proclaimed a national holiday to honor Martin Luther
King, Jr., and a conservative Republican president endorsed the idea.

And, in the most significant display, the first black presidential candidate (or the first with a serious following), King's disciple, Jesse Jackson,
sits side by side in debate with the two white Senators running for the
Democratic nomination. Whatever errors he has made elsewhere in the
campaign (stupid private references to Jews as "Hymies," his close relationship to a poisonous character who heads the Nation of Islam), Jackson
has sometimes sounded in the debates like the only grownup in the race.
In any case, the spectacle of a young black man treated equally with two
whites in a fight for the most powerful office on earth would have been
unthinkable in the United States a generation ago.

During the seventies a powerful white politician in New York was discussing the realities of his trade. He shook his head in disgust. "Forget the black vote," he said. "Blacks don't vote." They do now. George Wallace learned the lesson and found himself out courting the blacks whom he had once symbolically blocked at the schoolhouse door.

It is fitting that Jackson should be the man to inspirit the black electorate. For years he has been the one black leader whose attention was focused clearly on the dramatic stage on which the last act of the American racial melodrama will eventually be enacted. That stage is located in the black mind.

The journey of American blacks has been a series of epic passages: the middle passage from Africa, the long passage through slavery to the Emancipation Proclamation, the false dawn of Reconstruction, the terrorist Klan era with its nightriding death squads, the passage north to South Side Chicago and Detroit and Harlem, then *Brown* vs. *Topeka* and desegregation and the Martin Luther King era and the Great Society. What is unfolding now may be thought of in years to come as the Jesse Jackson era for black America. Whatever Jackson's role in the journey, the ultimate passage to be accomplished is the internal passage, the psychological passage.

To say that the last battle must be fought in the minds of blacks themselves strikes some as a perverse exercise of white man's jujitsu, a way of blaming the victim. If psychology is involved, surely it is the white mind that must change, not the black. Anyway, the problems of blacks are not psychological but harsh and external, and if anything, getting worse. There are many black Americas of course, and it is difficult to make large generalizations, psychological or otherwise. But statistics can take the overall readings. The median income of blacks is only 55 percent that of whites. Black unemployment is, as usual, twice that for whites. Many black families are stable, but more than half of black babies are born to unwed mothers. The lives of American blacks are sicklier and shorter than those of whites. And so on.

Yes. But as Jackson knows, the ultimate victory over the problems begins in the will and morale and imagination of blacks. The residue of the slave mentality still eats at that morale, still drips acids on the self-esteem. The external arrangements of things (Jim Crow and all the rest) seeped many generations ago into the heart and left there an annihilating anger and, sometimes, a self-loathing. Blackness has found it difficult to esteem itself in the imperiously white contexts of things. Besides, some of the arrangements designed to help poor blacks have simply replicated the patterns of the plantation. It is the same old configuration of subservience and *noblesse oblige,* of dependence and resentment and contempt, the part of the (benevolent) master played by the federal government, and the blacks still living in the slave quarters (ghettos) on the white man's dole.

In the service of black morale, symbols are immensely important. "Tokenism" has a bad name, but tokens have their uses. People become only what they can imagine themselves to be. If they can only imagine themselves working as menials, then they will probably subside into that fate, following that peasant logic by which son follows father into a genetic destiny. If they see other blacks become mayors of the largest cities, become astronauts, become presidential candidates, become Miss Americas and, more to the point, become doctors and scientists and lawyers and pilots and corporate presidents—become successes—then young blacks will begin to comprehend their own possibilities and honor them with work.

For years Jesse Jackson has stood in front of high school audiences and led them in psychological cheers: "I am . . . somebody!" The theme is not original with Jackson. Marcus Garvey, for example, thundered the idea: "Up, you mighty race, you can accomplish what you will!" That is a perfectly American thought, although usually addressed to individuals, not races. The United States has always been an immense struggle of the wills of the people who came here, a struggle of cultural and moral energy and discipline. The American Indians' story represents an immense tragedy, a catastrophic demoralization, almost a cultural extinction. Then one sees certain Korean Americans, with their sharp commercial energy, their Confucian family discipline and, often, very rapid rise (in one generation) from vegetable stand to Harvard Medical School. American blacks still struggle between the two states of mind, the one leading toward disintegration, the other toward success and acceptance.

It may be many years before the United States elects a black president—or, for that matter, a Mexican-American president or a Korean-American president. But it now becomes thinkable for a black child to entertain a fantasy that used to be advertised as every white boy's dream: that he might grow up to be President.

Hunger and joblessness are not psychological, but the beginning of the solution is. Symbols can bring change. They have real power in the world. "Firsts" proceed and become seconds and thirds, until they are no longer phenomenal but routine. As that happens, more American blacks will become, in a sense for the first time, citizens of the United States.

Bringing the Vietnam Veterans Home

For a long time now, the chief ceremonial function of Memorial Day has been simply to inform Americans that their summer has begun. Of course, residual touches of drum-thumping Americana still cling to the occasion—men in deep middle age parading up and down the holiday, strutting the flag. It is a formal rite of remembering, but remembering at a major distance. In their V.F.W. or American Legion caps the old soldiers have long since made peace with their generation's war. They have worn their memories of combat smooth with the retelling. They have grown easy with what they did for their country as young men; they won, and they are proud of it. The horrors that they saw—or performed—so long ago in other countries have been effaced by time, by the approval of history and of the nation they fought for.

The soldiers who fought America's latest and longest war, in Vietnam, do not participate very often in Memorial Day parades. The United States has not developed a moral context for them yet, and no one parades without a moral context. A nation does not fondly celebrate the memory of its convulsions.

Vietnam arrived in the American mind like some strange, violent hallucination, just when the nation was most prosperous and ambitious, shooting spaceships at the moon. Sweet America cracked open like a geode. The bizarre catastrophe of that war shattered so much in American life (pride in country, faith in government, the idea of manhood, and the worth of the dollar, to begin the list) that even now the damage has not yet been properly assessed. When the country came to, some time in the mid-seventies, it was stunned. In moral recoil from the military failure and the huge, lurid futility of the excursion, Americans did a humanly understandable thing: they suppressed the memory of Vietnam. They tried to recover from the wound by denying it.

But of course the veterans of Vietnam were tangible evidence, the breathing testimony, that it had all been humiliatingly real. Whether walking straight or riding wheelchairs, whether prospering at their work or glaring out at the rest of the nation from a daze of rage and drugs and night sweats, they reminded America that the war had cost and that it had hurt. For years, at least some part of every Vietnam veteran has inhabited a limbo of denial—the nation's or his own—often overcome by guilt and shame, and almost always by anger. Among other things, he has tended to think of himself as an awful sucker to have risked so much for so little. Most veterans (contrary to stereotype) have readjusted reasonably well to the civilian world. But many found that coming home was harder than fighting the war.

After World War I and World War II, the soldiers returned together with their units; they had the long trip back in which to hear each other's confessions and apologies. And of course the piers in New York or San Francisco were crammed with waiting wives and children, the grateful nation craning to get a look at its boys, its heroes. During Vietnam, in keeping with an almost sinister government tendency to treat the war as an elaborate bureaucratic illusion, the military shipped people out alone and brought them back alone. The process caused surreal dislocations: one day in a firefight in I Corps, the next day standing on the American tarmac somewhere, as if nothing had happened. One veteran remembers the awful solitude of homecoming: "They let us off on the Oakland side of the Bay Bridge. I had to hitchhike to the San Francisco airport because of a transit strike." The Americans who fought in Vietnam responded when their country asked them to give up their freedom and possibly their lives to do violence in the name of something the government deemed right. Veteran Ron Kovic's painful book *Born on the Fourth of July* described how the image of John Wayne unreeling in the adolescent mind functioned as recruiting poster and subliminal role model. In any case, they went. But psychically at least, the country did not want them back.

Now that may be changing. A new attitude seems to be developing, in both Vietnam veterans and the nation at large. Americans seem more disposed than at any time in the years since the Tet offensive to admit that the Vietnam veterans have borne too much of the moral burden for a war that went all wrong. If there is a burden to be carried, it should be assigned to the men who conceived and directed the war; or, more broadly, it should be shared—in the most profound explorations of which they are capable—by all Americans, including those who went to Canada.

The denial has been peeling away slowly for several years. An odd breakthrough occurred in January 1981 after the extravagantly emotional, almost giddy welcome home that America staged for the fifty-two hostages from Iran. The nation was an orgy of yellow ribbons and misting eyes. But then, a few days later, a countertheme surfaced. Vietnam veterans watched the spectacle of welcome (the routes of motorcades lined with cheering, weeping Americans, the nation glued to its TV sets, the new president doing the hostages proud in the Rose Garden), and their years of bitterness boiled up to a choked cry: WHERE THE HELL IS MY PARADE? The nation, flushed from its somewhat too easy outpouring over the hostages, began acquiring the grace to admit that the Vietnam veterans had a point.

Perhaps, too, enough history has passed to allow the country to proceed to the next stage, to acknowledge the Vietnam veterans without setting off a civil war or a national nervous breakdown. Fresh history has added a few new perspectives. Ronald Reagan, who in 1980 described Vietnam as a "noble cause," nonetheless proposed to eliminate $691 million in benefits for the Vietnam veterans, including $30 million for the ninety-one valuable and even lifesaving storefront veterans' counseling centers around the country.

It is difficult to generalize about the Vietnam veteran. The TV scriptwriter's vision in the seventies pictured him as a damply sweating crazojunkie who would erupt toward the end of the plot line and grease half of Southern California. A veteran named Glen Young took an elevator to a job interview recently and had a fellow passenger ask: "Are you one of the baby killers?"

A comprehensive group portrait of the veterans is available. The Veterans Administration published a five-volume study of Vietnam veterans by the Center for Policy Research in New York City. Vietnam veterans, the study concluded, have been paying a disproportionate social price for their experience. The war tore loose the wiring in many of their lives.

But it is a mistake to view all Vietnam veterans as profoundly troubled, as walking wounded. About half of the veterans, the study found, still carry disturbing, unsettling psychic baggage from Vietnam. Even so, most cope pretty well. Americans may now be too quick to indulge in a "Lo, the Poor Vet" rhetoric. Dr. Arthur Egendorf, a Vietnam veteran and a psychologist who was a principal author of the study, points out that those who pity Vietnam veterans simply relegate them to the role of victim (which is not much help to the veterans). Liberals use their pity to help prove that the war was wrong. Some veterans, denied respect, make do with pity, and even trade on it. But that is sad.

Was the Vietnam experience unique for those who fought it? History would have to go on a manically inventive jag to top Vietnam for wild, lethal ironies and stage effects—"a black looneytune," writer Michael Herr called it in *Dispatches*. Indochina became the demented intersection of a bizarrely inventive killer technology (all of those "daisy cutters" and carpet-laying B-52s and mad swarms of choppers and infrared night-scopes) with a tunnel-digging peasantry in rubber-tire sandals: the amazing, night-dwelling Victor Charlie.

Still, Vietnam was not unique in its effects upon the men who fought there. From Odysseus onward, almost all soldiers have come back angry from war. And they have had problems. In Elizabethan England, a disbandment of armies automatically meant a major increase in the number of thieves and highwaymen preying on civilians. In fact, veterans are almost always treated badly after a war, even if the brass bands do turn out for a ceremonial welcome home. During the twenties, the windows of the nation's pawnshops were filled with soldiers' medals for heroism from the Great War. Catiline, Hitler, and Mussolini constructed their power bases upon the grievances of veterans.

The fact is that fighting a war, any war, is a grisly, shattering business. Many men take years to recover from it; many never do. Curiously, societies almost always neglect their veterans for the first ten years after a war. Then the veterans get themselves organized into a political force (like the Grand Army of the Republic after the Civil War or the VFW and American Legion after World War I) and politically extract the benefits and pensions that civilian gratitude or pity never got around to bestowing.

But Vietnam was different from other American wars in one crucial respect: the United States lost it. When a man soldiers on the winning side, the social contract of arms holds up; the young conscript is asked to endure all discomforts of the field, including death, but if he returns, the grateful nation (though it may soon grow indifferent) promises at least a ration of glory, a ceremonious welcome, the admiring opinion of his fellow citizens. Sometime between Tet and the last helicopter off the embassy roof in 1975, America threw away its social contract with the soldiers and left them to straggle back into the society as best they could. A lot of them have still not made it.

But Americans can renegotiate the contract, can extract lessons and meaning from the disaster. They might begin by trying to help Vietnam veterans restore their lives. Many veterans say that it is too late for rhetoric, too late for symbols such as the Vietnam Veterans Memorial built not far from the Lincoln Memorial. Such vets want concrete help: more assistance finding jobs, more time to use the GI Bill. There is something notably irresponsible about a government that dispatches its young to be chewed up in an obscure land and then does not know their names when it all goes bad. Among other things, that sort of disloyalty may make it difficult to recruit the young for future military enterprises.

But symbols and rhetoric are also incalculably important. The hostages' return, with its powerful, complex effects, was all ceremony and TV. Many veterans want chiefly to be thanked for what they did, for doing as their nation asked. They crave an acknowledgment, a respect from their fellow Americans that they have never had and may never get. The victor always gets respect, even if it is of a shallow and predictable kind. The veterans of Vietnam are entitled to a different respect: the kind that goes to someone who has endured deep anguish, even failure, and survived.

Vietnam still chokes Americans. The nation will not recover from it, or learn from all of that slaughter and guilt, until it acknowledges that the men who fought the nation's first teenage war (average age: 19.2 years) did not cook up that war themselves in a mischievous moment. That was all of America out there. "It was a collective enterprise," says Dr. Egendorf, "and we were *all* damaged by it. A family melodrama is still going on. Sometimes a psychologist cannot treat the individual alone; he must see the whole family together."

America lost 56,480 men in Vietnam. The nation also misplaced many thousands of men and women who did make it home. To embrace them now may be a complicated, belated, and awkward exercise, but it should be done—done with a clear historical eye, without pity or jingo or other illusions. It would mitigate an injustice and might even improve the nation's collective mental health. It would help to settle America's tedious quarrel with itself. Americans should be able to repeat Robert Lowell's line: "My eyes have seen what my hand did."

The Poetic License
to Kill

In E. B. White's lovely fable *Charlotte's Web,* the literate spider Charlotte saves a pig named Wilbur from execution by spinning blurbs about him in the barn doorway: SOME PIG, RADIANT, and so on. The astonished farm folk put away their thoughts of slaughter; they no longer regard Wilbur as pork, but as a tourist attraction, and even a celebrity who enjoys the favor of higher powers. Sweet Wilbur will survive to grow old in the barnyard. He gratefully sighs, "It is not often that someone comes along who is a true friend and a good writer."

Soak the story in reality, bad luck, stupidity, and evil for a while, and it might turn into the parable of Jack Abbott and Norman Mailer (1982): the redemption of the distinctly uninnocent. In one sense, the tale is merely a particularly sensational item of literary gossip. But buried amid the blood and chic is an interesting question of principle. Almost everything, as Thomas De Quincey noticed, has either a moral handle or an aesthetic handle. Which handle do you reach for in the Abbott-Mailer case?

In the beginning, Mailer spins publicity for convict and murderer Jack Abbott, helps get Abbott's prison book published and Abbott paroled. The con with the prose style of a Doberman (all speed and teeth) obeys his muse again. Six weeks after parole, Abbott kills a man in New York City's East Village. Mailer must concoct another redemption. He proposes a principle: "Culture is worth a little risk," Mailer tells reporters. Abbott should not be punished too harshly for this murder. It is true that he is not in any condition just now to walk around loose, but he is a talented writer. Being put away in prison for too long, says Mailer, might stifle Abbott's creativity.

Attempting to spook the bourgeois sensibility, of course, has been Mailer's vocation for a quarter of a century. He has rarely done it so effectively, perhaps because in this case the blood is real, for the first time since Mailer stabbed his second wife with a penknife in 1960 (and got off with a suspended sentence). A fierce outrage cascaded down on him last week. It was common to hear New Yorkers say that he should be tried as an accessory to murder. Mailer barged around giving interviews and suing a newspaper for libel, looking truculent and stricken.

In one way it was unfair: Mailer had had the courage to sponsor a talented pariah, and then something in Abbott's transition from prison went disastrously wrong. Mailer was personally aggrieved and pained, not only for Abbott but for Abbott's victim. It is true that certain writers adopt convicts: criminals, sinister, romantic and stupid as sharks, become the executive arms of intellectuals' violent fantasies. For some reason, intellectuals rarely understand that they are being conned: convicts are geniuses of ingratiation. Still, Mailer after all was not promoting a killer but a prose stylist and what he judged to be a salvageable human being. He miscalculated: he overrated the writer in Abbott and underestimated the murderer.

It was not so much ideas as their loudmouthed idiot cousin—publicity—that helped soften the verdict. It began to seem that it was not Abbott and his admitted homicide that were on trial but, in a vague and sloppy way, the entire American criminal justice system. The jury decided that the system had just been too much for Abbott. So the verdict was manslaughter. Abbott had been acting, the jury decided, under "extreme emotional disturbance." A judge of Solomonic gifts might condemn Abbott and Mailer to be shackled together with molybdenum chains, inseparable ever after, like Tony Curtis and Sidney Poitier in *The Defiant Ones,* to clunk, snarling, from one literary dinner party to another.

Amid the travesty and pathos, however, Mailer had advanced an interesting proposition: the idea that a writer, or presumably any artist, deserves a special dispensation under the law. You can talk your way out of anything; Mailer suggested that a man ought to be able to write his way out of anything as well, including murder. Articulation leads to redemption; language can pick locks.

Mailer's principle—art should redeem or rather, more important, exculpate the artist—reached its full blossom as a tenet of Romanticism.

The artist, for centuries regarded as merely a liveried servant of church and aristocracy, sprang up out of the bourgeoisie in the early nineteenth century as a dashing hierophant whose work connected him to the divine. It excused everything, from rudeness to homicide. "The fact of a man's being a poisoner," proclaimed Oscar Wilde, "is nothing against his prose."

It is a confused and essentially stupid doctrine. W. H. Auden's memorable lines about W. B. Yeats describe a sweet metaphysical arc: "Time that is intolerant/ Of the brave and innocent/ And indifferent in a week/ To a beautiful physique/ Worships language and forgives/ Everyone by whom it lives." Yes: time grants pardon. But the law is not in the trade of metaphysics; the law's only hope of survival lies precisely in its struggle to be impartial. The Mailer doctrine suggests that somehow the law should set up separate standards for artists. There are grotesque possibilities here. Who judges the literary merit? What if a literary convict is really a terrible writer? String him up? Will we need a panel of literary judges to meet the first Monday of every month at Elaine's in Manhattan to hear its cases? If the perpetrator of the Texas chain-saw massacre shows a certain flair for the short story, do we let him off?

What distinguishes man from the animals is language, articulate consciousness. What distinguishes Jack Abbott from millions of other convicts is a prose style that was capable of catching a famous writer's attention. It is interesting that, as psychologists have noted, some hopelessly inarticulate teenagers have committed murder because they simply lacked the verbal skill to communicate their anger in any other way; Abbott has at his command both the sophisticated and the more primitive forms of communication.

If Mother Teresa of Calcutta should commit murder, any court might weigh her amazing life's labor against the evil of the one deed. The murder would be the exception in a life that otherwise displayed merit and extravagantly claimed mercy. But Jack Abbott's vividly ranting book, brutal and brutalized, should have made the jury wonder which was more characteristic of the man: literature or murder. In a long and essentially tragic perspective (in which all consequences are endured, all debts paid), literature performs its redemptions. Mailer's formula is a shallow little mechanism. "Culture is worth a little risk," he says. The world of that sentence is upside down: you defend culture, do you not, by locking up the people who try to kill it.

"Forgiveness to the Injured Doth Belong"

The American trajectory generally arcs into the future, not the past. The nation's promise tends to override its memories. The best life lies ahead, like a highway heading west. There are American ghosts, of course, haunted rooms, secrets in the attic. But the virtue of the New World has always been its newness. "Why drag about this monstrous corpse of your memory?" Ralph Waldo Emerson asked. Henry Ford never looked back. "History," he said, "is more or less bunk."

The spring of 1985, however, was the season of the past. It was the anniversary of almost everything. Americans were pitched back into unstable regions of memory, back into Vietnam and wartime Europe. Sometimes the experience has been disconcerting. The past only looks dead. Ronald Reagan, quintessential American and oldest president, did not seem entirely to grasp that. He displayed a curious insensitivity about the past, as if he did not know how important it is, or how dangerous it can be. As if he did not know that the past has monsters in it. His eyes accustomed to sunshine, Reagan did not peer carefully enough into the shadows.

Once the prospect of his visit to a German military cemetery at Bitburg stirred a violent storm, Reagan, clearly pained, insisted repeatedly that while "we will never forget" the Holocaust, the gesture was a matter not of forgiving and forgetting but of moving forward, of trying to achieve a genuine healing, a reconciliation, of celebrating the forty years during which the United States and West Germany have been strong allies. In a thoroughly American way, Reagan wanted finally to clear the past off the highway, as if it were some sort of old wreck. He wished to proceed, as

Lincoln said in his second inaugural address, "with malice toward none, with charity for all."

Yet the symbolism of his visit to the Bitburg cemetery, where forty-nine SS men are buried, clouded Reagan's goal of bringing about a healing. Before the trip, Reagan made matters worse when he said that young German soldiers were just as much victims of the Third Reich as the Jews were—a grotesque equation even if inadvertent. That statement, coupled with the visit to Bitburg, left an impression that the President of the United States was conferring a sort of official forgiveness upon the German army that did Hitler's work.

That is not how forgiveness operates. Once in the middle of the war, Simon Wiesenthal, a prisoner in a forced-labor camp in Lvov, found himself on a work detail in a hospital where a young SS officer lay wounded and dying. The Nazi made Wiesenthal sit and listen while he confessed his atrocities, including burning down a houseful of Jews in the Ukraine and shooting those who tried to escape by leaping from the smoking windows. The SS trooper, tormented by guilt, begged Wiesenthal, as a Jew, to forgive him. Wiesenthal turned and walked away. He survived the camps and has spent the past forty years hunting Nazi war criminals. But he remained troubled by doubts that he had done the right thing in refusing to forgive the SS trooper. "Forgetting is something that time alone takes care of," he later wrote, "but forgiveness is an act of volition, and only the sufferer is qualified to make the decision."

Christians are taught to turn the other cheek, to forgive. The eye-for-an-eye formula of the Old Testament does not rule out mercy and forgiveness, which are highly valued in Jewish teaching as well. But in Judaism, there are two conditions for repentance: one must go in genuine contrition to the person sinned against, and one must do one's best to compensate for the wrong done. But how can a Nazi, say, compensate a Jew for exterminating his entire family? In that sense, some crimes simply cannot be forgiven.

The summary power of forgiveness resides with God alone. After that, forgiveness gets personal. Pope John Paul II could forgive Mehmet Ali Agca, the man who shot him. The bullet hole in his abdomen gave him the authority to do that. So, in a sacramental way, did his ordination as a priest. Ronald Reagan can forgive John Hinckley (the Pope and the President both being members of the brotherhood of the shot). But Ronald Reagan cannot forgive Agca for shooting the Pope. Nor can he forgive SS men for what they did in Europe while Reagan was making Army training films in Hollywood. Wrote the poet John Dryden: "Forgiveness to the injured doth belong."

There is a difference between forgiveness and reconciliation, but the distinction between the terms never was very clearly made during the President's trip. Forgiveness implies a kind of moral embrace, a clearing of the books, that is difficult if not impossible in the context of Nazi Germany. Reconciliation is a transaction that can occur between two nations. But forgiveness is between individuals, or between an individual and God. Just as one rejects the notion of collective guilt, so one recoils at the idea of collective absolution. Deeds are done by individuals and must be judged individually. One of the evils of the twentieth century has been the practice of totalitarians who create collective categories of people (the "bourgeoisie," for example, or "enemies of the people") in order to legitimize expropriation, imprisonment, and mass slaughter.

If Reagan meant to set the past to rest, Bitburg brought it back to angry life. Yet there were many voices muttering, "Must we hear about the Holocaust again?" There have, after all, been other great tragedies in history—the Turkish slaughter of the Armenians, Stalin's liquidation of millions of kulaks and the enforced famine in the Ukraine in 1932–33, the destruction of perhaps two million Kampucheans by their own Khmer Rouge countrymen.

One cannot engage in a contest of comparative horrors. Yet there is about the Holocaust a primal and satanic mystery. And no cheap grace can redeem it. The Third Reich was the greatest failure of civilization on the planet. In Freudian terms, it was as if the superego had gone crashing down into the dark, wild id.

Germany represented one of the furthest advances of the culture, yet the Third Reich profoundly perverted the entire heritage of Western achievement. It was as if Goethe had taken to eating human flesh. The scientific method, perfected over centuries, fell into the hands of Dr. Mengele and the engineers of the ovens. Hitler was not alone responsible. More than a few Germans enthusiastically followed him, saluted him and died for him. They seized the accumulated trust of three thousand years and distilled it into unimaginable evil. They sought to extinguish not only Jews and gypsies and the rest, but all the lights of civilization. That is not easy to forgive.

Living with the
"Peculiar Institution"

In his novel *Love in the Ruins,* Walker Percy imagines the Lord leading
white people to North America and bestowing that Eden on them with
only one strange injunction: There are some people in a place called
Africa. Be careful that you don't enslave them. Otherwise . . . But
one day in 1619, a Dutch frigate landed at Jamestown, Virginia, and
traded twenty black Africans for food and supplies. That was the
beginning.

If slavery was America's original sin, *Roots,* for all its soap opera, sex,
and violence, seems to have had a certain expiatory effect. From the
various mythic provinces of TV, which may be the densest core of American imagination now, are gathered a virtuous and likable group of heroes: Pa Cartwright from the Ponderosa, Lou Grant from *The Mary Tyler
Moore Show,* affable Sergeant Enright from *MacMillan and Wife,* and
sweet Sandy Duncan from the apartment upstairs. But in *Roots,* they all
turn counterfeit—treacherous, violent, and contemptible. Only one white,
Old George, is sympathetic. The blacks are noble and enduring, even
forbearing when given a chance for revenge (Tom's opportunity to whip
one of his white bosses). However unintentional, an apology from white
America is contained subliminally in all of this—the blockbuster week-
long programming, the parade of villainous white stars. It is a kind of
ritual sacrifice of pop heroes, a small but formal self-abasement.

But how accurate is television's *Roots* as history? Novelist William Styron (*The Confessions of Nat Turner*) is harsher than most critics. *Roots,* he says, "is dishonest tripe. It took a crude mass-culture approach. It shows how dismally ignorant blacks and whites still are about slavery." As a number of critics have noted, there were, to start with, some errors of setting. Styron objects that "counties in Virginia, North Carolina, and Tennessee which are as flat as Ping Pong paddles look as if they were shot on a back set used for horse operas with a background of the San Bernardino Mountains."

Another reviewer pointed out that two white men would hardly have dared to venture near Kunta Kinte's African village to capture him because at that time a war was brewing between the English and a local chief, who would probably have slaughtered any whites he found in the area.

Alex Haley and the TV producers had the Lorne Greene character farming cotton in Spotsylvania County, Virginia; it should have been tobacco. Harold Cruse, author of *The Crisis of the Negro Intellectual,* observes: "When you see Leslie Uggams and her long polished nails, you just have to laugh." Although Cruse liked *Roots,* he thought "the ending was contrived, commercialized, and romanticized. For one thing, under those conditions, you don't just tie up a plantation owner to a tree and then get into a wagon and casually drive away as if there weren't bloodhounds and night riders who would track you down."

There are more substantive complaints. Historian James Brewer Stewart says, "The master/slave relationship was ridden with ambiguity. Plantation overseers and owners were not all-powerful. They were tied by a system of reciprocal rights and obligations." *Roots* often has a flattened, cartoon quality: the whites nearly all villainous, the blacks uniformly heroic. Africa is romanticized to the point that it seems a combination of third-century Athens and Club Méditerranée, with peripatetic philosophers afoot and Claude Lévi-Strauss expected for dinner.

Yet as a psychological event, if not as history, *Roots* surely transcends its mistakes. Haley called his saga "faction," and it cannot be evaluated merely as history or merely as an entertainment. As either one of those, it fails. Yet as both, in resonance with the long, complex American experience on the subject, *Roots* is extremely powerful.

The distinction between cathartic melodrama and historical events needs attention, however, if only because professional historians themselves have so much trouble respecting it. Slavery, so obvious in its lurid immorality, is apt to become especially distorted in the hands of American historians.

"What is it about the black experience," asks author Michael Novak, "that produces in so many good minds, black and white, a positive lust for corruptions of elementary sense?" The answers are probably 1) guilt and 2) ideology.

It is useful, though not extenuating, to point out that Americans did not invent slavery. Their form of chattel slavery, however, was uniquely ugly. Still, slavery has a long, dishonorable history. The Sumerians of Mesopotamia kept slaves before 2000 B.C., and the Code of Hammurabi laid down rules governing the practice. In eight years, Caesar sent back some 500,000 slaves from Gaul to work mines, plantations, and public projects; some, of course, became gladiators. The *Domesday Book* recorded 25,000 slaves in England. Races from the Mayans to the Muslims to, notably, black Africans have kept slaves for many centuries, in varying degrees of misery and servitude. The Malays sometimes paid their debts by giving, say, a child into slavery.

There are even some perversely approving things to be said for slavery: that in its earliest form, it actually marked a humanitarian improvement in the laws of war, since it involved the capture of prisoners instead of their slaughter. Oddly, it was not a primitive practice, in one sense, because it required a stable and settled society in order to take root.

Only by the nimblest sophistry could slavery be countenanced in a "civilized" society like eighteenth- and nineteenth-century America. Slavery has tortured American historians for generations: slavery theses and revisions of them writhed through the stream of historiography for one hundred and fifty years or longer.

Writers like Frederick Law Olmsted, a Northerner who traveled through the South in the 1850s and wrote three books about Southern life, emphasized the lurid, brutal and simply inefficient aspects of slavery in order to promote the abolitionist cause. This was a Simon Legree approach to the subject—and there are aspects of such simplism in *Roots*.

The trends that followed:

The Magnolias-and-Banjos School. This interpretation, promoted in the late nineteenth and early twentieth centuries, was elaborated by the Southern historian Ulrich B. Phillips. The premise, which influenced historians well into this century, had it that blacks were innately lazy and incompetent, capable of working only under compulsion. In this view, blacks were childlike innocents, perhaps biologically inferior; slavery, whatever its excesses, was a generally benign means of giving the colored people civilized ways. *Gone With the Wind* carried that general message.

Blacks as Devastated Victims. This view predominated from the late forties through the Kennedy Administration. Historian Stanley Elkins, building on black sociologist E. Franklin Frazier's work in the 1930s, detailed in *Slavery* (1959) a view that whites had done to blacks what the Nazis did to the Jews. Blacks were—and are—acted upon; they do not themselves act, because their culture was broken by slavery and its racist aftermath. The view awakened liberal guilt and paralleled the rise of the white civil rights movement. The Moynihan report described the devastation of black family life and asked for government aid to try to invigorate it again.

Blacks as Strong, Proud, Culturally Cohesive. The trend began with the Lyndon Johnson years and the rise of militant blacks who scorned the devastated-victim theory as unworthy and abject. The Moynihan report was rejected, if not disproved. Historian Herbert Gutman began work on the view of the black family as shrewd, strong, not nearly as weakened as it had seemed. The extended family had resources unsuspected by whites.

Yet if blacks had not indeed been broken by slavery, why did they put up with it? (One answer is that they did not, but responded with thousands of acts of sabotage, from nuisance to insurrection.)

There is a withering crossfire of pedantries in nearly all academic discussions of slavery and American blacks. In a book called *Time on the Cross,* economist-historians Robert Fogel and Stanley Engerman accumulated a mass of data on antebellum life in the South. They fed their statistics into computers and came up with a portrait of slavery as a highly rational and efficient system that gave the South considerable economic growth and a high standard of living for all Southerners, both black and white. While admitting the immorality of slavery, Fogel and Engerman found that blacks in the South, propelled by self-interest and the work ethic, outfitted with a Victorian code of middle-class behavior learned from their masters, did remarkably well under the "peculiar institution."

The Fogel and Engerman thesis, rather weirdly cheerful, seemed a relapse back to something like the banjo school. It brought a fusillade of rebuttal, most of it convincing. Fogel and Engerman argued that blacks were willing collaborators in an unfair but workable capitalist system: owners got free labor, blacks got economic rewards and family stability if they played along. This was one attempt to explain how blacks could be strong and cohesive and yet still be slaves.

Gutman, in one of his counterarguments, came up with this formula: family stability among black slaves—now widely accepted, despite the breakup of many families by sale—was a strong anti-insurrectionist force. *Roots* seems to agree with this explanation. When Kunta Kinte plans to run away for a second time, despite his partially amputated foot and his love for Bell, she tells him that her first husband was killed for running away and her children sold off, and that now she is pregnant again. If slaves revolt or run away, the family is broken or killed. So Kunta stays. Thus Haley squares with the current theory.

One of the great problems of all this history is thesis mongering, the intertwining of ideology and fashion with academic evidence. The black experience in the United States, from slavery onward, has been rich, immensely varied, extremely complicated, and often difficult to lay hold of. Blacks in slavery were kept illiterate and so left almost exclusively their oral tradition—which, of course, is what *Roots* is.

During the thirties, as part of the Federal Writers Project of the New Deal, scores of very elderly blacks who had lived under slavery were interviewed all across the South. Selections of the interviews, collected in *Life Under the "Peculiar Institution,"* prove that generalizations about slavery are nearly impossible. Some slaves were well fed and happy. Some were beaten to death. Some slave women were raped and others treated with kindness. A slave named Frank Bell in New Orleans was often kept in chains; his master discovered that Bell had married and, in a drunken rage, cut off the girl's head.

A former slave named Andrew Boone described how runaways were beaten: first with a "cobbin" paddle with forty holes in it to raise blisters, then with a cat-o'-nine-tails. "When de whippin' wit de paddle was over, dey took de cat-o'-nine-tails and busted the blisters. By dis time de blood sometimes would be runnin' down deir heels. Den de next thing was a wash in salt water strong enough to hold up an egg." Then an ex-slave named Lindsey Faucette reported: "Marse never allowed us to be whipped. . . . We worked in de day and had de nights to play games and have singin's."

In a sense, it does not matter whether what Haley has to say in *Roots* is literally true—and much of it undoubtedly is. What matters is that, despite a certain mythic stereotyping, *Roots* is plausible. The only pertinent generalization about slavery may be that it was an immense evil.

Roots gives that evil a brutal immediacy. In that process, the years of bondage have assumed a new psychological pertinence for both blacks and whites. Oddly, many whites seem to feel not guilt but an unexpected shock of identification with blacks, while blacks experience a larger shock of pride at glimpsing a complete vision of where they have been and what they have overcome. Neither race has ever seen it quite that way before.

The Fascination of Decadence

> *I like the word "decadent." All shimmering with purple and gold. It throws out the brilliance of flames and the gleam of precious stones. It is made up of carnal spirit and unhappy flesh and of all the violent splendors of the Lower Empire; it conjures up the paint of courtesans, the sports of the circus, the breath of the tamers of animals, the bounding of wild beasts, the collapse among the flames of races exhausted by the power of feeling, to the invading sound of enemy trumpets.*
> —Paul Verlaine, circa 1886

It was partly the spectacle of Western decadence that aroused the Ayatollah Khomeini to orgies of Koranic proscription. Alcohol, music, dancing, mixed bathing all have been curtailed by the Iranian revolution. Americans find this zealotry sinister, but also quaint: How can almost childish pleasures (a tune on the radio, a day at the beach) deserve such puritanical hellfires? But Americans are also capable of a chill of apprehension, a barely acknowledged thought about the prices that civilizations pay for their bad habits: If Iran has driven out its (presumably polluted) monarch and given itself over to a purification that demands even the interment of its beer bottles, then, by that logic, what punishment and what purification would be sufficient for America? The Ayatollah residing in some American consciences would surely have to plow under not just the beer bottles, but an uncomfortably large part of U.S. society itself.

The very idea of decadence, with all its fleshly titillations and metaphysical phosphorescence, excites that kind of Spenglerian anxiety. A lot of Americans seem inclined to think of themselves as a decadent people: such self-accusation may be the reverse side of American self-congratulation. Americans contemplate some of the more disgusting uses to which freedom of expression has been put; they confront a physical violence and spiritual heedlessness that makes them wonder if the entire society is on a steep and terminal incline downward. They see around them what they call decadence. But is the United States decadent? Does the rich, evil word, with its little horripilations of pleasure and its gonging of the last dance, really have any relevant meaning?

Decadence is a wonderfully versatile idea—like a perfume that gives off different scents depending on a woman's body chemistry and heat. It arouses pleasure, disgust and bombast. And sometimes elaborate denial. The critic Richard Gilman published *Decadence* (Farrar, Straus & Giroux) in 1979. His elegant treatise argues that the term is almost impossible to define, is constantly misinterpreted and misused, and quite possibly should be deleted from the language.

Gilman makes a persuasive, if somewhat pedantic, point. He argues that Americans overuse the word decadent; without knowing what they mean by it. They use it to describe a fifty-dollar bottle of Margaux, a three-hour soak in the tub, a forty-hour-a-week television habit, the crowds that tell the suicide to jump, a snort of cocaine. And yet Americans mean *something* by it. The notion of decadence is a vehicle that carries all kinds of strange and overripe cargo—but a confusing variety of meanings does not add up to meaninglessness. Decadence, like pornography (both have something of the same fragrance), may be hard to define, but most people think they know it when they see it.

They think it might cover, say, the Aspen, Colorado, fan club that grew up to celebrate murderer Ted Bundy with, among other things, T-shirts that read TED BUNDY IS A ONE-NIGHT STAND. Or the work of photographer Helmut Newton, who likes to sell high-fashion clothes with lurid pictures of women posed as killers and victims, or trussed up in sadomasochistic paraphernalia. One of his shots shows a woman's head being forced into a toilet bowl. The school of S-M fashion photography may, of course, be merely a passing putrefaction.

People informally play a game in which they compile lists of the most decadent acts not in practice. For horrific sensationalism, they might start with the idea of the snuff film (pornography in which an actress performing sex is actually murdered on screen). In the same awful category, they might include Viennese artist Rudolf Schwarzkogler, who decided to make a modernist artistic statement by amputating, inch by inch, his own penis, while a photographer recorded the process as a work of art.

The list would have to mention Keith Richards, a member of the Rolling Stones, who, by one account, in order to pass a blood test to enter the United States for concert tours, had a physician drain his own heroin-tainted blood from his body and replace it with transfusions from more sedate citizens. Some of the sadomasochistic and homosexual bars in New York and San Francisco, with their publicly practiced urolagnia, buggery, and excruciating complications thereof, would strike quite a few Americans as decadent.

In a less specialized realm, disco and punk songs like "Bad Girls" and

"I Wanna Be Sedated" have a decadent ring. In fact, the entire phenomenon of disco has a certain loathsome glisten to it.

Extravagance has always been thought to have something to do with decadence. Some lists might mention Tiffany's $2,950 gold-ingot wristwatch, or a pair of $1,000 kidskin-and-gold shoes, or Harrod's $1,900 dog collar, or Zsa Zsa Gabor's $150,000 Rolls-Royce with its leather, velvet, and leopard interior. But be careful. Extravagance may actually be a sign of robustly vulgar good health. The man buying His and Hers Learjets from the Neiman Marcus catalogue was helping to keep a lot of aircraft workers employed.

Decadence is a subjective word, a term of moral and psychological recoil. It expresses quite exactly those things that the speaker finds most awful, most repugnant; most dangerous and, as a Freudian might point out, most interesting. So a question arises: Are aberrant tastes decadent in themselves? Does the decadence consist in the fact that such tastes can now be openly practiced and even tolerated? Surely, tolerance is not decadence, unless it is a symptom of moral obliviousness.

Players in the game can pile up examples but still have difficulty arriving at any generality. Decadence, in one working definition, is pathology with social implications: it differs from individual sickness as pneumonia differs from plague. A decadent act must, it seems, possess meaning that transcends itself and spreads like an infection to others, or at least suggests a general condition of the society. Decadence (from the Latin *decadere,* "to fall down or away," hence decay) surely has something to do with death, with a communal *taedium vitae;* decadence is a collection of symptoms that might suggest a society exhausted and collapsing like a star as it degenerates toward the white dwarf stage, *"une race à sa dernière heure,"* as a French critic said.

Americans forget how violent and depraved other cultures have been. There is something hilarious, in a grisly way, about George Augustus Selwyn, the late eighteenth-century London society figure and algolagnic whose morbid interest in human suffering sent him scurrying over to Paris whenever a good execution was scheduled. Americans may have displayed an unwholesome interest in the departure of Gary Gilmore, but that was nothing compared with the macabre fascinations, the public hangings, the *Schadenfreud* of other centuries. In the seventeenth century, Londoners sometimes spent their Sunday afternoons at Bedlam mocking the crippled and demented.

In Florence during Michelangelo's time, countless victims of stabbings by hit men were seen floating under bridges. In London during the Age of Enlightenment, gangs roamed the streets committing rape. Says critic George Steiner: "Our sense of a lost civility and order comes from a very short period of exceptional calm—from the 1860s to 1914, or the interlude between the Civil War and World War I."

One of the problems with the concept of decadence is that it has such a long moral shoreline, stretching from bleak and mountainously serious considerations of history to the shallow places where ideas evaporate thirty seconds after they splash. For all the range of its uses, decadence is a crude term. It houses fallacies. People think of decadence as the reason for the collapse of Rome, but the point is arguable. Rome at the height of its imperial power was as morally depraved as in its decline. Perhaps more so.

A second model is the metaphor of natural decay, the seasons of human life, for example. Animals, people, have birth, growth, periods of vigor, then decline and death. Do societies obey that pattern? The idea of decadence, of course, implies exactly that. But it seems a risky metaphor. Historians like Arnold Toynbee, like the fourteenth-century Berber Ibn-Khaldun and the eighteenth-century Italian Giovanni Battista Vico, have constructed cyclical theories of civilizations that rise up in vigor, flourish, mature, and then fall into decadence. Such theories may sometimes be too deterministic; they might well have failed, for example, to predict such a leap of civilization as the Renaissance. Ultimately, the process of decadence remains a mystery: Why has the tribe of Jews endured for so many centuries after the sophisticated culture of the Hittites disappeared?

Richard Gilman can be granted his central point: "that 'decadence' is an unstable word and concept whose significations and weights continually change in response to shifts in morals, social, and cultural attitudes, and even technology." But the protean term is still tempting. It seems the one word that will do to point toward something moribund in a culture, the metastasis of despair that occurs when a society loses faith in its own future, when its energy wanes and dies. It would probably be more narrowly accurate to use words like corrupt or depraved to describe, say, punk rock, or murder in a gas line, but decadent is more popular because it contains a prophecy. To be decadent is to be not just corrupt, but *terminally* corrupt. "Decadence" speaks with the iron will of history and the punishment of the Lord. It is an accusation. "Woe to those who are at ease in Zion," wrote the prophet Amos, "and to those who feel secure on the mountain of Samaria. Woe to those who lie upon beds of ivory, who drink wine in bowls, and anoint themselves with the finest oils."

One could construct a kind of "worst-case scenario" to prove that the United States, with the rest of the West, has fallen into dangerous decline. The case might be argued thus: the nation's pattern is moral and social failure, embellished by hedonism. The work ethic is nearly as dead as the Weimar Republic. Bureaucracies keep cloning themselves. Resources vanish. Education fails to educate. The system of justice collapses into a parody of justice. An underclass is trapped, half out of sight, while an opulent traffic passes overhead. Religion gives way to narcissistic self-improvement cults.

There is more. Society fattens its children on junk food and then permits them to be enlisted in pornographic films. The nation subdivides into a dozen drug cultures—the alcohol culture, the cocaine culture, the heroin culture, the Valium culture, the amphetamine culture, and combinations thereof. Legal abortions and the pervasive custom of contraception suggest a society so chary of its future that it has lost its will to perpetuate itself. Says Malcolm Muggeridge: "What will make historians laugh at us is how we express our decadence in terms of freedom and humanism. Western society suffers from a largely unconscious collective death wish." Alexander Solzhenitsyn, who shares with Muggeridge an austere Christian mysticism, has been similarly appalled by Western materialism.

And yet, oddly, the United States probably seemed more decadent, or at any rate, considerably more disturbed, eight or ten years ago than it does now. In the midst of the Vietnam War, the ghetto riots, the assassinations, the orgasmic romanticism of the counterculture, the national rage was more on the surface. Says Milwaukee sociologist Wayne Youngquist: "There is decadence in our society, but it is an ebb, not a rising tide. Our institutions are healing, the age of moral ambiguity and experimentation is in decline."

Americans must beware, however, of looking for decadence in the wrong places. The things that can make the nation decay now are not necessarily what we think of when we say decadence: they are not Roman extravagances or Baudelaire's *fleurs du mal,* or Wilde's scented conceits. Nor, probably, do they have much to do with pornography, license, or bizarre sexual practice. It is at least possible that Americans should see the symptoms of decadence in the last business quarter's 3.8-percent decline in productivity, or in U.S. society's dependence upon foreigners' oil, or in saturations of chemical pollution. It is such symptoms that betoken "a race which has reached its final hour."

But the word decadence, like an iridescent bubble, can be blown too large; it will burst with too much inflation of significance. In any case, decadence is too much a word of simplification. The United States is too complicated, housing too many simultaneous realities, to be covered with one such concept. Subcultures of decadence exist, as they have in all societies. The amplifications of the press and television may make the decadence seem more sensational and pervasive than it really is. A sense of decay arises also from all of society's smoking frictions of rapid change, the anxiety caused by a sense of impermanence. The nation's creative forces, however, remain remarkably strong—in the sciences, for example, where achievements in physics, mathematics, biology, and medicine rank beside anything so far accomplished on the planet. Before anyone tries to use too seriously the awful and thrilling word decadence, he ought to distinguish between the customary mess of life and the terminal wreckage of death.

The Lure of
Doomsday

The Jonestown story, like some Joseph Conrad drama of fanaticism and moral emptiness, has gone directly into popular myth. It will be remembered as an emblematic, identifying moment: a demented American psychopomp in a tropical cult house, doling out cyanide with Kool-Aid. Jonestown is the Altamont of the seventies cult movement. Just as Altamont destroyed Woodstock, Jonestown has decisively contaminated the various vagabond zealotries that have grown up, flourished, and sometimes turned sinister.

All new religious enterprises, of course, are liable to be damned and dismissed as "cults." The term is pejorative: cult suggests a band of fierce believers who have surrendered themselves to obscure doctrine and a dangerous prophet. Yet some religions that are institutions now, more permanent and stable than most governments, began as cults.

Although Jonestown has prompted a widespread revulsion against cults, both fairness and the First Amendment suggest that one standard of judgment can still be applied: "By their fruits ye shall know them." Visionaries, even when they operate from a cult, can bring dimensions of aspiration and change to religion, which otherwise might be merely a moral policeman. But the historical record of cults is ominous and often lurid. Jonestown, for all its gruesome power to shock, has its religious (or quasi-religious) precedents.

Jonestown has even been rivaled as a mass suicide. The Jewish Zealots defending the fortress of Masada against besieging Roman legions in A.D. 73 chose self-slaughter rather than submission; 960 men, women, and children died. The event occupies a place of some reverence in Jewish memory and is not really comparable to Jonestown; the Zealots faced the prospect of slaughter or slavery, and their choice therefore possessed a certain passionate rationality. In the seventeenth century, Russian Orthodox dissenters called the Old Believers refused to accept liturgical reforms. Over a period of years some 20,000 peasants in protest abandoned their fields and burned themselves. In East Africa before World War I, when Tanganyika was a German colony, witch doctors of the *Maji-Maji* movement convinced tribesmen that German bullets would turn to water; they launched an uprising, and the credulous were slaughtered.

Religion and insanity occupy adjacent territories in the mind; historically, cults have kept up a traffic between the two. The medieval Brethren of the Free Spirit, the heretical Beghards and Beguines who practiced in Cologne and other Northern European cities, became nihilistic megalomaniacs. They began in rags but then, in the conviction of their spiritual superiority, which they eventually believed to surpass God's, adopted the idea that the general run of mankind existed merely to be exploited, through robbery, violence, and treachery. In 1420 a cult of Bohemians called the Adamites came to regard themselves, like the Manson gang, as avenging angels. They set about making holy war to cut down the unclean; blood, they said, must flood the world to the height of a horse's head. They were finally exterminated after committing uncounted murders. In 1535 an army of Anabaptists under Jan Bockelson proclaimed its intention "to kill all monks and priests and all rulers that there are in the world; for our king alone is the rightful ruler." They, too, had to be forcibly suppressed. Cultists, of course, are sometimes the victims of persecution. The heretical Albigensians, or Cathari, were broken by church crusade and massacre in the thirteenth century.

The United States has had its bloody moments. Mormons were slaughtered in Illinois and persecuted elsewhere. But it was some sixty Mormons disguised as Indians who, in September 1857, committed the Mountain Meadows Massacre. With the help of three hundred Indians, the Mormons killed more than 120 men, women, and children in the Fancher party that was passing through Utah on the way to California. It was, says historian William Wise, "the logical and culminating act of a society whose leaders believed themselves superior to the rest of mankind and who maintained that their own ecclesiastical laws took precedence over the laws of their country."

The tendency to join cults seems to come roughly in fifty-year cycles in the United States. A wave broke in the mid-nineteenth century, then again after World War I, and in the seventies. For several thousand years, the rule has been that cults flourish in times of great social change. The success of cults today is based partly upon an edifice of unhappy sociological clichés: the breakdown of the family and other forms of authority, the rootlessness and moral flabbiness of life.

At their worst, the cults acquire a psychosis of millennialism. This chiliasm, playing at the drama of the last days, flourishes when life is no longer seen as ascendant. But no matter how democratically advertised, visions of the New Jerusalem, Utopia, or an Edenic Jonestown are bathed in a totalitarian light. And they are shadowed by glimpses of enemies: Antichrist, Gog and Magog; paranoia is often a cult's principal instrument of discipline. One catches whiffs of an old dementia and witchfire.

Traditional religions allow people to live inside history, but still give sacramental expression to their spiritual longings. Cults strain to escape from history, through the reconstruction of Eden or a vision of the Second Coming. Experiments in earthly paradise have a way of ending in horrible irony. Zealots become infected with a fierce nostalgia for a mythical lost wholeness, an ecstasy of spiritual servitude. In Jones's cultish socialism, the spiritual and political were joined. In their terrific surrender, cultists reduce a multiform, contradictory world to cant formulas, and thus they become as dangerous as anyone whose head resounds with certainties. Cults are apt to become miniatures of the totalitarian systems built on Nazi or Hegelian and Marxist foundations. There are eerie similarities of style: intolerance, paranoia, submission.

Such movements, wrote historian Norman Cohn, strive to endow "social conflicts and aspirations with a transcendental significance—in fact with all the mystery and majesty of the final, eschatological drama." To be human is to live inside history, to accept a reality that does not respond to dogma or a megalomaniac's discipline. One escape is that found by the people in Jonestown.

The Lebanese
Dance of Death

In the Arab world, there is a widespread belief that if a child is too beautiful or brilliant, he may attract the evil eye. Parents were once known to disfigure especially pretty babies in order to protect them. God should have arranged some such mild, preemptive mutilation for Lebanon. He did not, however.

Lebanon was always as sweet and cunning and ancient and beautiful as the world. It was literate, rich, fabulous, chic as Atlantis in better days. No land was ever luckier, more cosmopolitan. If you drove in from the east, out of the deserts of Jordan, Iraq, or Syria, Lebanon was the coolest, greenest, richest land in the imagination of Allah. You climbed the Lebanon Mountains, and suddenly beheld the Mediterranean. Its deep blue waters played in the eye against the snow on the tops of the mountains. The air was dense with the scent of thyme and cedar.

It was a profoundly favored place. No oil, of course. Oil was the geological dumb luck of certain desert peoples. But Lebanon had beauty and protective fastnesses in its mountains. Shrewd and unusual people found refuge there, sects like the Maronite Christians and the Druzes. Lebanon was never really a nation in the ordinary sense, but a sort of charmed collection of tribes. Its pace in the old days was a delight. *Time* correspondent Wilton Wynn, who has written about Lebanon since 1946, remembers the hospitality of the countryside, the farmers in their fruit groves forcing a stranger to accept gifts of grapes and white figs and apples and pears. He remembers the magnificent village breakfasts of arak, kebab, grilled liver, tomatoes, yogurt, onions, eggs fried in pottery pans and flavored with sumac.

The merchant genius of the Phoenicians seemed to linger over the land that Lebanon inherited from them. Beirut, a bright, amiable amalgam of beach resort and international bank and world-class shopping mall and neon whorehouse, was invariably called the Paris of the Middle East. It may have been more like Monte Carlo, crossed with Miami Beach and Zurich. The Lebanese were cultured and vividly commercial. They stood precisely at the intersection of Western and Middle Eastern culture, and took a handsome profit by mediating between the two. They have the highest literacy rate and the only real parliamentary democracy in the Arab world.

Desert sheiks banked their oil wealth there, took their pleasures there. Money poured in. Multinational companies installed their regional headquarters. Lebanese lawyers would know more about Iraqi law than Iraqi lawyers, or more about Saudi law than Saudis. The Lebanese were cheerfully prepared to do anything for a price.

Life may have been a little too beautiful. The evil eye arrived. Half a dozen years ago, the evil burst up through the floor boards of the civilization. It came in gangs, the clockwork orange, and shot the Holiday Inn to pieces. It came up shaking Kalashnikov rifles, blazing away, shattering a culture. Sweet Lebanon became the repository for all of the bitterest hatreds of a region deeply talented at hating. The amalgam of tribes grew viciously tribal. Everyone in the country got a gun, and, as a despairing doctor said last year, since "everyone has arms, there's no reason to reason. People use guns now to get a parking space." Someone ruefully published a *Bullet Dodger's Guide to Beirut,* giving instructions on how to pass from one neighborhood to another without getting killed. Among the almost gleefully homicidal tribes mingled refugees, foreigners and, after them, foreigners' armies. Once, it could have seemed a charmed Rousseauian state of nature. It became the one that Hobbes described.

We usually construct our cultures on some predictable order. No society is self-confident otherwise. The Lebanese have by now developed a weird talent for living with the Hobbesian beast; their banks are even flourishing. So instinctive is the Lebanese commercial spirit that the people have learned how to profit handsomely from war. But it still is life in the ruins: strange, inspiring, depressing.

If the fate of Lebanon moves us, it is because the country has become a late twentieth-century fable of the end of civilization. The story of Lebanon carries at least a slight reverberation of every aboriginal myth of the fall from paradise. One feels an eerie premonition and vulnerability before the spectacle. What happened to Lebanon seems both a reversion and a forecast. It is a glimpse of the skull beneath the skin of civilization.

Part of the horror unleashed by the fate of Lebanon arises from man's fear of going crazy. Although it was outsiders (Palestinians, Syrians, Israelis) who destroyed the peace, still the factions of the Lebanese themselves have for several years given an operatic performance of sheer, violent lunacy. It is a madness practiced sometimes with savage gaiety: Kalashnikov fever, blowing people apart just for the hell of it, to hear the guns go off, to feel the kick, to watch the woman crumple half a block away, and spill her groceries and bleed to death in the middle of the street.

Lebanon, of course, suffers from a thousand unique vulnerabilities; it is, for one thing, preposterously unlucky in the people whom geography has chosen for its neighbors. But if an accomplished culture like the Lebanese can disintegrate so suddenly, a little gust of foreboding must pass through other societies. "All that will be left of these cities," in Bertolt Brecht's dark words, "will be the wind through [their streets]." Lebanon comes to seem a strange twentieth-century version of feudal Europe: when the larger armies depart, the law comes again to reside in the trigger finger, or in the authority of certain warlords with sectarian demons eating at them.

For all the fatalism and almost weird resilience of the Lebanese, the awful pageant of their land pains the imagination. It is a dance of death. It expresses a myth of ominous speculation. Lebanon comes to seem a model of postnuclear society: culture and law in rubble, the citizens withdrawing into tribes, into paranoia, darting from street to street, furtive, terrified, quick to kill.

The Start of a Plague Mentality

An epidemic of yellow fever struck Philadelphia in August 1793. Eyes glazed, flesh yellowed, minds went delirious. People died, not individually, here and there, but in clusters, in alarming patterns. A plague mentality set in. Friends recoiled from one another. If they met by chance, they did not shake hands but nodded distantly and hurried on. The very air felt diseased. People dodged to the windward of those they passed. They sealed themselves in their houses. The deaths went on, great ugly scythings. Many adopted a policy of savage self-preservation, all sentiment heaved overboard like ballast. Husbands deserted stricken wives, parents abandoned children. The corpses of even the wealthy were carted off unattended, to be shoveled under without ceremony or prayer. One-tenth of the population died before cold weather came in the fall and killed the mosquitoes.

The plague mentality is something like the siege mentality, only more paranoid. In a siege, the enemy waits outside the walls. In a plague or epidemic, he lives intimately within. Death drifts through human blood or saliva. It commutes by bug bite or kiss or who knows what. It travels in mysterious ways, and everything, everyone, becomes suspect: a toilet seat, a child's cut, an act of love. Life slips into science fiction. People begin acting like characters in the first reel of *The Invasion of the Body Snatchers*. They peer intently at one another as if to detect the telltale change, the secret lesion, the sign that someone has crossed over, is not himself anymore, but one of *them*, alien and lethal. In the plague mentality, one belongs either to the kingdom of life or to the kingdom of death. So the state of mind glints with a certain fanaticism. It is said that

when children saw the telltale sign during the Black Death in the fourteenth century, they sang "Ring around a rosie!" That meant they saw a
ring on the skin around a red spot that marked the onset of the Black
Death. "A pocket full of posies" meant the flowers one carried to mask
the ambient stench. The ditty ended in apocalypse: "All fall down." The
Black Death eventually took off half the population of Europe.

During the American Civil War, more soldiers died of typhoid than
died in battle. The epidemic of Spanish influenza in 1918–19 killed more
than 500,000 Americans. Before the Salk vaccine, nearly 600,000 Americans were infected by poliomyelitis, and 10 percent of them died. The
polio epidemic caused memorable summers of trauma, during which
swimming pools and shopping centers across the United States were
closed.

From a statistical point of view, AIDS is not yet a major plague. Still,
one begins to detect a plague mentality regarding the disease and those
who carry it. Paradoxically, homosexuals are both victims of the plague
mentality and themselves perpetrators of it. Because 73 percent of those
who have AIDS are homosexuals, the general populace tends to look with
suspicion on all homosexuals. Because the virus is transmitted by homosexual intercourse, homosexuals themselves bring to their intimate lives
a desperate wariness and paranoia.

The mentality was most evident last week in other quarters, among the
mothers of New York schoolchildren, for example. A plague mentality
results from ignorance and fear, but not in the way that is usually meant.
When medicine is ignorant about a lethal disease, then the only intelligent
approach, by mothers or anyone else, is to be fearful and intensely cautious. But, like a plague itself, a plague mentality seems an anachronism
in the elaborately doctored postindustrial United States. The discussion
in recent years has gone in the other direction: Has medicine got so good
that it is keeping people alive past their natural time? At a moment when
rock fans of the First World undertake to cure a biblical scourge like the
Ethiopian famine with twenty-four hours of music bounced off a satellite,
AIDS, implacable and thus far incurable, comes as a shock. It arrives
like a cannibal at the picnic and calmly starts eating the children.

Cancer used to be the most dreaded word to be uttered in a doctor's
office. But cancer no longer means a virtual sentence of death. AIDS
does. AIDS therefore sounds with a peculiar and absolute resonance in
our minds. It catches echoes of the voice of god and of nuclear doom.
AIDS carries significances that go beyond the numbers of those afflicted.

In many minds, AIDS is a kind of validation of Judeo-Christian morality. The virus is a terrible swift sword in the hand of God, a punishment for transgressions against his order. Thus the disease partakes, so to speak, of the prestige of the infinite. AIDS becomes a dramatically targeted refinement of the doctrine that all disease is a form of God's retribution upon fallen and sinful man. "Sickness is in fact the whip of God for the sins of many," said Cotton Mather. AIDS renews in many minds, sometimes in an almost unconscious way, questions of the problem of sin: Is there sin? Against whom? Against what? Is sex sometimes a sin? Why? And what kind of sex? And so on.

The psychological reaction to AIDS, apart from the real fears it engenders, represents a collision between the ordered world of religious faith—God presiding, Commandments in force—and a universe that appears indifferent to the Decalogue or the strictures of St. Paul, one in which a disease like AIDS, a "syndrome," is as morally indifferent as a hurricane: an event of nature. Beyond that argument, which itself now seems ancient, it is probable that in most minds a vague dread of the disease is accompanied by a sympathy for those afflicted. Sympathy, alas, is usually directly proportional to one's distance from the problem, and the sentiment will recede if the virus spreads and the sympathetic become the threatened.

In a way, AIDS suits the style of the late twentieth century. In possibly overheated fears, it becomes a death-dealing absolute loose in the world. Westerners for some years have consolidated their dreads, reposing them (if that is the word) in the Bomb, in the one overriding horror of nuclear holocaust. A fat and prosperous West is lounging next door to its great kaboom. It is both smug and edgy at the same time. Now comes another agent of doomsday, this one actually killing people and doubling the number of its victims every ten months as if to reverse the logic of Thomas Malthus. The prospect of nuclear holocaust may be terrible, but the mind takes certain perverse psychological comforts from it. It has not happened, for one thing. And if it does happen, it will be over in a flash. AIDS is much slower and smaller, and may not add up ultimately to a world-historical monster. But the bug has ambitions, and is already proceeding with its arithmetic. Meantime, science, which dreamed up the totalitarian nuke, now labors desperately to eradicate its sinister young friend.

Thinking Animal
Thoughts

The dogs would die anyway. They would be strays, caged in shelters, ready to be "put to sleep." The idea was that the Defense Department's new Wound Laboratory would pay about eighty dollars for each dog. When the time came for research to proceed, the dogs would be anesthetized with pentobarbital, suspended in nylon mesh slings and shot with a nine-millimeter Mauser from a distance of twelve or fifteen feet. The dogs would then be carried into a lab, and people studying to be military surgeons would examine the damage and learn something about gunshot wounds, which might some day save human lives on a battlefield.

It is a harsh moral configuration. The Wound Laboratory is perfectly designed to bring on a confrontation between the zealot and the omelet maker (the omelet maker being the one who always insists that you can't make an omelet without breaking a few eggs). The issue is framed exactly: animal life is forfeit to the potential gain of human life. An ironist would point out that the Wound Laboratory would put animals to death in order to perfect the human talent to make war—and that war is humanity's most dramatic bestiality, Inevitably, the idea of the Wound Laboratory received publicity, and it stirred up the fury of what is becoming one of the more aggressive American constituencies. The Defense Department decided that it would not start shooting dogs there until it had studied the question further.

The notion of an Animal Rights Movement can be faintly satirical, especially if it is seen as the *reductio ad absurdum* of other rights movements. It smacks of a slightly cross-eyed fanaticism that might have amused Dickens, of battle-axes who file class-action suits in behalf of canaries. The movement has its truncheon rhetoric. Its ungainly equivalent of racism and sexism is "speciesism." Just as there is the male chauvinist pig, there presumably must be (so to speak) the human chauvinist pig.

But the animal rights issue has developed a peculiar power. Although a candidate running on an animal liberation ticket might provoke witticisms about dark horses and fat cats, he or she would receive a respectably serious share of popular sympathy, if not of the popular vote. It is not some revolution that has suddenly come to critical mass, but it is there, a presence.

The situation of animals stirs people in a profound way that is sometimes difficult to explain. Thoreau wrote, "It often happens that a man is more humanely related to a cat or a dog than to any human being." Sometimes the love of animals bespeaks an incapacity for the more complicated business of loving people; mental patients who react to other humans with fear and loathing can develop calm, tender relationships with puppies. Animals are usually perfectly themselves, not the elaborately perverse psychological mysteries that people seem to become. Animals, if not rabid, have a certain emotional reliability. But being on the side of the animals does not always make one a good guy. It is wise, when beginning a discussion of the subject, to remember that Hitler was a vegetarian.

And yet the matter of animals and their claims in the world is morally fascinating. What are animals for? What is the point of animals? To ask such questions is mere speciesism, of course. The human race walks around enveloped in an aura of narcissism that would be laughable to any other animal bright enough to appreciate it. Privileged to possess presumably the highest, undoubtedly the dominant intelligence on the planet, humans assume that the rest of creation was provided for their convenience. But people are not merely predators with a taste for meat. The relationship between humans and animals is deep and primitive and ambiguous, both violent and sometimes deeply loving. People admire some animals, and shoot them precisely because they admire them. They wish to kill the tiger to take on his powers, to kill the deer to feel some deep, strange beauty in the deed, a fatal oneness. People fear some animals and devour others.

One medical theorist, Dr. Paul D. MacLean, has suggested that when a man lies down on a psychiatrist's couch, a horse and a crocodile lie down beside him. People, according to MacLean's theory, have not one but three brains: neomammalian (the human), paleomammalian (the horse), and reptilian (the crocodile). Certain primitive tribesmen make no distinction between human and animal life but assume that all life is roughly the same. It simply takes up residence in different forms, different bodies. Higher cultures do not make that organic assumption; they are haunted by the animal in man, by the idea of animals as their lower nature, the fallen part, the mortal. The clear blue intelligence of civilization, they think, is imprisoned in the same cell, the body, with its Caliban, the brute undermind.

That assumption is a bit of a slander upon the animal kingdom, of course. It arises from an egocentric and spiritually complicated habit of mankind. People use animals not only for food and clothing and scientific experiment and decoration and companionship, but also, most profoundly, for furnishing the human mind with its myths. Victor Hugo wrote, "Animals are nothing but the forms of our virtues and vices, wandering before our eyes, the visible phantoms of our souls." We become those elaborately varied creatures, we take their forms. Odysseus' companions were transformed into swine, but in the metamorphosis, their intelligence remained human, unaffected. In reality, when men are transformed into beasts, for whatever reason (anger, greed, lust, drugs), their intelligence is usually very much affected, for the worse. Unlike Odysseus' men, they keep their human forms but assume the character of beasts.

Animals, being so specifically themselves, so characteristic, have always been a powerful source of metaphor with which to describe human behavior. The lion is courage. The bull is strength. Christian allegory codified creatures and thus abstracted them: the hyena was impurity, the deer was the Christian longing for immortality, the pelican was redemption. Animals inhabit every corner of human fantasy and literature. They come bounding up out of the subconscious like tigers in a child's nightmare. They come in the form of snakes in Eden and albatrosses and white whales and in other forms purely fanciful, like dragons and unicorns.

Human beings sometimes have difficulty seeing animals dispassionately and according them the dignity of an objective existence. Animals tend to be either embodiments of ideas and phantasms or else cellophaned food units. As there is a can of soup, so there is a leg of lamb. The mind does not linger on what the leg of lamb used to be attached to or the messy process by which it was detached and turned into groceries. The technique, both physically and psychologically, is one of dissociation.

The lamb that owned that leg had life once. The issue of animal rights poses the complicated question of why one life—the lamb's, for example, or that of the dog destined for the Wound Laboratory—should be sacrificed for the nourishment or medical interest of another life, that of a human being. Every year research of one kind or another kills more than sixty million animals, including 161,000 dogs and 47,000 monkeys. Many of them die in the cause of presumably worthy medical study. Animal rights people become more militant when they ask questions about some other experiments: Why should rabbits be killed, for example, by having a new mascara tested on their eyes?

If human beings assume that they were created in the image of God, it is not difficult for them to see the vast and qualitative distance between themselves and the lesser orders of creation. The Bible teaches that man has dominion over the fish of the sea, the fowl of the air, the cattle, and every creeping thing. Perhaps the rise of the animal rights movement is a symptom of a more secular and self-doubting spirit (although that could not be said of another animal lover, St. Francis of Assisi).

The human difference is known, to some, as the immortal soul, an absolute distinction belonging to man and woman alone, not to the animal. The soul is the human pedigree—and presumably the dispensation to slay and eat any inferior life that crosses the path. But in a secular sense, how is human life different from animal life? Intelligence? Some pygmy chimps and even lesser creatures are as intelligent as, say, a severely retarded child: if it is not permissible to kill a retarded child, why kill the animals? Self-awareness? Some creatures, such as chimpanzees, notice themselves in the mirror: others, such as dogs, do not. Laughter? (Max Eastman said that dogs laugh, but they laugh with their tails.) Conscience? The gift of abstract thought? An institutional memory that permits them to record experience and develop upon it, generation upon generation?

Descartes said that animals are mere "machines." If that is true, dropping a lobster into a pot of boiling water is about the same as dropping in an automobile transmission. The question of how to treat animals, how to think about them, usually revolves around the mystery of what animal consciousness is like. Is it all mere surface, pure eyeball and animal reflex, season and hunger and adrenal spurts of terror or breeding lust, a dumb, brute, oblivious ritual of the genes? Researchers occasionally find disconcerting evidence that animals are capable of unexpected intellectual feats, like the chimps at the Yerkes Regional Primate Research Center at Emory University who are learning a form of language. In any case, it may be risky for human beings to insist too much on the criterion of self-awareness; people are fairly oblivious themselves. Socrates said that the unexamined life is not worth living. If that is true, half the world's population should be suicidal.

But even if the lobster feels no pain in the pot, or the steer is just a dumb brute lumbering into the abattoir, they do have life. The offense against them—if there is one—is not essentially the pain we inflict upon them, but the fact that we deprive them of life. Albert Schweitzer constructed many saintly paragraphs about "reverence for life." He would lift an earthworm from a parched pavement and place it tenderly on the grass: he would work in the stuffy atmosphere of a shuttered room rather than risk the danger that a moth might immolate itself in his lamp.

The rest of the race is not so fastidious. The world has its hierarchy of tooth and claw, that savage orderliness one watched as a child in Disney nature films, all those gulping, disgusting ingestions by which the animal kingdom proceeds on its daily rounds. It is a slaughterous ripping, the hunt and kill, that is also somehow dreamy and abstract. The big fish eat the little fish, and the folks eat the chickens. Various living things are destined to perish in the jaws of others, and the best that our civilization has been able to do is to draw the line at cannibalism. "Nature is no sentimentalist," Emerson wrote. "Providence has a wild, rough, incalculable road to its end, and it is of no use to whitewash its huge, mixed instrumentalities, or to dress up that terrific benefactor in a clean shirt and white neckcloth of a student in divinity."

The Animals of Africa

Africa

The animals stand motionless in gold-white grasses—zebras and impala, Thomson's gazelles and Cape buffalo and hartebeests and waterbuck and giraffes, and wildebeests by the thousands, all fixed in art naïf, in a smiting equatorial light. They stand in the shadowless clarity of creation.

Now across the immense African landscape, from the distant escarpment, a gray-purple rainstorm blows. It encroaches upon the sunlight, moving through the air like a dark idea. East Africa has a genius for such moments. Wildlife and landscape here have about them a force of melodrama and annunciation. They are the book of Genesis enacted as an afternoon dream.

In Amboseli, under the snow-covered dome of Mount Kilimanjaro, a herd of elephants moves like a dense gray cloud, slow motion, in lumbering solidity: a mirage of floating boulders. Around them dust devils rise spontaneously out of the desert, little tornadoes that swirl up on the thermals and go jittering and rushing among the animals like evil spirits busy in the primal garden.

Later, in the sweet last light of the afternoon, a lion prowls in lion-colored grasses and vanishes into the perfect camouflage—setting off for the hunt, alert, indolent, and somehow abstracted, as cats are. A rhinoceros disappears: the eye loses it among gray boulders and thorn trees. The rhino becomes a boulder.

To the human eye, the animals so often seem mirages: now you see them, now you don't. Later, just after dusk, Abyssinian nightjars discover the magic wash of the headlight beams. The birds flit in and out of the barrels of light, like dolphins frisking before a boat's prow. The Land

---

267

Cruiser jostles, in four-wheel drive, across black volcanic stones toward the camp, the driver steering by the distant light-speck of the cooking fire.

And then the African night, which, more than elsewhere, seems an abnegation of the conscious world. MMBA, "miles and miles of bloody Africa," and it all falls into black magic void.

The world stills, for the longest time. Then, at the edge of sleep, hyenas come to giggle and whoop. Peering from the tent flap, one catches in the shadows their sidelong criminal slouch. Their eyes shine like evil flashlight bulbs, a disembodied horror-movie yellow, phosphorescent, glowing like the children of the damned. In the morning, one finds their droppings: white dung, like a photographic negative. Hyenas not only eat the meat of animals but grind up and digest the bones. The hyenas' dung is white with the calcium of powdered bones.

Africa has its blinding clarities and its shadows. The clarities proclaim something primal, the first days of life. The shadows lie at the other extreme of time: in the premonition of last days, of extinction. Now you see the animals. Soon, perhaps, you won't.

Africa is comprehensive: great birth, great death, the beginning and the end. The themes are drawn, like the vivid, abstract hide of the zebra, in patterns of the absolute.

The first question to ask is whether the wildlife of Africa can survive.

The second question is this: If the wild animals of Africa vanish from the face of the earth, what, exactly, will have been lost?

The Africa of the animals is a sort of dream kingdom. Carl Jung traveled to East Africa in 1925 and wrote of a "most intense sentiment of returning to the land of my youth," of a "recognition of the immemorially known." Africa, he said, had "the stillness of the eternal beginning."

Earliest man lived in these landscapes, among such animals, among these splendid trees that have personalities as distinct as those of the animals: the aristocratic flat-topped acacia, the gnarled and magisterial baobab. Possibly scenes from that infancy are lodged in some layer of human memory, in the brilliant but preconscious morning.

While visiting Africa I decided to ask people about the way that animals come to them in dreams. My five-year-old son in New York City has nightmares about animals he has never seen. He dreams, for instance, of lions. What does an African boy dream about? I collected dreams from Masai and Kikuyu schoolchildren, from schoolteachers, from witch doctors, from Masai warriors and safari guides, from white ranchers and game catchers and naturalists, and from myself. It was a way of seeing the animals.

The Masai elder sat in the Lord Delamere Restaurant in the Norfolk Hotel in Nairobi and explained that all animals are left-handed. It is true, said the elder, named Moses. Never get onto a lion's left side. A lion attacks to his left. All animals instinctively lead with the left paw, the left hoof, the left horn. Even cows are left-handed, said Moses.

The Masai are pastoralists who have always lived among the wild animals, lived amicably enough, with some violent exceptions that come with the territory. Moses lives in the remote Loita Hills in southwestern Kenya. On this day he wore his Nairobi clothes: two sweatshirts, one over the other, and dark trousers and sneakers. There were holes in his earlobes where ornaments might fit, but they were austerely empty. Handsome, thoughtful, impassive, answering questions like a visiting lecturer, Moses conjured up wild animals. His gaze was sleepy and distant.

On the table Moses demonstrated how the rhinoceros thinks. He used the saltshaker to represent the American visitor, me. The pepper shaker would be the rhino. The sugar bowl would be the boulder that stood between them. "Be careful," Moses warned. He moved the rhino in an ominous drift to its left. The rhino began to circle the sugar bowl, using the bowl as cover in order to ambush the saltshaker (me) from behind. I became a naked and oblivious wanderer on the white linen plain. I stood frozen and defenseless as the rhino came on.

"Rhino will always go to the left, like this," said Moses softly. He knocked down the saltshaker with a sharp crack of the pepper shaker, like a chess master toppling the king. I went down. White grains of salt spilled out of the holes in the top of my head, and I expired on the flat white linen. The expanse of tablecloth had become for an instant dangerous, in a surreal way. I had been run down by a pepper shaker from the Pleistocene in a restaurant named for the paramount white colonial of British East Africa, Lord Delamere (1870–1931).

I did not believe Moses' left-handed-animal theory. Perhaps Moses meant it to be mere entertainment. I could not be sure, but gave way to it anyhow. I shook my head in appreciation, my mind for the moment numb and hospitable and superstitious. It had ripped across time zones for twenty-three hours, across the Atlantic Ocean and the breadth of Africa, and had dropped out of the sky into Nairobi. It was dislocated. My soul vibrated. I thought of a soap bubble's elongation when its iridescent membrane is drawn swiftly through the air by a child. My soul began now to float slow-motion in the strange, bright medium of Africa. I felt suspended, drifting through layers of time.

The Africans run Kenya now. Lord Delamere's dream of an African "white man's country" ended twenty-four years ago with black independence. From other tables in the Lord Delamere Restaurant came the low music of Swahili, like a dark stream of syllables rushing over rocks. I heard both the deep molten music and the undersong of baby talk that bubbles through Swahili, the lingua franca that came up from the coast with the Arab slavers.

Moses in his tutorial passed on now to the subject of lions. He told about how he had killed a lion in the Loita Hills not many days before. He and another Masai were herding cattle in the upland pastures. A lion sprang at his friend and clawed him on the shoulder. Moses came running and drew the lion away from the other man. The lion charged Moses, and when the animal was six feet distant, Moses hurled his spear. The spear went into the lion's left eye and crashed through its brain. The animal came to rest at Moses' feet. It was the sixth lion that Moses had killed in his twenty-nine years.

There was trouble with the authorities after that. The rangers came and told Moses he could not kill a lion because it is against the law in Kenya to kill one. "I told them, 'The lion attacked my friend!' They said, 'You should have reported the attack first and asked for a permit to kill the lion.' " In the Lord Delamere Restaurant, Moses threw back his head and laughed, and cried, with an oddly Yiddish intonation, "Ai-yi-yi-yi-yi!"

Moses was asked about a Masai child's dreams. "I do not know what a Masai child has nightmares about," he said. "I will tell you what my bad dreams are about. I have bad dreams about Nairobi, and bright lights and speeding cars and lorries crashing. And all the noise of a thousand radios playing." He made a face and clutched his head: "All of that noise crashing out of the air!" Then, "Ai-yi-yi-yi-yi!" In the Loita Hills, said Moses, "we sing, but we sing without instruments. It makes some sense."

Many of the paved roads in Kenya are crumbling. They look as if a large tar-eating animal had been chewing at them from the shoulders, inward toward the center line. A vehicle therefore speeds demonically down the dead center of a two-lane road, like a rhino charging. The driver waits until the last instant to flick the steering wheel to the left (British rules, drive on the left—Did Moses derive the left-handed theory from that?) to swerve around the onrushing bus. The wildest animal on the road is the *matatu,* a jitney designed to carry about eight passengers. Instead, it customarily holds twenty Africans or more, some spilling out the back door, hanging on with one arm. The *matatu* is a hurtling metal beast with people in its belly, an event of nature on the highways. "Aieee! Aieee! *Matatu!" Matatu* owners have a witty taste for apocalypse. One of them named his *matatu* the *Enola Gay.* Another proclaims itself the *Stairway to Heaven.* Not reassuring.

Dreaming: Shirley Strum says that there came a time when the baboons spoke to her in English. They came to her in her dreams and asked for her help. For twelve years Strum, an anthropologist from California, had been studying a baboon troop at a ranch called Kekopey, near Gilgil. Then the ranch was turned into an agricultural collective, and the new farmers menaced the baboons and tried to kill them off.

The baboons were Strum's friends. She had given all of them names, and she sat among them every day. They were accustomed to her and accepted her. She came among them like a ghostly premonition of their evolutionary future, a benevolent spirit out of the time warp, another civilization. She came from space. She sat among them, holding her clipboard, and made silent notes.

Strum understood the dangers of anthropomorphism, of coming to love the animals too much and to hate the people endangering them. Strum, the least violent of creatures, said that if she had had a gun, she might have shot the farmers who were threatening her baboons. Now, in Shirley Strum's dreams, the baboons asked her for help, and she searched for a ranch that would accept them. The ranchers mostly thought she was insane. Baboons raid crops. Importing baboons to a ranch made as much sense as transplanting cockroaches to a New York City apartment. But at last Strum made an arrangement with the Chololo Ranch on the edge of the Laikipia Plateau north of Nairobi. She had the baboons trapped and sedated and brought to a new home where they would be safe, and she went on silently studying them.

"Watching the baboons is like watching a soap opera," Strum says, "except that the baboons are much nicer people than you see on *Dallas* or *Dynasty.*" I walk out with Strum among the baboons at eight A.M. in Laikipia. They are feeding on the buds of an acacia tree not far from the granite kopje where they sleep. Strum knows all the baboons. "That is C.J. and Ron," she begins. "The female is Zilla. C.J. and Ron have a conflict of emotions." Ron is new to the troop, and so is Ndofu.

Baboon life, says Strum, is an endless series of negotiations. The drama of their lives revolves not around sex or male intimidation but around alliances, around friendships. Baboons have a Japanese complexity of deferences and dominances. They live, it seems to a newcomer, in a constant state of distracted tension, as if caught in an elastic web of attractions and repulsions, a web constantly in motion, in adjustment of distances. I study their hands, which are so human, so adept and articulate that they could be trained for neurosurgery, if good hands were all that a neurosurgeon needed.

Now a magic evening light comes across the Laikipia Plateau, and the baboons straggle in from their day's browsings among the acacia flowers. They sit and socialize on the lower rocks of their high kopje, grooming one another with a sweet absorption, playing with their babies. Like almost everyone and everything in Africa, they seem profoundly tribal. Another troop of baboons arrives, a hundred yards away, and each tribe stares at the other with a nervous intensity across the lovely evening light.

It is time to begin the six-hour drive from Nairobi to Moses' *enk'ang* (small village) in the Loita Hills. The Land Cruiser travels for three hours over paved road to the dusty frontier town of Narok, then follows a rutted washboard road across an empty and chokingly dusty plain until it shifts into four-wheel drive and begins the slow climb up into the hills. It is lovely in the hills. They look somewhat like the Sangre de Cristo Mountains of New Mexico. Part of their beauty is their pristine remoteness. One rarely encounters a white man there.

I came first to the *enk'ang* of Moses' older brother Joseph, who, surrounded by children and dogs and friends, strode out from the *boma*—a tall thorn-and-cedar enclosure, the feudal African fortress against lions and leopards—to meet me. Joseph was smaller and more delicately boned than Moses. He had the fine, intelligent head of a Talmudic scholar, I decided, an Ethiopian head, a fastidious head, given to complex distinctions. Joseph and I set out in the evening light to walk across the hills to Moses' *boma*. Joseph wore a handsome red blanket hung over his shoulder like a toga and, oddly, a suede golf cap that suited him well. He was barefoot, his feet tough and thick as they trod upon rocks and twigs and thorns and dung indifferently.

I asked Joseph if there were any wild animals close by. He did not carry a spear just now, only a thin wand of olive wood. The spear was not necessary at this time of day between *bomas,* Joseph explained. People passed back and forth; the lions would stay away.

Joseph talked, when asked, about the Masai diet. Milk, tea. Some maize. Goat or beef on special occasions. Do the Masai ever eat the wild animals? Joseph answered, "Sometimes we eat the gazelle, because the gazelle is close to God."

Joseph's accent had a strange geographical range, with pronunciations in English that sounded as if they had come from either India or Germany. *God* came out sounding like the German *Gott.*

I (the roundheel quester from America) gave a sigh of discovery. "Ah." Long pause.

"Are there other animals that the Masai consider to be close to God?" I had decided, in vague tracery, that the gazelle's grace was associated in the Masai mind with God's grace, a profound though punning link, and that by eating of the flesh of the gazelle, the Masai thought to partake of the grace of God. A pagan chinking of the altar bells, a transubstantiation.

I walked on through the hills, my hands behind me, like an abbot. Then I glanced up at Joseph and saw that the elder was looking at me in consternation.

"Close to God?" asked Joseph.

"You said the gazelle is close to God," I prompted. Something in Joseph detonated minutely, and then he waved it off with a snort.

"Oh, no! I said that we eat gazelle because it is close to goat! The gazelle tastes like goat! We like goat!"

Gott and goat. It was a lesson learned. East Africans see no spiritual significance in the animals, even though each of the Masai clans claims an unsentimental relationship with one animal or another.

Llewelyn Powys, a young English poet, came out to settle in Kenya early in the century. He wrote that Africa was a "country frequented by clawed creatures with striped and gilded pelts, where nettles sting like wasps and even moles are as large as water rats. . . . The sun, naked as when it was born, sucks out one's life blood, and nourishes savagery long since made dormant by the pious lives of one's ancestors. Kill! Kill! Kill! is the mandate of Africa."

A drowsing lioness at midday stirs in the grasses under a flat-topped acacia tree. She yawns, and her mouth is an abrupt vision of medieval horrors, of ripping white spikes. And then the mouth closes and she is a smug, serene Victorian dowager. She complacently surveys her young, who sleep nearby, and subsides again into her torpor.

Sometimes it seems that there are no straight lines in Africa or that Africa at any rate resists them. Things curve and undulate: the landscape, the rivers, the gaits of the animals, the design of the *enk'ang,* the trajectory of the spear (although the spear itself is straight). Logic is also curved. At the same time everything in Africa seems sharp and pointed, given to punctures and ripping. It is a land of teeth and thorns. The whistling-thorn acacia has spikes that can penetrate a six-ply tire.

It is easy to fall in love not only with the shapes and colors of the animals but with their motions, their curving and infinitely varied gaits. The zebra moves with a strong, short-muscled stride. It is a sleek, erotic beast with vigorous bearing. The zebra's self-possession is a likable trait. It is human habit to sort the animals almost immediately into orders of preference. The animals are arranged in people's minds as a popularity contest. Some animals are endearing, and some repulsive. One wants to see the lion first, and then the elephant and after that the leopard, then rhino . . . and so on. One wants to see some animals because they are fierce, and some because they are lovable and soft. It is hard to explain the attractions and preferences. It is possible that human feelings about wild animals reflect the complexities of sexual attractions. Certain animals are admired for their majestic aggressions, and others for softer qualities. The lion is a sleek piece of violence, the waterbuck a sweet piece of grace.

Some of the animals move in deep slow motion, as if traversing another medium, previous to air, and thicker—an Atlantis of time. The elephant goes sleeping that way across the spaces. The medium through which it moves can be seen as time itself, a thicker, slower time than humans inhabit, a prehistoric metabolism. The giraffe goes with undulous slow motion, a long waving that starts with the head and proceeds dreamily, curving down the endless spine. The giraffe is motion as process through time. It is delicate, intelligent, and eccentric, and as Karen Blixen said, so much a lady. Each of the animals has its distinct gait. The Grant's gazelle's tail never stops switching, like a nervous windshield wiper. The hartebeest moves off, when startled, in an undulous hallumph.

For days in Masai Mara, I watched the wildebeests. Ungainly and pewter colored, they are subject to sudden electric jolts of panic, to adrenal bursts of motion that can make them seem half crazed as a tribe. Now they were engaged not so much in migration as in vagrancy, wandering across the plain on strange but idiotically determined vectors. Wildebeests smell monsters on the afternoon breeze, take sudden fear and bolt for Tanzania or Uganda or the Indian Ocean, anywhere to get away.

Sometimes, of course, the monsters are there. The veldt is littered with the corpses that the lion or cheetah has killed and dined on. But sometimes the herding wildebeests seem to be caught in a collective shallow madness. A fantasy of terror shoots through a herd, and all the beasts are gone: hysteria of hooves. The wildebeests thunder by the thousands across rivers and plains, moving like a barbarian invasion. They follow their instinct for the rains, for better grass. And they mow the grass before them. If they know where rain is, the wildebeests are relentless. Otherwise, they march with an undirected rigor, without destination, like cadets on punishment, beating a trail in the parade ground. The wildebeest's bison-like head is too large for its body, its legs too thin and ungainly. It looks like a middle-aged hypochondriac, paltry in the loins and given to terrible anxiety attacks, the sort of creature whose hands (if it had hands) would always be clammy. God's genius for design may have faltered with the wildebeest.

In Masai Mara, vultures wheel dreamily in the air, like a slow-motion tornado of birds. Below the swirling funnel, a cheetah has brought down a baby wildebeest. The cheetah, loner and fleet aristocrat, the upper-class version of the hyena, has opened up the wildebeest and devoured the internal organs. The cheetah's belly is swollen and its mouth is ringed with blood as it breathes heavily from the exertion of gorging. A dozen vultures flap down to take their turn. They wait twenty yards away, then waddle in a little toward the kill to test the cheetah. The cheetah, in a burst, rushes the vultures to drive them off, and then returns to the baby wildebeest. The vultures grump and readjust their feathers and wait their turn, the surly lumpen-carrion class.

The skeleton of an elephant lies out in the grasses near a baobab tree and a scattering of black volcanic stones. The thick-trunked, gnarled baobab gesticulates with its branches, as if trying to summon help. There are no tusks lying among the bones, of course; ivory vanishes quickly in East Africa. The elephant is three weeks dead. Poachers. Not far away, a baby elephant walks alone. That is unusual. Elephants are careful mothers and do not leave their young unattended. The skeleton is the mother, and the baby is an orphan.

One day in Meru, the Land Cruiser glides through the lion-colored grasses. It is late afternoon, and lions everywhere are rising from their long day's slumber to think about hunting. The driver, a Masai named

Simeon K. Londaga, sees the lion and stops and points. Poking my head like a periscope through the roof of the Cruiser, I follow the line of Simeon's finger and get lost out there in the grasses. I squint as if dialing my eyes to better focus, as if trying to build the platonic lion out of grass. Still the lion will not come. The beast is hidden in the grass like the number in the dot test for color blindness. Rake your gaze into the grass again, staring deeply into it, and slowly the scene develops like a Polaroid picture, taking color and form. The eyes discover that they are staring straight, deeply, into the eyes of a lion—only the eyes. And the lion is staring straight and deeply back. The eyes in the grass are yellow-black eyes, cat's eyes, emitting rays of measurement and judgment and hunger. "Only you, *mzungu!*" say the eyes. *Mzungu* is Swahili for white man. I feel the chill of a savage attention. At last the Polaroid develops itself fully. The lion turns and lies in full view, spreading the beige grass and lying precisely in the posture of the woman in the grass in Andrew Wyeth's painting *Christina's World*. The grasses in Wyeth's dream and the grasses garnishing the lion have the same color and texture. But whereas Wyeth's Christina was crippled and lay in an unforgettable posture of longing, of groping, the lion, his hindquarters lazing off on one side, is a masterwork of indolent power. All utterly what he was, all lion.

One night around a fire inside the *boma,* Moses recounted some of his dreams. In one of them, he runs up a ravine with steep rock walls on three sides, pursued by a rhino. He claws at the rock walls, trying to escape, hanging by his fingertips. He wakes up screaming. In another dream, a lion is dragging Moses through deep grass. Moses desperately clutches at the grass with his fingers, but the grass comes up in clumps, and Moses is dragged on.

One afternoon Moses and I went to the Morijo Loita Primary School, a windswept arrangement of tin-roofed buildings on a bare hillside a few miles from Moses' *boma.* Several dozen schoolchildren were gathered in a classroom of the sort that made me think of the places where Abraham Lincoln went to school on the Indiana frontier. The children sat in rows at long crude benches. They were asked about their encounters with the wild animals, in reality and in dreams. A boy named Seketo told of being chased by a lion once while he was herding cows. But he said normally when a boy meets a wild animal, the solution is simple: the boy runs one way and the animal runs another, and both are happy.

In dreams, the children were paralyzed by fright. A girl named Hyinka dreamed that when she went into the forest for firewood, a Cape buffalo attacked her and tried to push her down with his horns. She could neither run nor scream. The buffalo pushed her into the water with his nose. Memusi had a dream about a lion's attacking and biting, and she tried to scream but could not. Lekerenka could not scream, either, when bitten in his dreams by a spitting cobra. He woke up crawling on the ground.

I conceived a modest theory about dreams. The difference between the Kenya nightmares and the scary dreams of a five-year-old boy in New York City might be that the beasts of primal fantasy live just outside the Masai huts. The Masai reside, so to speak, in the psychic forest, where the wild things are. The beasts there were not invented by an illustrator. They are the originals. The lion roars in the Masai's sleep, and roars when the Masai awakes as well.

So to some extent, the world inside the skull corresponds to the world outside it, an interesting reconciliation. The inner eye and the outer eye may sometimes see the same image, the same dreamy beast standing under the fever tree. The sleeping and the waking become interchangeable. The actual and the psychic coincide.

The pen where Moses and his family kept their goats at night was covered with a grid of heavy wire. When I wondered about it, Moses explained, "Leopard comes at night to take the goat." Around every Masai *enk'ang* is built a sturdy fence of thorn and cedar to keep the lions out. One day, walking in the forest, Moses shouldered an enormous slab of cedar to add to his *boma*. "The lion makes me do a lot of work," he remarked. Sometimes the barricades do not hold, and the Masai wake to the bawl and crashing of cattle as the lion struggles to carry off his beef.

Reality and dreams dance round to bite each other. One night when Joseph was still a boy, he and his friend dreamed the same dream, about a leopard attacking the calves. "We both woke up at the same time, screaming and fighting the leopard," Joseph said. "We both roared like the leopard, and then the whole *boma* woke up screaming"—shouting about the leopard the boys had seen—but had seen only in their dreams. And in the morning, by the goats' pen, the people found leopard tracks. "You know," said Joseph thoughtfully. "There *are* scary animals. And they eat people. Sometimes people never learn to be brave, and even as old men, they are still afraid."

One afternoon in the Loita Hills, there were three Masai warriors, called *ilmurran,* sitting in the shade beside a dung-walled hut. Their hair was long and greased with fat. They were barefoot and wore only the *shuka,* a bright-patterned piece of cloth, like a tablecloth, draped as a short toga around waist and shoulders. Their spears leaned against the wall of the hut, with their *rungu*—knob-ended clubs that the Masai can throw with a fierce accuracy. One of the warriors, named David, spoke halting English. He was about twenty years old, although the Masai pay little attention to precise ages, since a boy's real life does not start until he is circumcised in mid-adolescence and thereby, with great ceremony, becomes a man.

David translated for the others. David said that, yes, the warriors still obeyed Masai tradition by raiding other tribes for cattle. The Masai believe that in the beginning, God (*Enkai*) bestowed all the world's cattle upon the Masai. Therefore, when Masai warriors go down into Tanzania to raid a Kuria village and steal cows, they are merely taking back what already belongs to them.

How is a cattle raid carried out? "We come at dusk to the Kuria village," David said, "and make a lot of noise. There is a big fight, with spears, with bows and arrows. I have lost friends in raids, and think I have killed six or seven Kuria, although I cannot be sure because we leave quickly. We do not wait to see if they are dead. We take the cows away and drive them all night so we can be across the border in the morning when the army might come to start looking for us."

The government has often tried to domesticate the Masai, to get them to give up the path of the warrior. Some years ago, a colonial district officer named Clarence Buxton decided to try to substitute manly sports for cattle raiding. He conceived the idea of encouraging Masai warriors to play polo while mounted on donkeys. The plan did not go far.

The government forbids long hair and warrior business and lion hunting, but it is a huge country, and sometimes the government can manage to be only wistfully authoritarian.

I asked one of the warriors, "Is it easier to kill a man or a lion?"

The young man immediately answered, "Easier to kill a lion."

Why?

"It is hard to fight a man, because he is as clever as you are. He has arrows and a spear. He is as tricky as you are. And besides, a person has friends, and if you kill him, his friends can kill you! It is more complicated."

The young warrior is asked his name and replies, "Lord Delamere." His parents had named him Lord Delamere. I tear a page out of my notebook and walk thirty yards away and place the paper on the ground, weighed down by a stone. His lordship is asked to demonstrate his accuracy with a spear. Lord Delamere shrugs and stands and hurls his spear, impaling the blank page. I ask to borrow the spear so that I might try. Alas, I do not straighten my arm, as in a javelin throw, but start the motion somewhere behind my right ear, as if throwing a fastball. The spear sails up, too high, and at the apex, points straight skyward, and then collapses in the air, subsiding downward on its butt, ignominiously, like one of the early failed rockets from Cape Canaveral. Lord Delamere would not wish to hunt lion with the American.

That night, while sleeping inside Moses' *boma* in the Loita Hills, I dreamed that I raided cattle on West 57th Street in Manhattan. I loaded four stolen cows into a cattle trailer towed by an old Chrysler Imperial and drove them up across the Connecticut border.

Fifty Somali poachers armed with automatic weapons came nosing around the rhino refuge at Lewa Downs. "But we put out the message that if they came in, a few of them would have to die along with us," says Anna Merz. Under the driver's seat in her car, she carries a spike-headed club. She is not licensed to carry a gun, but she employs guards with old Enfield rifles to patrol her fenced-in 7,500-acre refuge, where approximately sixteen rhinos live.

"Poor buggers!" says Merz, talking about her rhinos. Her eyes now flash bright indignation. "It is a sin and a crime that animals should be driven to the brink of extinction, especially by something as idiotic as a dagger handle!" The situation of the rhino is bleak. In 1970 there were 20,000 of them in Kenya. Now there are considerably fewer than 500. It strikes me that Merz's rhinos live like a child kept in a germ-free bubble because of some defect in the immune system. The germs are the poachers. With rhino horns worth about $65,000 each now, to be sold for use as medicines in the Orient or as dagger handles in North Yemen, Anna Merz has about one million dollars stomping around inside her fences.

Merz, an Englishwoman who has lived in Africa much of her life, began the refuge two years ago. A sign at the front gate reads ALL RIGHTS RESERVED FOR RHINOS. She is now raising an orphaned baby rhino named Samia, almost two years old and up to about five hundred pounds. Merz tenderly caresses her and calls her "my darling." Samia, feeling frolicsome, knocks Merz over into the mud. Merz rises, muddy and laughing, and prehistoric Samia knocks her over again. Once again, Merz laughs.

I thought of a passage of bully rhetoric in Theodore Roosevelt's *African*

Game Trails, the record of his 1909 safari. The rhino, wrote Roosevelt, "seemed what he was, a monster surviving over from the world's past, from the days when the beasts of the prime ran riot in their strength, before man grew so cunning of brain and hand as to master them."

Hugh Lamprey, of the World Wildlife Fund, flies in to Merz's sanctuary that morning to ask her to accept another baby rhino, which was just orphaned by poachers in the Masai Mara. Lamprey is a mandarin who urbanely calls down apocalypse in a voice that sounds the way the finest, oldest brandy tastes. I privately bestow a title upon him: the Duke of Extinction.

The duke speaks of many things African and animal, and warns at the end of each paragraph that such things should not be written about because publicity is fatal. Now you see the duke. Now you don't. He concludes with a flourish of suave obliteration, "If there was one species you could remove to the benefit of the earth, it would be man." Among the animal lovers, it is not unusual to encounter that misanthropic streak. The animal lovers seem to feel themselves to be just as besieged as the animals are.

Sometimes, when talking to the older Kenya whites, people who had been around in the colonial days and stayed on after independence, I caught the vibration of a nostalgia so radical that it strained all the way back to the Pleistocene. They had no use for people anymore. They seemed to wish to cleanse the earth of the human stain, and restore it to preconscious innocence.

One night Moses announced a goat feast in honor of his visitors.

The goat was slaughtered outside the *boma* just after dusk. I held the flashlight. Young Olentwala did the killing. He threw the goat on its side and seized it by the muzzle with his right hand and placed his knee against the goat's throat and thus strangled it. Joseph said this was the kindest way, but I doubted it. It was done, anyway, rather tenderly. Joseph and Olentwala chatted easily in Ol' Maa as the goat spasmed and spasmed and spasmed, and at last expired.

Joseph borrowed my Swiss army knife. The moon came up, and Joseph, with an easy precision, relishing the job, began smooth surgery on the goat. He peeled away the hide from the clean inner sack. Halfway through that part of the operation, he and Olentwala leaned down and captured a pool of blood in a pocket of the hide, and drank deeply and loudly, slurping. After a draft, Joseph remembered his manners. He looked up from his drinking and offered me some fresh blood, which I declined.

The sky was now full of brilliant stars. Joseph was happy with his work. He squatted by the rich bag of goat and sliced it with the Swiss knife, working like a surgeon toward the animal's inner pleasures. After five minutes, he came to an item that looked like an enormous cold-remedy capsule. Joseph with great precision peeled away the skin of the capsule, and then took the bright red little salami of it and popped it in his mouth. He made a sound of relish. "Kidney," he explained. He gave the second kidney to Olentwala.

At last the goat was butchered up neatly in the flashlight beam and deposited on its own still wet inner hide. Joseph festively carried the meat into the *boma*. A good fire burned there, and he skewered the thighs and shoulder pieces, hanging them over the flames, and dumped the innards into boiling pots of water. Joseph and Moses took relish in the feast. Among the Masai, the goat was profoundly appreciated. It was a holiday. For the Masai the goat had died well.

Two mornings later, Moses came to the campfire just after breakfast. He looked grave. He led me to the hut where the Masai kept the baby goats at night, out of reach of leopards. Moses went inside and emerged with a baby goat in his arms. The goat was no more than a week old. It was thin and shaking, and its fur was wet and slick. The animal was clearly almost dead.

"What happened?" I asked.

Moses shook his head, wearing a look of elegant forbearance.

"The driver Davis did it," said Moses.

"Did what?"

"I don't know why. He said the goat had too many flies. He sprayed the goat with insect spray from the can, all over, and now the goat is poisoned and is going to die."

The cook kept a bug bomb near the kitchen hut to drive off flies. Davis seems to have been seized by a purifying impulse.

The flies that attend the Masai are sometimes overpowering. They come with the cattle and are a fact of life. Masai and flies live in symbiosis. Walking among the Masai, one keeps a forearm waving in front of the face like an irregular windshield wiper chasing off the densities of flies.

The Masai are a handsome and arrogant and elegant people, filled with a serene self-satisfaction that amounts to a collective narcissism. Whites in East Africa for generations have been infatuated with the Masai. Yet certain details of their lives, like the flies that sometimes cake their lips and eyelids, can be disgusting. The Masai dwell in the world's most magnificent spaces. Yet to stoop at midday to enter one of their dung-walled huts to share a cup of tea is to be plunged immediately into an impenetrable, claustrophobic gloom, choked with smoke. A laser beam of sunlight fires through the darkness from a window the size of a Kenya five-shilling piece. It takes three minutes for the eyes to adjust and make out the dim outlines of one's friends sitting on short stools, knees near their chins, their eyes fixed dreamily on the coals of the cooking fire, their ruminative conversation interrupted by long silences.

The driver Davis was a Luo from Lake Victoria, a hearty man of middle age with a smiling open face and the public manner of a gregarious bishop. Davis considered himself a Roman Catholic priest. Into a notebook that he always carried, he had inscribed the text of the Latin Mass, copied from a missal that he had borrowed somewhere in his travels. Davis sometimes donned a long white alb and, all by himself outside the *boma,* performed services beside his Land Rover, chanting the Latin in a rich bass.

The collision between Catholic faith and morals on the one hand and Masai tradition on the other is spectacular. Perhaps the flies had come to seem to Davis the outward sign of the devil's presence here in the Masai *enk'ang,* home of polygamists and breezy pagan fornicators. But the goat was an ancient symbol of the devil. The theology was confusing. Perhaps Davis merely intended to endow one fly-free little life in the dense air of the *boma.*

Davis was at his prayers next evening at dusk when the witch doctor came to speak to me. The witch doctor, Ole Loompirai, sat in a dark, dung-walled hut and drank beer with me and explained the work that he did. The *laibon,* or witch doctor, spoke in a low, murmurous voice in Maa, sucking frequently on an oversize bottle of Tusker, a faintly smoky Kenya beer brought up in the Land Cruiser from Narok. Moses impassively translated.

As the witch doctor talked about charms and animal sacrifices, Davis's rich, deep Latin poured through the small window of the hut: *"Pater noster qui es in coelis, sanctificetur nomen tuum . . ."* The *laibon* explained the uses of animals in his work. He employed the warthog, for example, to cast a spell to keep the government out of Masai business. Good choice, I thought. The warthog is a strutty little beast, a short-legged peasant with a thin tail that stands straight up like a flagpole when it runs. It backs into its hole and pulls dirt on top of itself and, if cornered there, comes out of the hole like a cannonball. Perfect for ambushing bureaucrats.

The *laibon* used a Dik-dik, that small lovely antelope, to thwart some-one's plans. It works thus: he places charms upon the animal and then releases it in the direction of the person who is the target of the spell. For help with childbirth, he drapes the skin of an eland on the woman— the eland being much like the cow, which possesses magic powers. In order to bring rain, the *laibon* places a dead frog on the ground, belly up, with a charm upon it. Within twenty-four hours, before the frog de-cays, the rain will fall.

The *laibon* drained his Tusker and asked for another. From outside, in the failing light: *"Ecce agnus Dei. Ecce qui tollit peccata mundi . . ."* ("Behold the Lamb of God. Behold Him who takes away the sins of the world.") Of course, it all works, said the *laibon,* irritated that the doubt-ing question was asked. If there are sick cattle, sacrifice a sheep, and take the undigested grass found in its stomach, and stretch the skin over the entrance to the *boma*. The cattle will pass beneath the skin and grass, which will draw the illness out of the cows.

Of all animals, said the *laibon,* cows have the greatest power, the great-est importance. "The cow and the Masai came from the same place in the creation, and they have always been together." I thought of the cattle-raiding warriors and asked the *laibon* if it is all right to kill a man. The *laibon* thought, drank, blew his nose onto the dirt floor, and replied, "It is not so bad to kill a man. If you do it and are successful, it is not so bad, because God allowed the man to die. God agreed, and so it hap-pened."

Asked if he liked the wild animals, the *laibon* answered, "I like the animals, but they do not like human beings. That is the problem. But the eland is a friend. You can eat an eland, and use his skin for many things." Not long ago, the *laibon* dreamed that a spitting cobra bit him. He cried in his sleep and leaped out of his bed, shaking, and awoke.

The *laibon* has been chased by lions many times. The worst attack came one evening when he was walking to another *enk'ang* to see his girlfriend. (I savored the idea of a witch doctor going to pick up his girlfriend for a date.) The lion stalked and menaced him for a long dis-tance, the *laibon* jabbing with his spear, the lion never quite attacking. Odd.

It happened a year ago in the Chalbi Desert, in the Northern Frontier District. John Hall and his daughter Susan were camping in the open. It was eleven at night when the hyenas came, screaming and laughing, their eyes flashing in the moonlight. There were six or seven hyenas in the pack, and even after Hall opened up on them with his shotgun, they kept coming at him. Hall and his daughter raced for their vehicle, which was open at the sides, and still the hyenas came on, working as a pack, snapping hungrily. Hall plunged the vehicle at them repeatedly and finally chased them off into the desert.

John Hall has been a cattle rancher on the Laikipia Plateau for twenty-three years. The safari guide, Chrissie Aldrich, brought me up from Nanyuki to Hall's Enasoit Ranch. Hall's neighbors regard him as an eccentric because he gives the wild animals the free run of his ranch. At one time, he and his wife, Thelma, had a large lovely garden in their front yard, but the elephants systematically demolished it. Hall says cheerfully that he decided to enjoy watching the elephants instead of watching his flowers.

"The elephants are quite considerate, really," says Hall. There is a cabbage tree next to his house. "The elephants pushed down all of the other cabbage trees here, but they left that one standing, because they did not want it to fall on the house." A pride of seven or eight lions lives on his spread. Hall says that the lions do not have a strong appetite for beef, and besides, if they should kill a cow, it is a tax write-off. Twenty years ago, he did have to shoot a lion, one that had killed forty-six of his cows. The lion's skin hangs on the living room wall.

Hall could make more money if he chased the wild animals off his land. "But this is the last of the game," he says, speaking intensely. "So at all costs you must forfeit money to save it. It doesn't look very hopeful for the game, but you mustn't give up. I will fight to the last." That vibration is heard again and again: "Cattle can be replaced anytime, but the game cannot. What right have we to eliminate game? I would eliminate all humans and leave it to the wildlife."

Hall began farming years ago in Nottinghamshire, England. He is a rangy, bearded man who looks like D. H. Lawrence without the haunted introversion. "I always craved wilder conditions," Hall says, matter-of-factly. "I just don't like civilization in any form." The sight of a paved road incenses him.

A wounded Cape buffalo once chased Susan and John Hall into the house. One day a large male baboon pursued Thelma Hall down the veranda and into the house. The baboon came inside after her. She remembers its awful yellow fangs. John Hall came after the baboon with his shotgun, but the gun jammed. Hall jabbed with the gun butt, and the baboon started chewing it up. Finally, Hall whacked the baboon on the head with the gun butt, and it ran under a bed, where Hall finally shot it.

Thelma Hall has begun writing poems about the animals, especially about the elephants. One of the poems ends: "I was always taught/There are fairies at the bottom of the garden./At the bottom of our garden/ There are elephants!''

Moses and Olentwala and I set off from the *boma* one morning to spend the day out in the hills with 140 head of high-humped Boran cattle. Moses carried his long-bladed lion-killing spear. Olentwala, a man in his early twenties who had never been a warrior, carried a less lethal-looking spear, lighter, with less metal on the killing end. They held in their left hands the club-shaped *rungu* and a walking stick of olive wood.

Moses, like all other serious students of African bushcraft, is a reader of droppings, an analyst and commentator on dung. As he and Olentwala whistled the cattle along, he remarked now and then on the evidence that lay in the forest paths and meadows. Here a Dik-dik passed in the early morning. There a waterbuck had paused. Everywhere in East Africa such expertise is encountered.

Moses moves through the forest reading signs. He and Olentwala keep up an easy undulous whistling dialogue with the cattle. Moses explains that the whistles have meaning. The cows know by the Masai's whistle whether they are headed back home.

A sign: Moses kneels and looks at a patch of sandy earth for a moment. He spits a mist upon his palm, *pssht-psssht-psssht,* and then he pats the ground. He shows what sticks to the moisture: some dirt, but also a minute bristling of golden tiny hairs. A shedding. "Lion," says Moses. "Last night."

Moses stays downwind of the cattle. He says that the lion, if it is there, will know to keep downwind, and not give the cows its scent. So Moses and his spear will stay between the lions and his cows. Most students of the lion say the lion pays no attention to wind, but one does not argue with a man who has killed six of them.

In an easy loping walk through the meadows, Moses sings a warrior song. There is a falsetto line of rapid narrative in these songs that is interrupted with a chorus of bass organ tones fetched from deep in the chest—low, menacing warrior iterations, animal noises proclaiming war

beneath the almost soprano narration. Moses is performing both the falsetto and the deep, sinister chorus. The deep tones of the chorus are like
the lowest register of a fierce harmonica. The song is about the Masai
clans, about old drought and famine. An old *laibon* says, don't worry,
because the warriors will go and raid and get cows from other tribes.

There is a warrior lope that goes along with the song, although Moses
does not give it the full treatment now. Chin and chest jut forward at the
assertion of organ tone: *Hunnnnnnh! Hunnnnnnnnh!* The Masai know
how to look dangerous, and sound dangerous. And the history of East
African warfare confirms that they are dangerous. But I wonder why the
hands of the men are so oddly soft.

The Boran cattle wear bells that thock and dong and clatter through
the forest. The Masai and the cows are so intimately connected that each
herdsman knows every cow individually (even, as now, when we are
bringing along 140 head) and knows where each will be in the line of
march. Moses says the same two white cows always lead the herd, and
they do. And the same white cow always comes in last. Moses now
and then quite tenderly browses with his hands over one of his animals
and pulls off ticks, an act of love. Herding cows is infinitely pleasant for
the Masai. It is a matter of walking their money around the grounds.
Their cows are dear, animate wealth.

At midmorning the Masai pause. The cows graze, and the herdsmen
shelter lazily under a grove of olive trees. Moses and Olentwala joke in
Ol' Maa. I stretch out and make notes: "Moses has killed six lions, more
than 60 buffalo. A buffalo wounded his brother last year, and he wants
to kill lots of buffalo. He points to a buff skull on the forest floor and
says he killed that one there several months ago. Cows grazing all around
me now. M. shows me a 'buffalo's house'—a hollowed out space among
the olive trees where the buffalo shelter. Moses: 'We like the animals. I
am very sad if we don't see them.' "

Then, after we have resumed our herding, the notebook again: "Cows
(11:45 A.M.) smell lion and start bawling loudly. They smell fresh lion
urine. Moses sees it, pts to spot with spear. Still wet. Lions must be
downwind from us now. Cow horns all went up exactly at once when
they smelled. Hot noon sun. Moses laughing. Cows still afraid, horns up,
smelling. WE CHASE THREE LIONS through forest. One growls. They get
away thru bush and olive trees. We chase for 150 yds. and they have
slipped away. This is somewhat dangerous business."

What happened was that we saw three lions, and Moses suddenly came alive in the purest spontaneous act. The presence of the lions brought Moses electrically alert. The damndest thing. The lions brought me electrically alert as well, though with less self-confidence.

Moses seemed to become, all at once, everything that he ought to be—which was what the lions were as well: exactly lions. Moses vibrated with a current that contained no thought or premeditation. There was nothing in him of the third eye or the conscience or the sense of sin, but only an animal impulse to kill the lion. Moses went springing after the lion as the lion springs after the wildebeest.

We saw the lions running through the trees. Then they vanished. On general principles, lions are afraid of the Masai. They scurried ignominiously into the forest, not wishing to test Moses. Moses strode back from the olive trees and remarked, "Lucky lions."

Moses and Olentwala practiced throwing the *rungu*. Then they lazed for a time under the trees. Out of the sun, East Africa cools by ten or fifteen degrees Fahrenheit. Altitude and breeze and shade. Moses, showing off, undertook to make a fire. He found a piece of cedar, planed the top, and with his Masai *sime* (short sword) bored a starting fire hole. He cut a twirling stick and found the seedpod needed to catch and preserve the fire. Then he and Olentwala set about the rubbing, and soon they had a little smoking seed of flame in Moses' palm.

East Africa is a paradise, but one capable of ominous effects: nature's sweet morning, but also an awful mess, a killing field. The peaceable kingdom is dung covered and bone littered, its graceful life subject to sudden violent extinctions. A high turnover. Life is to be stalked and slain, almost abstractly, and ingested. These days, the death is also to be photographed. The tourist minibuses cluster around a cheetah kill. The late twentieth century forlornly suckles on the Pleistocene. The whites popping through the roofs of the vehicles like blossoms from a vase will glare at one another with the hatred of one whose dream has been interrupted.

Among the wild animals, individual life has no claims. What matters is something collective, the species, the tribe, the march of genes: the drive of life, and its dreamlike indifference to the details of individual death. The Great Chain of Eating. Nature at this level is bloody and sloppy, faintly horrifying and very beautiful.

Life and death coexist with a unique ecological compactness. Nothing is wasted. First the lion dines, and then the hyena, and then the vulture, then the lesser specialists, insects and the like, until the carcass is picked utterly clean, and what is left, bones and horns, subsides into the grass. It has been an African custom to take the dead out into the open and leave them unceremoniously for the hyenas.

What is the point of wild animals? If lions and leopards and rhinos and giraffes are merely decorative, or merely a nuisance, then the world will no more mourn them than it mourns the stegosaurus or the millions of buffalo that once wandered across the American plains. Is all animal life sacred? How would one react to the extinction of, say, the rattlesnake?

A farmer named Jim Trench was driving around his place near Mount Kenya one day in a rainstorm, showing me the giraffes that share the land with his livestock. He remarked, "Africa would not be Africa without the wild animals."

There are parts of Africa that are less and less Africa every day. Kenya, for example, has the highest rate of population growth in the world (4 percent). Half of the country's people are under the age of fifteen. The Malthusian arithmetic ticks away. Progress: fewer infants die, old people live longer than before. The population will double by the year 2000, to forty million, and then double again early in the twenty-first century. The human generations tumble out.

Those who live among the wild animals may be excused if they sometimes do not share the American's or the European's mystical enthusiasm for the beasts. Farmers like the Kikuyu, the Embu, and the Meru regard the wild animals as dangerous and destructive nuisances. Crop-raiding baboons are esteemed roughly in the way that coyotes are valued by West Texas ranchers. They are considered vermin. Elephants passing through a Kikuyu *shamba* (small farm) one night can wipe out a farmer's profit for a year. The law forbids killing them. If the elephants and giraffes and lions pay for themselves by bringing in the tourists and their dollars, if they prove their worth, then perhaps the governments of Africa will, before it is too late, organize the political will to protect them as a natural resource. But what do wild animals mean?

The wild animals fetch back at least two million years. They represent, we imagine, the first order of creation, and they are vividly marked with God's eccentric genius of design: life poured into pure forms, life unmitigated by complexities of consciousness, language, ethics, treachery, revulsion, reason, religion, premeditation, or free will. A wild animal does not contradict its own nature, does not thwart itself, as man endlessly does. A wild animal never plays for the other side. The wild animals are a holiday from deliberation. They are sheer life. To behold a bright being that lives without thought is, to the complex, cross-grained human mind, profoundly liberating. And even if they had no effect upon the human mind, still the wild animals are life—other life.

John Donne asked, "Was not the first man, by the desire of knowledge, corrupted even in the whitest integrity of nature?" The animals are a last glimpse of that shadowless life, previous to time and thought. They are a pure connection to the imagination of God.